I THINK I'LL DROP YOU OFF
YOU OFF
IN
DEADWOOD
A Hitchhiker's Story

I THINK I'LL DROP YOU OFF

IN DEADWOOD

A Hitchhiker's Story

TOM DETITTA

Cherokee Publishing Company
Atlanta, Georgia
1994

Library of Congress Cataloging-in-Publication Data

DeTitta, Tom.
  I think I'll drop you off in Deadwood: a hitchhiker's story/ by
Tom DeTitta. – 1st ed.
    p. cm.
  ISBN: 0-87797-167-6 : $17.95 (est)
  1. United States–Description and travel–1981- 2. United States –
Social life and customs –-1971 – 3. Hitchhiking – United States
4. DeTitta, Tom –Journeys – United States.
E169.04.D47   1969
917.304'92 --dc20   89-7368
                                                  CIP

Maps appearing on section opening pages were provided from the
Superior Wall Map © Hammond, Inc., Maplewood, NJ.

Copyright © 1994 by Tom DeTitta

This book is printed on acid-free paper which conforms to the American
National Standard Z39.48–1984 Permanence of Paper for Printed Library
Materials. Paper that conforms to this standard's requirements for pH,
alkaline reserve and freedom from groundwood is anticipated to last several hundred years without significant deterioration under normal library
use and storage conditions.

Manufactured in the United States of America
First Edition
ISBN: 0-87797-167-6

99 98 97 96 95 94   10 9 8 7 6 5 4 3 2 1

Edited by Alexa Selph
Design by Paulette Lambert

Some names have been changed to protect the privacy of individuals.

 Cherokee Publishing Company, P O Box 1730, Marietta, Ga 30061

To Ray, Pat, and John, the group I've been meeting with every Christmas

And to the people who will stop and give you a ride

CONTENTS

Acknowledgments

I want to express my thanks to

The island of Ocracoke, North Carolina, for always being a place to start; and the towns of Murphy, North Carolina; Hiawassee, Georgia; Young Harris, Georgia; and Blairsville, Georgia; the mountain communities where I came to write.

The restaurants that stay open till closing and don't allow music or video games, especially the Barrett House and Georgia Mountain Restaurant in Hiawassee; the Hardee's in Murphy; the Coffee Shop in Blairsville; and Breadman's in Chapel Hill—the places where this book was written.

The people who lent a hand, an ear, and some red marks on a manuscript: Debbie Edwards, my friend beneath the tallest sycamore tree in Young Harris; Nell Perry, who aided and edited; and Mark Barrett, who argued that even bad Scotch is better than good whiskey.

And Robin Mauney, whose courage, compassion, and dedication will always be an inspiration.

PROLOGUE

A DISTANT RADIO STATION

I have no interest in where I am going. As a recent college graduate, I just spent the whole of my senior year studiously avoiding applications or résumés. As a traveler, I have no destination, which is fortunate because, as a hitchhiker, I have no way of getting there.

It is a cloudy day in June, and I find myself heading west from Chapel Hill, North Carolina. A very familiar face is behind the wheel. Although there is not a whole lot she likes about what I am doing, my mother has decided she should be my first ride. We don't talk much about this because I am very busy flipping radio stations.

"Bringing you the best in country—WCCV, High Point—"

"Relaxing music, all the time. WRVP, Winston-Salem—"

This frantic finger rolling has become an obsession. I don't think I've heard a single song from beginning to end in a year.

"The hottest rock: WQDR, Raleigh, Durham, Chapel Hill—"

Turning, turning, turning the dial, as if there were something between stations—

"Hit radio, WCGG—"

"Relaxing music—all the time—"

—that moved around constantly—

"It's five minutes after four o'clock on a cloudy—"

—and was always just out of my grasp.

"Sherry, Sherry, Baby . . ."

Then, a message broke through my activity with an urgency that forced me to pause.

"Severe thunderstorms forecast for the entire region. Heavy rains and strong. . . . Stay tuned until. . . . "

. . . until the station faded into the static that surrounded it. Outside the sky seemed to be greying to the north and the west. Severe thunderstorms were out there somewhere—but where? I dropped my hand from the dial, caught up in a wave of excitement I was absolutely sure of.

Imagine a whisper in an unknown language, an event out of context, a moment with no past and no future. Like a stranger in a small town or a wrong turn down an unfamiliar street, it at once frightens and excites you: Thunderstorms! Where are they? Will I cross their path?

Different somehow from "Severe thunderstorms with three inches of rain forecast for Chapel Hill between four and seven-thirty tonight," as though the whole thing were planned and all that was left was to sit through it.

I began moving the dial in search of a more complete message, but a distant melodic swell filled the space where it had been. It was music that I had never heard before, but it offered a beauty that a favorite song could never possess, as it faded in and out of my grasp, until it disappeared without a title, without an author—just a song.

In a moment I would be left alone on the side of the road with no place to go, no time to be back by, and with nothing in particular that I wanted to see. In a moment, I would be left to whatever would be waiting for me at the end of a thumbnail—searching for the wonder of a place between stations.

1

JUST A FOOL WIND BLOWIN'

You stand absolutely still on the side of the road, wanting only to be caught up in the motion that ignores you. Sometimes it seems as though you will never have motion; sometimes it seems as though you will remain still forever. This scares you tremendously. In stillness there is only you, alone on the side of the road.

From the fear of a moment, you establish your perspective. You watch the drone before you and wait, hoping only that you will be caught up soon.

By whom?

You strain to see faces. There is a bearded face inside a green pickup that looks as though it has chewed a lot of tobacco. It tightens its muscles to a narrow point in trying to get a better look. It doesn't seem to think you belong along the side of the road. Then WHOOSH—it is gone.

A middle-aged female face is absolutely surrounded by blonde curls, and then by a station wagon. Tilted slightly to the right, it takes a good long look until it realizes that the look is being returned. Quickly it turns away, then—WHOOSH—disappears.

A group of faces are packed tightly inside a car from Tennessee. Several younger ones pop up from the back seat and point while the older faces in the front seat strain to see through the distraction of limbs. WHOOSH! Who were they?

The road's collective vision seems mostly suspicious. Who is that person on the side of the road, and what is he doing there? Yet, deep, deep in their eyes, a wonder buried beneath pages of newspaper articles forces a brief glance in the rear-view mirror to ponder for a moment what was left behind.

From the side of the road, you think that perhaps if you make some sort of sign you can gain some control. You rip off the flap of a discarded box and scratch out a message: "WEST." Like the equipment used by ancient sailors to keep from falling off the side of the world, the sign is an amulet. You hold it in your hand like a college degree.

How does it work? You tilt it one way, then move away from the Interstate; tilt it another way, then move closer to it. You tell yourself that there are things you can do that make a difference. You make that a rule; you call it Hitchhiker Rule Number One.

Should you smile or look serious?

Then for some reason, a car stops about fifty yards ahead. You run toward it, not knowing who, or what, or why. It will provide motion, and motion is the thing you are asking for. You try and remember the type of tilt it took to get it.

The van had carpeting squeezed into every inch of its interior. Even the steering wheel was carpeted. There was a person behind the wheel who was very involved with green polyester. He apologized because he was only going ten miles. That was all he said. He was my driver, but I knew nothing about him.

"You live in Burlington?" I asked.

"No, Graham."

"Graham a nice place?"

"It's not too bad."

There was a silence. We were not speaking the same language.

"Do you like living in Graham?"

"It's OK."

There was another silence.

"You work in Graham?"

"No, Burlington."

"What do you do in Burlington?"

"Sell carpets."

There was really nothing being said in the conversation that was part of my first ride across America.

"I hope all the rides I get are in air-conditioned vans with swivel chairs," I hinted.

"Uh-huh."

At least there was nothing inconsistent in his motion. It was steady and direct. There were no changes in speed, no variations to cause discomfort. And so I let it take me for mile upon mile.

On the other side of the window, I could see the trees swaying back and forth from a wind that I couldn't feel. In front of them, open, grass-covered hills whispered to be sat upon. The side of the road that always gets passed on the way to somewhere else.

As a young boy, I had often wanted my parents to stop the car and let me out. But even after I drove my own car, I never once paused from where I was going.

Suddenly the motion stopped. My driver looked at me in an end-of-the-line sort of way. Evidently we had come to my stop.

"Thanks for the ride," I said.

Then, before I closed the door, I simply had to say, "You know I'm hitchhiking around the country and you were my first ride."

"No kidding! All the way to California?"

"Maybe."

"Well, how much time do you have to do it in?"

"As much as I want."

"No kidding! Just said the hell with it and left, huh?"

"Sort of."

I waved, then placed my pack against a reflector pole. Things looked different somehow, and then I realized: Suddenly, I was no longer where I had been.

That alluring roadside serenity is much less inviting when you have no other choice. People pass, and you are alone; they are all going somewhere, while you are still.

In the stillness, you start to notice things: Ankles bend only forward and backward; a heart cannot stop beating if you grow tired of the noise. There are powerful thoughts seeping through this stillness that you don't want to know about.

You want motion.

You want a job, a religion, a wife and kids.

Somewhere to go; something to do.

From the fear of a still moment, you find the motivation of a lifetime.

What was the right way to hold the sign? What was the distance needed to stand from the road? Shifting, shifting, shifting, until it all feels safe again. Patterns were beginning to emerge: certain things must be done.

Another car stops. It could be anyone, but anyone is better than no one.

The son drove while the father sat beside him in some struggling state of Chrysler Newport.

"It's a good idea to wear bright clothes like you got," the younger one said. "That's something I noticed, I'd get rides faster wearing bright clothes."

"I'll be a lot quicker in picking up a hitchhiker who's got on bright clothes and holding a sign," the father added. "I've never had a bad experience with one like that."

The age difference between the two was most apparent in their hairstyles. The father had short hair forced into a wave by a hair product you could smell, while the son had random long hair batched together in a ponytail with a red, white, and blue elastic band.

Neither paid much attention to where they were going. Seventy-five percent of their concern was directed over their shoulders into the back seat.

"I used to travel quite a bit when I was your age," the old man continued. Now he wouldn't stop. "The nice thing about it is that people always remember you. Why, just a while back I happened into Reidsville, an old town in my territory when I was selling. Down at lunch, in a restaurant in town, a fella I thought I'd never seen before came on up to my table.

" 'Say, you're Joe Nelson aren't you?' this fella asked. 'Well, my dad used to buy tonic from you since I was so big!'

"When he said his name, I remembered. We talked for a while and just had a good time of it. The young fella even insisted on buying my lunch. Wouldn't have it any other way.

"It's nice when you can go someplace else and people know who you are."

The topic of conversation accumulated into the back seat and couched a place for me within the car's environment. These things would not have been thought of without a little random direction along for the ride. I felt as though I belonged, at least for a while.

Beneath me the engine turned and churned to someplace new. I could feel the inches swell into feet, then yards and miles—all toward a place I was going to be, when moments ago there was stillness.

"Thing about hitchhiking, is that you never really know," the young man continued.

"I got into a car once just the other side of the Tennessee line. There were two guys up front, just as cool-looking as they could be. Never thought a thing about getting in between the two of them. Never thought a thing about it. Next thing I knew I felt a butcher knife in my belly. They took everything I had, including my shirt and jacket, and left me freezing up on some mountain road, waiting for someone to pick me up."

"Did you call the police?"

"Not much the police will do for a hitchhiker. You're pretty much on your own out there."

That was a good point.

"Well, did you have a lot of things happen to you like that?" I asked.

"You're gonna have him turned back and heading home if you keep talking like that!" the old man mused with a chuckle.

Then it was over, again, and I stood alone waiting for another ride:

"I remember the day me and a friend decided to up and hitchhike to Oklahoma," this man wearing a grey flannel shirt said to me. "That was fifteen years ago, and I remember it like it was yesterday.

"Just a fool wind blowin' was all it took. Just a fool wind blowin'. Fifteen hundred miles to the sign that said 'Welcome to Oklahoma,' and we turned around and headed back."

The same gale was lifting me through yet another ride: "Just a fool wind blowin'."

On the side of the road again, I was beginning to feel like a symbol for that spontaneous moment that is held tightly forever. I was beginning to feel like "a hitchhiker," and that was a feeling I had to legitimize at the gas station near the bottom of the exit ramp.

With a pack upon my shoulders that distinguished me from everybody else, I eased into the front office, past the attendant at the cash register, past the customer hanging the key back on the wall, right straight up to the machine that said "Cigarettes," banged me out a pack of Marlboros, and headed off into the sunset.

Sunset?

As best as could be expected on a cloudy day: a red glow in the sky was saying, "That's all folks!" to a day that had brought me fifty miles to buy a pack of cigarettes when I didn't even smoke.

On the road again, another driver hesitated to say he was only going another fifteen miles down the road. (Didn't anybody in North Carolina go anywhere?) I accepted, and then tried to remember the name of a woman I had dated briefly two years ago who was from Winston-Salem.

We stopped for gas, and directory assistance.

"I'm sorry, there's no Lisa Glenn here. . . . "

"Lisa? You must have the wrong number. . . . "

"No, there's nobody here by that name. . . . "

"Lisa? Lisa's in Cambridge."

"Cambridge, Massachusetts?"

"May I ask who's calling?"

"My name is Tom DeTitta, I used to date Lisa a while back."

"Oh, yes, I've heard of you."

There was a pause.

"Well, Lisa is at Harvard studying to become a doctor, and I don't expect her back for a while."

"Oh . . . well, I was just hitchhiking across the country and happened to be passing through Winston-Salem when I thought to myself, 'I know somebody there!' and so I figured I'd give her a call."

"Really? How long have you been hitchhiking?"

This was going to sound really dumb, I thought.

"Well, actually today's my first day. . . . "

I don't remember much of my conversation after that. I just remember concentrating on the part where I heard myself say, "Well, I've really got to get going now, the guy who I'm getting a ride with is in a hurry," and then listening for a click that I had been waiting on desperately.

Five miles later, the day was churning hard toward dusk at the place where I had been deposited. There was another person I could call, a college friend who had been the singer in our band, and who I had heard was trying to make it in Nashville. But that was still four hundred miles away. Home was about a hundred miles too far to walk. My tent was lying in wait. Behind me, I could feel a lonely wind approaching through the grass and trees long before I felt it through my hair.

A man stood beside a Chevy Malibu that blared out-of-date music from an open door. He was tall, young, and his hair had a military cut.

"Knoxville?" I bargained, "I'd like to get as far as Knoxville."

"Well, you just got yourself a ride to Knoxville."

I hesitated. Afraid of disappointment, I had made Knoxville my goal.

"Actually I'd really like to get to Nashville."

"Well, you just got yourself a ride to Nashville!"

With all that I owned fitted snugly in the car trunk of an army private on three-day leave to Kentucky, I slammed the door on the impending quiet, and listened with an irrational joy to a scratchy recording of "Sergeant Pepper's Lonely Hearts Club Band."

2

OFF-RAMP

In Nashville, bright colored lights line streets that bustle with all-night-and-into-the-morning music and beer; music, beer, and women; music, beer, women, and song. Crowds flock to and set themselves in front of the stage where dreams are always found. Although I'd never been, everyone knows that Nashville is this stage.

A rest-area set of directions from my friend's roommate ushered us to the back of the upper-upper mezzanine overlooking this stage. On this fringe of Nashville, the bright lights led to hamburgers: Krystal burgers were proud to be the nation's smallest.

There were no pools or tennis courts decorating this sprawling apartment complex. Inside of 4103–H, there was only that same roommate, Martha, staring right at me, serious as a heart attack.

"Julie's gonna be a star," Martha said. "There's nobody in this town who can sing like her."

This last-minute ride had led right to Martha, who was much bigger in person than she had been on the phone—pushing 250 in faded jeans, 260 including her long, thick, straight hair. She made her assertion as if she dared me to think otherwise. Not only was she Julie's roommate, she was also Julie's manager.

"Julie is definitely gonna be a star."

She sat in a chair across from me. Everything in the room matched because everything was green. Off to the side, there was this other guy who introduced himself as Hank—or perhaps Frank. His words sputtered almost indistinguishably from a severely deformed face that looked as though it had half-melted.

Kittens appeared and re-appeared, although a mother cat never did.

"Julie's gonna be a star and she's not gonna have to screw everyone in town to do it," Martha continued.

Julie slept in the next room—couldn't be awakened by my arrival because she had to be up by ten for a restaurant job.

"I've got her hooked up with some real names in this town, and they think she's gonna be a star, too."

At this point Frank/Hank found some dishes in the sink that needed cleaning.

"She's got nowhere to go but up."

Julie's career and our friendship began at the same time, the night the two of us were locked in the college radio station together. One of the seemingly infinite array of things a college freshman can be when he or she grows up is a disc jockey. It just so happened we were both checking out that possibility late the same night. The station had just signed off the air, and the last guy out locked the door that would not open from within without the key he went home with.

If we had been locked in a chemistry lab, we probably would have found a way out. But there were at least ten thousand records in the school's collection. After a lifetime of waiting for our songs to come over the air, that night we were the airwaves. Each took a turn at playing a next-favorite—listening, singing, dancing—until the morning DJ found us surrounded by nearly a hundred albums.

From that night on, Julie decided she could sing. I had always been a drummer. In between multiple-choice questions and sorority rush, we played in bands that fought over whose favorite songs would be performed.

Julie had the type of looks that didn't need a voice, and that was fortunate for the band. Nobody was listening to the words anyway; frat boys just needed an excuse to dance.

We always talked about a life that would allow music without having to study in the bathroom between sets. But when senior year rolled around, "all-you-could-ever-be" had been narrowed considerably by the college placement office.

It seemed we were each ignoring this fact in our own way. About a half-year ago, Julie packed her economics degree and followed the road to Nashville. I was just following the road.

"I've seen more people come into this town having to sleep with everyone before they sung a note," Martha said. "I've got her a good gig—a new band—not like that last bunch. You'll see tomorrow."

Julie was asleep—would not be disturbed—because she would have to practice after she had served lunch.

Eventually, 5 A.M. brought a room at the end of the hall. There was a mattress on the floor that was not going anywhere, and so neither was I. Somewhere back in North Carolina, I had felt night approach in a dark and heavy cloak of uncertainty unlike anything I had known since childhood.

Hitchhiking meant that I would never know where I would be sleeping. No matter where I stood in the morning, once I stuck out my thumb, it was up to a bunch of total strangers to determine where I would be lying that night.

As I searched for the switch toward a more gentle darkness, I saw Julie for the first time on the wall, posing behind a microphone, smiling, wearing a cowboy hat, and next to a picture of Marilyn Monroe.

Morning had taken Julie without leaving any explanations. The guy with a deformed face had apparently slept on the couch and had just awakened. When Martha tried to continue where she had left off, her audience of two made a beeline for the concession stand.

"There's a fish place down the street," Frank (Hank?) said, and I followed.

The sidewalk looked like the wake of an Antarctic icebreaker. It led to about a hundred different restaurants where we wouldn't have to leave a tip. The place this guy liked had a pink Cadillac with fat, white-wall tires parked in front. It offered deep-fried from the sea. We both ordered some special fried sample-dinner that was advertised cheap and for a limited time only.

As we sat, I needed a special malt syrup across the table that I wasn't able to get without the help of my companion.

"What did you say your name was again?" I asked.

F was particularly hard to understand. Was it Frank or Hank?

"How'd you get here?" I asked. "What brought you to Nashville?"

Fr(H)ank woke up fourteen days ago and thought he'd died and gone to both heaven and hell.

The day had started in Cleveland, Ohio, at a going-away party that was to have been a grand send-off for his new life down south. He barely remembered driving anywhere. When he awoke, he was surrounded by white. There was no telling where the walls ended and the ceiling begun. It was like being trapped inside a ping-pong ball.

There was no one around to provide an explanation. Just a white that he tried to knock down with all his might, until his shoulders and arms started to bleed.

Much later, a door opened from the white, and a man in uniform told him about the DUI, and the pummeling he had given a cellmate who had tried to molest him. After the lawyers processed these two inextricable events, he had surrendered his car and whatever money he had for getting a two-thousand-dollar fine reduced to one thousand dollars, plus legal fees of twenty-five hundred.

After hitchhiking to Nashville, he found a job at a pizza place where he met Martha, who, for her whole life, seemed to always have room on the couch. He quit his job a few days ago to prepare for a ride to the West with a woman he knew would be arriving just any day.

"She'll be here soon and then I can leave," he said.

"What's this business with Julie and Martha?" I asked.

The way it looked from the outside, Julie's random sense of stardom landed her in the most accessible means to that end. Nashville wasn't as expensive or as far away as either New York or Los Angeles. As Martha said so many times, "Julie is going to be a star!" and I guess we just all assumed something like that was going to happen.

But as Frank/Hank knew, there weren't any welcoming committees for strangers to this city. The hotels charge by the day, and the temporary jobs last for a week at a time.

There is nothing in a hotel room to call your own. You begin the day with borrowed towels. Gazing out, the light outside your window hums a lonesome song that keeps you up all night. The maids wake you up too early. Cost-by-the-day is always more than you expected.

At some place and through someone, Julie stumbled upon Martha, who made her a deal on the extra room in the apartment. At the time, Martha's only means of income was finding discarded washing machines and selling them for forty dollars more than they cost to fix.

The relationship mushroomed from landlord to manager after Martha dug deep into her list of former couch guests to find an old family friend who had written a song that Willie Nelson sang once. Martha's daddy had let the friend stay at the house during a particularly extensive drunk.

With this connection for her roommate's ambition, Martha thought she finally had what it took to make it in this town.

"Does Julie think Martha can help her?" I asked.

My companion mentioned the pictures of this person with Martha's family that Julie just had to see. That one record label really did have his name next to the words "Written By."

Apparently, there are stories that Martha plays over and over about the time this guy woke to find himself tied to his bed; there are stories about massive consumption of liquor.

Martha offered Julie a wall to accumulate those few pictures of her life in Nashville. After the first gig Martha managed, the band somehow didn't get paid, and so Julie no longer had to pay rent.

"Julie won't sell washing machines," my friend said. "Martha got her a job waitressing."

We had to get back to the house because in another twenty

minutes, Martha was going to pick up Julie from work and drive her to rehearsal.

"Martha thinks Julie's gonna be a star."

"Yeah, I heard."

We each retreated into our own "crunch, crunch, crunch" and the search for fish in all that had been fried so completely.

The food was horrible; we ate every bite. On his way out, what's-his-name stuffed a couple of sugar packets into his pocket, and before I knew it, so had I.

"How about I just call you Fritze?" I offered.

He took that as the friendly gesture it was meant to be.

Martha's car had holes in the floor through which you could see the cracks in her driveway. Once behind the wheel, she began a calculated coercion with the ignition that consisted of three quick presses on the gas petal, wait three seconds, then one try at the starter — two tries at the starter.

Repeat.

After a few minutes, this gradually gave way to a more verbal form of coercion. The car finally responded to " . . . you shit-faced piece of crap."

"I hope Julie's not pissed that we're late," Martha said.

It was a three-block walk to where Julie worked. The car got us there in one-tenth the time it had spent deciding whether or not it would. There, for the first time in nearly a day at her house, I saw my hostess. Because Martha let me sit in front, Julie had to sit in the back. I reached behind me and shook her hand.

"Long time no see," I said.

"I couldn't believe it when Martha told me you were coming," she replied.

Martha turned the dial on the radio to a louder station.

"It's good to see you," I said.

"Yeah, good seeing you."

Then she paused.

"I guess you've met everybody, then."

Martha forged ahead like a Malibu steam engine. Later, she would be selling a used washing machine that somebody hadn't even bothered to try to fix.

It seemed that Julie's parents had given her a late-model foreign car to drive in college. If they didn't, they certainly could have. Like most college students, I doubt Julie had ever realized that washing machines broke. They just changed color when you moved into a bigger house, like the wallpaper.

There were a lot more questions lingering in the silence between us, which Julie seemed uninterested in pursuing. She just looked past it all through the window and onto the street. When this was not enough, she reached past the driver's seat and pressed the button that she knew would lead even further away.

"Some asshole guys from the talent agency were saying they'd get me a job at whatever club I wanted."

"Those sons of bitches!" Martha yelled. "They'll get you a job all right—after they get you in bed!"

Apparently one of the talent agencies in town had offices across the street from where Julie was working.

"They kept at me the whole mealtime. . . . I had to be polite."

"Damned men, think that they can rule the whole world 'cause of what they got between their legs!"

The tirade had generalized to an attack on all those stuck with something external between their legs—as if Fritze and I were somehow not a part of that club. Eventually what seemed like a wrong turn into an industrial part of town revealed a barbecue diner, and under that diner, a room barely big enough to accommodate amplifiers. At the far end, a few musicians were wiping the sleep out of their eyes at 3 P.M.

Julie immediately left Martha's rage to find another haven behind the microphone that was onstage. "Testing, one-two; testing, one-two." She continued way beyond what was necessary, asking questions of musicians, and occasionally tapping the drummer's drums in a feigned playfulness that brought a smile only because the drummer was male and Julie was so pretty. From back in the audience, I could only watch.

Martha had immediately gotten involved in negotiations with the only guy there who wasn't hunched over and drinking a cup of coffee. When she returned, the musicians and the rest of us instinctively huddled around to hear what Martha had to say.

"We've only got four free meals. Each one's a full dinner, but there's seven of us here, so Julie can have a sandwich, and the rest of us can split one, then whoever wants the French fries can have them, and whoever wants the cole slaw can have that, but you can't have both. We'll divide what's left."

"How come we only got four dinners?"

"They said only one for each musician. They wouldn't believe that Frank and Tom were with the band."

"But we've got five musicians in the band."

They all looked around to confirm this. Something wasn't right. "Where's Paul?"

A series of frantic phone calls led to an alcohol-rehabilitation unit at a local hospital.

"Does that mean he can't play tonight?"

After she realized this, Martha simply continued on the phone until about an hour later, there was another set of faded jeans behind a guitar.

"He might have played with them at one point," Fritze said.

Julie had never moved from behind the mike.

Throughout the rehearsal I was painfully reminded of why I had not yet chosen to become a professional musician. Julie, in the typical role of a lead singer, was complaining about everything—vaguely. *Something* didn't sound right, or *someone* was off. Everything would stop, and the band members would look around, try it again and again, but the problem would never get beyond pronouns.

None of the accused were from Nashville. In fact, the only two who could really identify with any one location were the drummer and one guitar player who both had left a small town in upstate New York to try and make it big in Nashville. Their wives and both of their children stopped in after cleaning rooms at a motor lodge. (A new guitar player, they might have noticed: wonder what happened to the old one.)

It was a whole different group from the one that had worked with Julie last week, and completely different still from the group Martha had fired three weeks before. But the band was doing the types of songs that everybody knew and most anyone could play.

Also appearing during the rehearsal was some ex-showgirl who had just driven thirty-two hours from Las Vegas. She was trying to see if any of the bass player's free dinner could be used to feed her child. She had some connection to him that wasn't genetic. This was the bass player who had been sleeping in a car parked outside the motel where the other two were staying. He had described this band as his twenty-fifth start-up band in the last five years.

"Wait, I'm telling you something is not right! Something is off somehow!" Julie interrupted.

At home, any approach to stillness was masterfully assassinated by Julie. The objects of her rage were numerous and moved from general to specific: music, living in Nashville, the new band, the car, the cats, and finally Fritze, who had just gone to the store to get something Martha needed.

"I'm not living with just whatever stray you happen to bring in here! It's my house too, and I don't even know Frank. I don't care what his problem is, I'm not the damned Salvation Army!"

"He's just gonna be here a few days till that ride comes for him."

"He's been saying that for two weeks now! He'll be saying that two years from now!"

"If his ride doesn't come in the next two weeks, then I'll have him find a place."

"What difference does it make then? In two weeks I'll be back home."

"You're not going to leave until you get your big chance in the studio."

"Yeah, well when is that going to be? I've been hearing about that for the last three months."

"When you're Dolly Parton, you can tell people when to do things. Right now you gotta wait till he has time. He's a very busy man."

"Well I don't have much more time any more."

"OK, we'll talk to him by the end of the week. I'll give him a call tomorrow, and we'll set something up."

Fritze returned with a half-a-chicken, which Martha slapped onto a pie tin, doused in water, and slammed naked into the oven. After the bird had been "et," Julie had to have a nap before performing. She was about to close the door to her room when Martha added:

" . . . and we're gonna have to get that contract signed between me and you before we go to any damned studio."

The door slammed shut.

Gigs were weekends, weekdays, well into a week of my prolonged overnight stay. Martha always managed to find places for the band to play. Most were places that didn't necessarily have to have a band; places that, in fact, didn't have to have anything more than cans of beer. But if you're playing for the hat, then it doesn't cost the owner anything to have you, and " . . . sure Martha, we could use some live music in here." Even the three-dimensional pictures of Elvis behind the bar seemed to agree.

The band was together, if not tight. In between sets, they talked to their wives or their girlfriends; they drank Coca-Cola that week as their friend lay alone in detox. During the sets, the wives would refuse others' requests to dance, but the girlfriend from Las Vegas didn't want to just sit there!

If the band members noticed the hat move too quickly through the audience—if the owner of the club kept forcing them to turn down the volume so people could talk—there were still thousands of fast-food joints and souvenir shops where some assistant manager stood ready to point out a sub-minimum-wage effort. Beneath the sound of guitars was always: "Take out the trash, asshole."

From anywhere in that city, you could always hear the rumblings of musicians from Kentucky and North Carolina who were pouring more sugar into that third miserable cup of coffee, thinking they should have asked for more money before the interband rivalry broke out, before the club owner said: "You're fired. I don't ever want to see any of your stinking faces again, ever."

Against this backdrop, from one gig to the next, a sax solo worked its way from the middle of the first set to the end of the first set, and then to the end of the second set. Somehow, the four guys who were just playing together made music on this one. Eventually, the band began to look for it at the end of each night. If the audience didn't ask for an encore—if there was no audience left—the wives were always on hand to provide the necessary justification for that one more song.

The bass player who doubled on sax would reach way back to something that managed to survive twenty-five start-up bands, and this guy you hardly noticed all night would come through with a sound that had all the rest of the band members bouncing and hopping and swaying like the Ted Nugent entry at the high school air-guitar contest. Against it all, and for the moment, these were working musicians in Nashville, Tennessee.

Fritze was always looking for women to dance—never approaching, never asking—always looking. The energy that should have sent him across the room instead settled into the ends of his fingers, the ends of his toes, and especially the whole length of his leg, which shook like a naked Floridian in Fairbanks when he spied a possibility.

As the night wore on and the unrealized opportunities accumulated, Fritze would become particularly agitated when that sax began to blow like a factory whistle that announced "five minutes till closing." Even then, Fritze remained looking out over it all like an accountant painfully trying to pick the right number on a spinning roulette wheel.

After hanging onto his chips for nearly a week, Fritze spotted a familiar face:

"Hey, Tina, come on over," Fritze said.

Tina was a nurse with curly red hair that had been worked into an Afro. She had come in by herself, and I could tell by the sudden excitement in Fritze's left leg that she was available.

"This is my friend Tom," Fritze said. "Want to dance?"

"Let me get a drink first?" she replied.

Tina would have been married to some guy Fritze knew, except that she demanded a little too soon that this prospective husband divorce his last wife before they marry. As a result, the almost-was-a-husband married yet another woman who wasn't so particular about things.

"Dave was a marriage waiting to happen." Tina said. "Have you seen him around much?"

"Sometimes," Fritze said. "Every once in a while."

Then Tina began talking about some guy she had met a few nights ago who had come over to her apartment, watched a television show, then left. She told this story in a tone that asked us to feel sorry for her. I had no idea why we were supposed to feel sorry for her until the frantic movement in Fritze's fingers and toes tipped off the possibility that was inherent in her disappointment. Then it was the end of the second set, and Fritze could hear the saxophone coming.

"Tina, come on, let's dance!"

"No, I think I might leave pretty soon. I'm kind of tired from work."

Fritze quickly processed the disappointment and implemented damage control.

"Dave comes in here you know . . . "

Dave was the almost-husband.

" . . . but he usually doesn't come until late," Fritze added.

"Oh," Tina said. "Well I'd love to see the expression on his face when he sees me."

Fritze was banking on the loosening effect of a few more pitchers a little further down the line. But three pitchers later, that loosening effect had nothing to pull it any direction and so it slid into despondency. Last call came around, and of course, Dave never had. At that point, Tina began to talk to me for the first time.

"How do you know Julie?"

"We went to school together."

"Oh, you went to college. . . . Where was that?"

"Duke, over in North Carolina."

Tina perked up around the thought of a couple of doctors she knew who had gone to Duke: Did I know them? Did I want to be a doctor someday?

Fritze left to answer "last call."

What year did I graduate? What courses had I taken? Why didn't I want to become a doctor when that was obviously an option?

"Well, maybe I might be a doctor someday," I said, sensing that was some kind of right answer.

"You want to dance, Tina?" Fritze came back.

Tina wanted to go for a drive.

Tina's M.G. sports car fit exactly two people, and there were three of us. There was a space behind the two seats big enough to fit a set of golf clubs. But a zipper along the roof created a makeshift passenger seat that sent my head and shoulders into the night air, ears flapping and nose into the 20-30-40-then-65-mile-per-hour wind like somebody's beagle.

People who drive sports cars like to go fast. At first all I could think about was that when she flips this doing 60 around a curve, I am inherently decapitated.

But when we hit the freeway, the lights of Nashville suddenly appeared ahead like nothing you've ever seen from behind a windshield. Where was I going? Who was I going with? Suddenly, I was hitchhiking again.

After about twenty miles, the conversation in front had resulted in one empty seat. Fritze had mumbled something about needing to see a man about a horse. Before walking off, he snapped, "See you later, Dr. Tom," and I really didn't know what he meant.

At Tina's apartment, I could still feel the wind in my hair as I walked into another life, glancing at personal notes on a refrigerator door, and sifting through the particulars of an album collection.

"Put on whatever you like," she said.

"Well, what do you like?"

I was introducing a long-stemmed glass of wine into a wide-mouth stomach of beer when Tina began presenting a deep and meaningful conversation about happiness being a state of mind, and about how all the terrible disappointments she had faced didn't bother her at all. The sharp ring of the phone at four in the morning made me wonder where I was and where I was going to sleep that night.

"It was my ex-husband. He wanted to know if I had given the dog a shot for whooping cough."

Then she said, "Don't worry. He usually knocks if he ever comes over."

In no way whatsoever would this be mine tonight. I might be cheap, but there was something even I couldn't handle about being a closing-time-last-ditch-effort of some woman who was rebounding from a husband, an almost-husband, and a failed one-night stand. This became increasingly clear to me as I saw that red hair and an Afro really don't work well together. Thanks for the ride and all, but holy cow, look at the time!

On the ride home, I watched as those same lights of the city melted against the coming of a new day. I wondered what I had said or done that could be used to create sympathy in the next conversation: ("He kept asking me how my dog got whooping cough!")

The only defense I could offer was a soft kiss good-night.

It was well into 1 P.M. Sunday, and all of Nashville that had seen closing time was wondering what they were going to do with a day they'd just as soon skip.

Mornings in the afternoon always come laden with questions: Why did I sleep so late? Why did I drink so much? Why did I go to bed with her?

Was I ever going to stick my thumb out again and continue?

This was not my house. It was not my mattress on the floor forever to keep. I had saved six hundred dollars for the first three months of traveling the country, not for three weeks of drinking beer.

What was I still doing in Nashville?

Julie met me trying to squeeze a cup of coffee out of her empty kitchen cabinets.

"Where were you last night?" she asked.

Julie sat straight up at the kitchen table and watched me with both eyes. Now that the question mark hovered over my head instead of hers, Julie had time for me.

"Out. I went out after the gig."

"I saw you leave with Frank and some girl."

"Yeah."

"Who was she?"

"I'm not sure."

"Tina," she said.

"What are we doing today?" I asked.

Julie mumbled something about Martha and a prayer meeting.

"You mean we're going to church?" I asked.

"I've never been to this church before," Julie explained. "Martha's been bugging me to go with her."

In addition, Julie was to perform a song she had written that she said had to do with the relationship between a pimp and a prostitute.

"But Martha and them think it has to do with God and man."

There was no coffee, which I needed so desperately, and so there was nothing else I needed to do. I sat at the table across from Julie, and she began to play with the spoon that would hold no sugar.

"So where did you go with Tina?" she managed.

"What time is this prayer meeting?"

The Madison Pentecostal Church was in the shopping mall section of town. We passed four of them in the few short miles it took to get there. The church was nestled in a lot across the street from Sears, Roebuck. The flashing lights and white brick exterior fit right in with the neighborhood. If you didn't look twice, you might think something was on sale there.

Inside the large arena, the seating was general admission and nearing capacity. You could hear the tap-tap-tap of drums, a squeak of a horn, and the ever-present "testing—one, two" that preceded every show.

When Martha's father saw us approach, he rushed over to grab

Julie by the arm and forward her to a well-dressed man who was smiling in the midst of a lot of people.

"Here she is, Reverend, this is the Julie we were telling you about."

Fritze had somehow disappeared when everyone was getting in the car for this.

"The Lord has put his song on her tongue, and tonight she wants to share it with us," Martha's father continued.

This reverend wore tinted eyeglasses that remained dark in this brightly lit interior.

"Well, what's the name of this song, child?" he asked.

"It's called 'The Painter,' " Julie replied.

"Well, I've never heard that song before. What's it about?"

"It's about God and man," Martha added quickly.

"Trust me, it's a good song for the people to hear," Martha's dad said.

"Well, why don't you come into my office and sing it for me real quick," the reverend suggested.

At that moment, the sound check had materialized into an opening number.

"No, doesn't look like we have time," preacher said and he looked like he had a dilemma on his hands until he added, "Tell you what, you sit tight, and if the Lord tells me to call you up, by golly, I will!"

As the reverend escaped upon the congregation that was his, the music broke into a drum solo that packed raw, hard-driving energy into his ascent upon the pulpit: bass, snare, bass, snare, cymbal crash, and then silence to make room for the Word.

Within moments, people were falling. Not a trip, not a slip, but down-for-the-count falling: eight-nine-ten—and nobody seemed to notice much.

They held up their hands before they dropped, raising their palms to the sky like mini-satellite dishes open to receive a spiritual communiqué.

Julie seemed upset by all the people falling, and so Martha leaned over and explained: "Filled with the holy spirit and overwhelmed."

The reverend began each sentence like a human being, but finished each like a man-beast. Even if he was talking about parking, he would suddenly YELL ABOUT HOW THEY WERE TOWING AT THE SEARS AND ROEBUCK!

And his congregation was dropping like flies.

Then I thought: "This is the ultimate."

This is the top of the heap.

Greater than any political rally where people wore donkey ears and red, white, and blue clothing; greater than hockey night in Canada. I'd never seen a play or movie that actually had them dropping in the aisles. Nobody ever fell down for Perry Como.

It was greater than anything Nashville country-music-capital could muster because the best they could do was two-for-one, and that ain't nothing compared with salvation.

It would have been over and done with in my mind right then and there, except that my good friend had a pending appointment on the sacrificial altar. When Martha finally dropped, Julie lunged toward the back of the hall and I quickly followed.

"You know you don't have to be here," I said.

"Yeah, I know . . . but Martha's been bugging me to come to her church."

"You don't have to do what Martha says," I snapped.

"I know I don't. I'll do whatever I want!"

"Julie, look at this! What are you doing here?"

"Yeah, well look at you! You're a fine one to talk! What are you doing hitchhiking just anywhere?"

At that moment, the reverend had become struck by the Lord. The girl who had God's song on her tongue was wandering astray, and so he was calling her forward. The whole group of nearly eight hundred strangers at some church in Tennessee had found their way between the only real conversation Julie and I had managed. They were clapping, chanting, calling her to come upon the altar.

Julie could only smile from ear to ear, as Martha's father made his way toward us.

"I really don't want to do this," she said only to me.

But in a few moments, she stood before all of those left standing, as the pianist read the music Julie handed to him.

I felt sorry for her at first, then confused, and even angry as she started singing. But with only the piano beside her, with her sex appeal negated by circumstance, I noticed for the first time that Julie's voice had become beautiful.

Not just beautiful, but powerful, too. A far cry from that scratchy, squeaky, uncertain attempt we tried to drown out with amplifiers.

Julie had become a singer.

I took a seat next to Martha, who had become unstruck, and sat upright to catch every note, as did most of the others who moments ago had been lining the floor.

I doubt Julie or any of us would be any more saved than we had been the day before. In time, she might very well find herself in another place altogether. But in between, Julie had stopped in Nashville to let the chaos of humanity seep through her vocal cords and emerge as music.

At this particular gig, well into my second week of beer, babes, and "Blue Eyes Cryin' in the Rain," I met a guy who was traveling across country and offering a ride to the West Coast for seventy-five dollars.

"You won't have to worry about getting rides with queers or having to listen to someone tell you about their grandmother who just died," he told me.

Hitchhiking had become this distant roll of thunder that lingered at every horizon over the past two weeks. There weren't any other friends to visit west of here. If I hitchhiked tomorrow morning, there was absolutely no telling where I would be sleeping that night. But if I stayed another day in Nashville, I might as well stop by Motor Vehicle and get a Tennessee driver's license.

"Hitchhiking sucks," he said. "You never know what's going to happen to you."

He was traveling in a self-contained van unit that served as a springboard for his two favorite forms of being: hiking and biking—alone. He had pretty much eliminated almost all of the human factor from the mechanization of his movement. I had to reach back beyond my fear of the moment to remind myself that his kind of travel had nothing to do with why I stuck my thumb out when I had enough money to take a bus.

He kept talking about walking alone in the woods; riding alone down a road.

"It's freedom, you know . . . *freedom!*"

Further into the beer, he began replaying parts of his "ultimate sexual experience," which was a chance meeting with an unknown woman on the Appalachian Trail in New Hampshire.

He described sex in terms of the setting and circumstances without saying much about the woman. The more he talked, the more it seemed like the "ultimate" was probably also the "only" because you got the sense that the only way this guy could get an erection was on top of a mountain with a woman he had just met, who would be continuing in the opposite direction the next morning.

"Freedom—you know? *Freedom.*"

Fritze had disengaged himself from our conversation and the possible ride it offered. He had a ride coming just any day now. In fact, he seemed generally uninterested that night, and so I was surprised to see the foot start tapping, which could only mean females—two young ones—wrapped in bright orange and green terry cloth.

They entered like lost cattle through the stockyards of Saint Paul, until they spotted the musicians' wives together in a group and headed straight for them. They were followed by an equally self-conscious male who accidentally tested the permanence of a few tables on his way over.

Each waved briefly at the guitar player and the drummer, who kind of smiled back at them.

From that point, Fritze lost all interest in what was being said at the bar. He liked the numbers life was offering at the moment, and so he concentrated on the big score. As the second set was coming to a close, Fritze sensed some kind of opportunity in Martha's big mother who happened in at that moment.

She was good-hearted and open for suggestions, so Fritze had her dancing before she could find a seat. She took it all with one of those smiles that knew other people were watching.

When Fritze danced, it just meant his quick-foot got more involved—real involved—while his upper body pretended not to notice. He danced like the ghost of Elvis Presley. His face and arms seemed coolly detached from the tremendous commotion his legs were making, as if he were being pulled by the legs into some kind of shake-rattle-and-roll machine.

Martha's mother just loved the Fritze-shake. So did everyone else. When the song was over, Fritze just naturally followed Martha's mother into the covey of wives/managers/new friends dressed in terry cloth.

The guy's name was Ed, and he and the two girls had driven all the way from that same upstate New York town, "... just to see our friends in the city of music," Ed said repeatedly. "Just to head out and see our friends playing guitar and drums in Nashville!"

The girls seemed only mildly interested in the whole idea, but looked at Ed like some crazy Indian chief who was mustering too strong a warpath for them to bother resisting.

When the guy from the bar came by and started talking about his California dreaming, Ed got even more excited about places even further down the road. The guy got to tell his stories all over again, while Ed sat wide-eyed and wondering.

The music started and Fritze wanted to dance. It seemed he was trying to tell some jokes as a prelim, then he asked each one of the prospects in turn: "You wanna dance now?" and each just giggled.

Fritze regrouped. He asked about upstate New York; had it been a long trip? Did they like it here—so far? and finally:

"You wanna dance now?"

They giggled some more, but began to mean it less.

The music, however, would not stop, and so neither would Fritze, until the girls weren't even giggling any more. One of the wives had overheard all of the conversation, and finally snapped at my buddy:

"Can't you see they don't know how to take you!"

All of a sudden, I remembered the guy with the deformed face whom I had left back at a fish house a few weeks ago.

Even the music couldn't drown out the silence after that. When Ed excused himself to go to the bathroom, we followed the momentum out and away, then into the fast-food world that lurked outside the bar.

Fritze parked it in front of one such counter and began to order junk without regard to cost or appetite.

"Why do you think that girl was afraid of me?" he asked.

"Don't worry about it," I said. "She's just a long way from home."

Again we fell randomly into the night. The beer and burgers were fighting to see which was going to get the better of us. When we were no place in particular, it started to rain. In fact, it started to pour. The cold rain felt incredibly lousy at that point, but the only shelter the world was offering was a phone booth.

Lightning struck hard again and again just a few feet from our narrow, improvised lodging.

"Would you please get off my foot?" I asked.

"Soon as you get your elbow out of my back."

Motorists passing by seemed to enjoy the spectacle that was spotlighted by an overhead white neon. Each time the lightning struck nearby, it would register as a kick in the shins or an elbow in the chest. One of us dropped a quarter, but neither of us even thought about trying to pick it up.

"What are we going to do now?" I asked.

"We're going to wait until this storm ends," Fritze replied.

"Then get your elbow out of my ear."

"You get your heel off my big toe."

We switched around and made it worse.

"Is Tina working tonight?" I asked.

"Yeah, I think so."

"You know where she works?"

"Uh-huh."

There was no change to be found in either of our pockets. We argued about who would look up the number and who would get the quarter, with neither side really winning. I just started thumbing through the phone book, and he tried to lift up the quarter with his feet. Finally he just dropped down and on his way up knocked the phone book out of my hand just as the pages got to "hospitals."

"Jerk!" I said.

"Got the quarter, didn't I?"

We both decided the safest call with one quarter would be the general nurses station at that particular hospital.

"Hello, is Tina? . . . "

I cupped the receiver over my hand.

"What's her last name?"

"George."

" . . . is Tina George there? WAIT—no, don't hang up! Can you transfer me there? No, you see we're in a phone booth in the middle of a bad storm and there's only a quarter between us. . . . Who's we?"

After a while, the phone started ringing toward this person whom I really didn't have much to say to. I quickly shoved the phone at Fritze.

"No . . . we were just in a phone booth in a storm and we thought we'd call," Fritze began. "Who's we? Me and Tom. Right, Tom from the other night . . . do you want to speak with him? Why not?"

The storm finally let up and we began to move toward something familiar. The motel that kept the musicians was at the bottom of the hill on the way to the house. It was as far as Fritze got, as he hesitated around a vacant '69 Pontiac. From under the passenger tire, Fritze came up with the key for what had been the bass-player's home.

"Martha kicked you out?"

"It's just for a little while. . . . Jim's found him a place with that girl. She said she wouldn't stay in a car with a kid anymore."

"Martha is afraid that Julie's gonna leave, isn't she?"

"I got that girl coming to pick me up soon," Fritze said.

Fritze locked himself in the back seat, and pushed the sun visors down in anticipation of at least a couple of hours sleep. He had gathered some dirty clothes as a pillow and stretched out beside an empty guitar case.

"You gonna be all right?" I asked.

"It's just for a little while," he said. "You gonna take that ride with the guy tomorrow?"

"I don't know. I might."

"Well, send me a card if you get somewhere."

"Where will I send it?"

"I don't know. Just send it here. . . . It'll get through somehow."

"I tell you what," I said. "If I get somewhere, I'll let you know somehow."

The hill from the motel to home was infinite, as the sun's growing presence forced me to see how tired I was. At the end of that infinite hill, the door to the apartment was locked, and Fritze wasn't around to open it.

I knocked and knocked and rang and rang. Finally I made my way through the apartment shrubbery to a bedroom window, spotted Martha sleeping, and knocked gently on the glass.

In one motion, Martha reached under her pillow, pulled out a revolver, and pointed it straight at me, as I saw my trip end before it had really begun.

II

INDIANA
OHIO
KENTUCKY
CHICAGO
DETROIT
Milwaukee
Indianapolis
Columbus
Cincinnati
Cleveland
Louisville
Lexington
Toledo
Dayton
Grand Rapids
Lansing
Ann Arbor
Flint
South Bend
Gary
Windsor
Evansville
Bowling Green
Owensboro
Frankfort
Springfield
Richmond
Muncie
Kokomo
Terre Haute
Bloomington
Kalamazoo
Battle Creek
Jackson
Fort Wayne
Lima
Mansfield
Akron
Huntington
Kingsport
Johnson City
MAMMOTH CAVE NAT'L PARK
CUMBERLAND MTS.

3

"YOU AIN'T GONNA GET AROUND THAT BEND..."

"You're doing something I always wanted to do. Out on the road with no place to go, no place to get to. I think that's even better than that guy from last night who was driving to California!"

I had decided to let that guy drive to the West without me. I decided to allow him his "freedom." It would have been an easy ride to take. Seventy-five dollars seemed the least costly way to continue after having stayed so long. It also seemed chicken.

In a compromise between never having to hitchhike again before the Pacific and having to thumb my way out of the city limits, I had latched onto at least two hundred miles of "north" that Ed and his two companions needed in order to get "northeast." Apparently five waking hours had been sufficient time at this destination. They had, in fact, *seen* their friends performing in the City of Music.

"You see people, caught up, just living their lives day in and day out. Not me. When I get up enough money, I'm heading out on the road like you. You won't catch me in that old nine-to-five all my life, no sir."

When I left, Julie and Martha had been talking about meeting with Martha's connection sometime in the future. Ed and company had stopped in to say good-bye to the friends they couldn't find, when I decided I could get packed in five minutes. Martha told the story about how she almost shot me that night, but only one of them laughed. I tried to get the group to stop by a particular '69 Pontiac on the way out, but they were looking at a fourteen-hour trip.

"We were all sitting around the bar a couple nights ago when I said, 'Hey, let's go visit our friends in Nashville!' and the first thing the next morning, we were on the road and heading south!"

Next to Ed, but far, far away, the two women had retreated into a photo album that offered pieces of a place they had been away from for nearly a day and a half: home.

"I like that one from New Year's," one whispered.

"I like it too."

Each had refused the ample space beside me to remain undivided against the hitchhiker type that rapes women on a road out of Nashville.

"They're just a long ways from home," I had told Fritze the night before, but how was he ever going to understand this now?

"That's just the kind of guy I am. I think you gotta go for it when you get the chance. That's how I want to live my life, not stuck in some nine-to-five. Travel, that's the key."

Ed's burly, workingman's build was struggling to possess his boyish face. The net result was somewhere around the age of nineteen. An oversized key-ring hung from his belt loop, suggesting factory or institutional doors that needed to be locked in somebody's nine-to-five.

"Just the best feeling: the open road and not a care in the world."

Ed continued like a voice-over to a commercial: "You've just been traveling the open road while avoiding any semblance of responsibility. Now it's time to head for the best tasting beer. . . . "

While on the other side of the window, I began to notice men alone and miles apart from one another, begging with one hand to go while their luggage remained quietly beside them.

Keeping slow time with closed guitar cases and duffle bags, they faced the many who were denying their single-handed request with a steadfast look that was absolutely and completely all they had to say.

They certainly didn't look as though they had the whole world before them. They looked as though they had been out there for a while. They tilted their heads at odd angles to keep the sporadic bursts of non-acknowledgment from shoving hair across their faces. They looked as though they'd been looking at the world that same way for months.

"I can't wait until I get the money. Once I get the money, I'm gone," Ed said.

"Look at Harold in that one," one of the girls whispered.

"Yeah, that's funny."

"Traveling is just the greatest thing in the world—just great!"

One of them just kept walking as if he had to. Occasionally, he would turn an unshaved face to offer that enduring look to all who passed.

"The only reason that I would ever want to be rich. . . . "

Another hitchhiker stood alone on the highway as we crossed the state line into Kentucky. Who would be picking him up, I wondered? What sort of things awaited him in America's passenger seat?

Eventually, the pages of the photo album had run out twice, and Ed couldn't find any more synonyms for "great" to describe the travel he had never done. Each of us was left to contemplate a landscape that changed at the rate of sixty miles per hour. I looked hard into the forests and fields, trying to make it all still for a moment.

Messages began to penetrate my reverie: billboards, neon, flashing lights—all having something to do with campgrounds, hotels, and restaurants around a place called Mammoth Cave.

Wasn't that one of the natural wonders of the world?

Then, through the silence rose a voice that could no longer be denied.

"Aren't you a-scared that somebody might beat you up or something like that?" one of the girls asked, while the other turned her neck completely to hear my response.

"Sure, you take your chances on the road—that's what it's all about."

Had I just said that?

"Has anything bad ever happened to you?" the other asked.

"Yeah, but you always get through it, you just gotta keep moving on."

Ed gazed heavily into his rear-view mirror: it was Miller time.

"What was the absolute worst thing that ever happened to you?"

"It's hard to say."

The sudden sound of tires over gravel and Ed's quick swerve to get us back onto the road ended my performance immediately. The disruption frightened the women away from their adventurous line of questioning, and the photo album was reopened. In another moment, I saw a sign that said "Next Exit for National Park."

"Could you pull over here?" I asked.

There was a gas station beside a place called Eats that would serve as my dropping-off point. The moment the car came to rest, Ed made a beeline for the office, and not much later he was carrying a key hung on a wooden stick in a calculated search for an opening along the side of the building.

The two girls giggled as they watched Ed struggle with the lock.

"What's so funny?" I asked.

"It's, well . . . it's . . . that's why we're going home now," one began, giggled, then stopped directly before giggling again.

"What do you mean?"

The two looked at each other as if they ought to be ashamed.

Finally the one continued, trying her hardest to be serious about something she thought was the funniest thing in the world.

"Well, you see Ed's got this problem," she began. "You see, he really wants to go to the bathroom, but. . . . "

The other one was biting the inside of her cheek.

" . . . Maybe he's nervous or something, but he can't do it—either way!"

Ed returned with a mollified look of anguish. The white metal door to the men's room had opened and closed, but apparently the only thing down the toilet was the status I had assumed just moments ago. Then Ed grabbed my hand and shook it exactly three times.

"You're doing something I've always wanted to do," he said, "and I admire you for it."

Ed looked as though he was genuinely moved, as they rode off toward a familiar toilet. Through the short hills of Kentucky he had come face to face with a man traveling the world and pissing at will—a step down the road from where he was, but still many miles from the steadfast, enduring look of the confirmed hitchhiker.

"The Eastern Bluebird is found from the Rockies to the Atlantic, and from Newfoundland to the Gulf of Mexico. It is one of several species of North American thrushes of the genus 'Sialia' and the family Turdidae, and is noted for its stunning . . . "

Restaurant placemats were made for hitchhikers who were just dropped off at a truckstop somewhere.

" . . . gentle and inoffensive in disposition, bluebirds are readily driven out by more aggressive species such as the house sparrow and . . . "

"Did you say 'water' with the roast beef?" the waitress asked.

"Yes," I said, "just water."

"Nests are lined with fine grass usually found in tree holes, but the birds can be attracted by special nesting boxes made from . . . "

There was a little roast beef in my sandwich of the same name; a little roast beef and a lot of gravy. The water tasted funny, somehow. Soon random streaks of brown were obscuring my "Bluebird Facts."

My pack slipped from its perch against the empty seat across from me. A dull thump resounded through the restaurant. All ten people there turned toward my bluebird article stained with gravy.

Several attempts to right this wrong led to the same "thump." Finally I just let the thing fall: "thump." The people in the restaurant looked satisfied.

"In many cultures as a symbol of fidelity, hope, and cheer . . . "

Anything else? No that's just fine, thank you. But have you seen any good movies lately and what's your favorite color?

Outside, the gentle Kentucky hills were pulling the day's scalding sun into their dark green fields and gently contoured hills. A thin cloud of humidity marked the transition and spread a hazy glaze over the land.

At the very edge of my sight, coming from the direction I was moving toward, I sensed a dark, vertical figure inching its way toward me. It looked like a moving stick, rounding the bend that I was yet to reach, moving ever so slowly.

Closer still, the stick had legs, arms, a face, and carried only a blanket; closer, then closer still. I watched with a strange fascination at the persistent way that the man barely continued moving—one step in front of the other, on and on.

The old black man's dirty shirt and pants were torn in so many places they hardly seemed like clothes anymore. His boots were entirely too small. The heels were worn hard at a forty-five-degree angle, while the outer side of each shoe had a hole from continuous contact with the ground.

His gaze was straight ahead, and his walk followed that gaze so completely that he seemed not to notice the pain his feet must have been enduring. It looked as if he would continue right past me without the slightest concern for my presence—as though there was nothing else in his life besides those steps—one in front of the other, on and on. Pop, scrruff; pop scrufff; pop scrrufff.

Then, as if remembering, he stopped.

"You ain't gonna get around that bend," he said. "Dere's cops round there tellin' everyone to just head on back. Dere's BEARS on da hill! They said it'd be best to just go on down to the truckstop, get a ride in the mornin'. You got a cigarette in dere?"

His most predominant feature was his eyes, stained with red and yellow cataract lines, and bulging from his face. Their complete domination of his boniness hinted that his build wanted to hold 250 pounds instead of just 80.

The cigarettes I had bought at the gas station in North Carolina were stale and crumpled, yet the man inhaled my offering with a sudden voracious consumption that contrasted severely with his steady, surviving demeanor. He finished the entire thing in about seven breaths.

"Know 'bout how far it is to Norff Keroline?" he asked.

"Couple days if you get good rides. But I think you're going the wrong way."

The cigarette completed, he began pop-scruffing away.

"Yeah, well you just might get a ride down there," he said without looking back. "You just keep a lookin'—you might just get one. . . ."

He continued an indistinguishable monologue that dripped into the impending night. Pop, scrruff; pop, scrufff; pop, scruff; one step ahead of the other, on and on; eventually disappearing into the hazy place where the sky met the land in the coming of night.

A motorcyclist came charging from the woods on a road I hadn't noticed. He was about to continue either right or left.

"Hey," I yelled with my arms, "are there any campgrounds or anything around here?" I screamed.

He took off his helmet.

"Whhatt?"

"I said, are there any campgrounds or anything around here?"

The "or anything" was in case there was a free hotel or open slumber party to match my seven-dollar-a-day budget. After Nashville, I had a little more than four hundred dollars left.

"Whhell, there's a campground back about a half a mile from where I just came from, but you don't want to go there."

"Why not?"

"There's snakes. Lots of 'em, especially this time of year."

"Ohh."

"But if you go down about a mile and a half on this road you're heading on, there's a big campground on the left. Can't miss it."

With that he popped his helmet back on, and buzzed off in the other direction, away from the snakes and the bears.

Unusual sounds emerged from the side of the road as the dusk camouflaged any movement the grass foretold. I walked in the center of the road holding a two-inch canister of chemical spray, ready to kill the first bit of uncertainty that lunged from a darkness that had come too soon. Around another bend, a fortress of black trees barely allowed a reassuring glow. The lights reflected some obscure message that signified commercial campground.

A heavyset, salt-and-pepper-haired woman circumstantially acknowledged my passing across her line of vision. She was wearing a hat that had many different types of plants on it, and her shirt bore that same, obscure message.

"Where's it you're hiking from?" she called.

I wanted to talk with her. I wanted to tell her a lot of things. But all I said was, "North Carolina."

"Wow, that's sure a long way to walk!"
I smiled and looked for the registration desk to give me a place.

The morning came in blue: bright, sunbaked, fluorescent blue, patched into quarter-inch, rip-stop squares, that magnified the late morning sun and held it ten inches away from my face in every direction.

Crusty brown pieces of goop clustered around my eyelids in a determined effort to keep me from exacting details. These remnants of my first altercation with the night air could not simply be rubbed out—they had to be picked out, with each wad taking three or four strands of eyelash along with it.

I strained to reach yesterday's blue jeans crumpled in the bottom of my sleeping bag, while the shirt of the same day lay balled up where my head had been. A thin layer of sweat growing thicker lubricated my every move within the extreme warmth of my goosedown sleeping bag: What had been comfortable at night had become excessive by day.

The man in 8-C took a moment from pumping something on his green Coleman stove to watch the blue cocoon next door collapse as its larva emerged. Behind him stood solid sheets of metal molded into something named "Airstream." The militaristic shape of "Airstream" was accented with a television antenna on its flank, wind chimes along the veranda, and a string of multi-fluorescent-colored lights, which by day were only plastic shells. It would have taken a major hurricane for his temporary residence to look the way mine did after a simple exit procedure.

When I returned his gaze, the man in 8-C immediately withdrew into the safety of camping procedures, and I quit trying to figure out exactly what he was doing to his stove as the glare from the Airstream was searing what was left of my eyelids.

In fact, there was a whole lot of glare coming from that general direction. Behind Mr. "8-C's" feeble attempt to blend in with the landscape, there stood another Airstream, then another, then another, then another.

It looked as though an Airstream convention was taking place to the west of the remains of a blue nylon pup-tent. I hadn't even had the opportunity to locate the zipper of my pants yet, and already I felt out of place.

Where was the bathroom?

As I escaped sheet-metal-alley, there suddenly appeared—between myself and one of the natural wonders of the world—a large, fake rhinoceros, colored pink. Next to it was a windmill, and then an alligator, and then a few more ceramic things that I was hesitant to identify so early in the morning.

What were these things doing on the morning of my great adventure across America?

Presenting obstacles for miniature golf.

Why?

The lifeguard wasn't on duty at the pool, yet.

Across from both, the souvenir shop nearby offered a million and a half mementoes of commercial campground, as well as jigsaw puzzles and basket-weaving kits to help their campers get through it all. In the gameroom next to that, Ms. Pac-Man was eating little dots.

Somehow I hadn't noticed all of these things upon my arrival. All that had mattered were the lights and the designated spot assigned to me — even at a cost of seven dollars a site.

What had been comfortable at night had grown excessive by day.

Not only that, but the excess was highly restricted. Beside the entrance to each of the outdoor recreational facilities were lists of regulations approximately the size of the New Testament.

At the pool: *Anyone caught running along the poolside will be asked to leave. Anyone caught with a lawn chair above their heads . . .*

And at the golf course: *Anyone caught trying to smash the ball through the windmill on hole number seven . . .*

I could pretty much accept the pool rules. There is a general assumption lurking within anyone who has ever been to a community pool or YMCA camp, that given the chance, ordinarily sane and healthy-spirited people, when brought within striking distance of a 35- by 50-foot cement tub of water, will suddenly lose that particular line of inhibitions that keeps them from walking in front of traffic and will immediately begin jumping on the heads and necks of other swimmers while poking each others eyes out with lawn chairs — had the rules not been there to advise them otherwise.

I did, however, have a problem with the rules restricting the actions of people tapping little balls over fake grass. Try as I might, I just couldn't fathom the hazards of miniature golf.

But when I saw an equally impressive list of standards for suitable behavior in the bathroom, it all made sense to me: obviously, this place often housed field trips from the state penitentiary. Civilized people wouldn't require such direction, and they certainly wouldn't tolerate its insinuations while on vacation. Would they?

At night, I had been afraid, and by day I was being told not to leave papers in the urinals. I felt like a moth who had been banging against a window toward the light in a small, small room, when behind him, the whole world was waiting for him to get used to the dark.

That same woman I remembered from the night before was sitting in the same spot she had been, wearing a different hat that was as excessive in its portrayal of bird species. That day's T-shirt possessed the same campground insignia in a somewhat different design. She was surrounded by similar-looking ladies who were all making baskets.

Once again, I had crossed her vision.

"I bet you're hungry this morning."

I hadn't had time to think about that yet, but it sounded all right in theory.

"You've got about ten minutes to rush over and get the 'all you can eat' pancake breakfast for only three dollars. It started at eight, but we keep it open till 10:30 just for you late risers."

She thought that was very funny. Some of the sleep must have been lingering in my eyes. I counted six different bird types pictured on one side of her hat.

"He's hiked all the way from North Carolina to come to our campground," she announced to all those making dried-flower vases.

I realized then that she was the proprietor of the establishment, and also that she had an accent that was unmistakably New Jersey.

"Just like that boy who wrote the book, he is walking . . . "

"Hitchhiking," I interrupted.

"Hitchhiking?"

They all stopped making baskets.

The proprietor looked as though she was going to accuse me of stuffing a Sears catalog into the urinal.

"You might make it in time. If you hurry, there might be something left for you. It's right down the hill."

She turned in search of conversation with her companions, who tried to find something to talk about with her, and certainly nobody was going to be talking to me anymore.

Hitchhiker Rule Number 2: Don't mess up people's basket-making sessions for a lousy clarification.

Hitchhiker Rule Number 2½: If a woman displaying half the nation's flora and fauna on her head misinterprets your existence, there's probably a good reason for it.

Behind the grill, a large black male wearing a small chef's hat gave my approach a look that almost sent me far, far away from what had been a pancake buffet. If not for the feigned hospitality of some tall guy who was sweeping the floor, I would have gone back to my tent and eliminated the space a can of tuna fish was taking in my pack.

"Well, you made it just in time," he said glancing at his watch to make sure there weren't any rules being broken one way or the other. "Glad to have ya."

The chef glared at me and poured three piles of pancake batter onto the hot grill: TKkisssss TKkisssss TKkisssss.

The guy with the broom was wearing yet another manifestation of the official insignia, something to the tune of "It's Always More Fun at. . . ." He set my place with a paper plate, plastic knife, and plastic fork. He took my three dollars and poured orange juice into a bathroom-sized Dixie Cup, then handed me two plastic pouches of syrup and a tiny round plastic tub of butter.

Within a few minutes he had placed three hot pancakes onto my paper receptacle — directly in the center of the plate, one right on top of the other.

"Will that be good enough for ya? If you want any more, just go ahead and call. We can fry them right up for you, just go ahead and call."

The chef rolled his eyes then stood watching.

"I think this'll be fine," I said.

The chef's hat lay crumpled on the floor where its former owner had thrown it in his haste to exit.

Batter oozed from the center of pancakes that could have used at least five more minutes of heat.

"So where are you from?" the guy asked as he swept up all around me.

"North Carolina."

"North Carolina! I used to work at a Baptist summer camp in North Carolina! Pretty state, pretty as a state could be. You know what they say, 'Nothin' could be finer.'"

He thought that was pretty funny, too.

"Well, what brings you out here? Bet it's to see the caves, isn't it?"

"Actually, I'm hitchhiking around the country and I just happened to stop here."

He stopped sweeping.

"Did you say hitchhiking?"

Packed up, and heading out with a capital O, I was stopped by a man who had a "Manager" patch pinned to his baseball cap.

"Why bother driving all the way to those caves when we've got our own caves right here? Tour starts at two o'clock."

I wanted out.

"I'm not driving, I'm hitchhiking."

His hair bristled from under his designated insignia cap.

"Oh, I see."

One, two, then three hours worth of sweat dripped off my face and took a moment on the ground before becoming a part of the ninety-degree, ninety-five-percent humidity that was trying to evaporate me. All the while, the people on their way to a national park not only passed, but when able, crossed the double yellow line in unmitigated avoidance.

With many different colors of license plates stuck to many models of vehicles, they all managed to have recreational equipment heaped high enough in their back seats to block any thought that might have come by way of their rear-view mirrors.

Perhaps they would have been more open to a roadside adventure had they been closer to home and without an agenda. But on the road to a national park, they were America on vacation, and they wanted only to see what they had planned on seeing.

The "genus superiorus" of these vacational bypassers was big enough to receive twenty of me without straining. Its inevitable passage buried me in a fit of artificial wind greater in magnitude than that mustered by even the largest Cadillac going fifteen miles per hour over the speed limit.

It had motion on the roadway like a vehicle, but its enormity suggested that it could not be. It was like a whale whose place of motion suggests "fish," while its sheer size claims "mammal." Its definition straddles the supposed contradictions between "travel" and "stability," "vehicle" and "home."

Though possessing similar nomadic migratory tendencies, "Winnebago" is a sworn enemy of the hitchhiker. The larger, more prolific species is found in particular abundance on the road to a national campground, whereas the endangered species of hitchhiker is particularly susceptible to long and unforseen periods of nesting along these same byways.

Site 26-A was the continuation of a bad chapter. Amidst the strings of multicolored porch lights, I felt out of place without possessing anything named Coleman. I sat at my designated bench to read the pamphlet given to me at the gate, while a television blared from 27-A.

How did I get here? Someone must have dropped me off again.

A ranger was going to be giving a talk at 7:30 that night on the etymology of the Kentucky word for fishes—or something like that. Then at nine, there was going to be a slide show about the park—this park.

I figured I'd build a fire if only to prove to myself that I really was in the great outdoors and not a Disney World replica. As I stalked the wilderness behind 26-A, however, I noticed that all the wood had green leaves at the ends of the branches.

"You looking for wood?" the man in 27-A called out.

It must have been a commercial.

"Well, you won't find any back there. You've got to go to the store and buy it. That's what we did. That's the only way you can get any out here."

Now I knew there were two places in the world where you had to buy firewood: Mammoth Cave and Manhattan. And so, with dollar in hand, I began my search for a good deal on kindling.

Behind the campsites, on the path that led to the general store, I came upon a man and his son crouched behind a bush.

"Shhh," the boy pointed into the woods: "There's a deer!"

Sure enough, not fifteen feet from where we stood, a doe fed on some low brush without the least bit of concern over humans' being so close.

The father left a hand on his son's shoulder and bent down far beyond comfort to leave quiet words under the rim of the boy's baseball cap. The father pointed out markings on this unexpected phenomenon, and whispered other points of interest into the boy's wide-eyed wonder.

Seeing the two of them together like that left me with an empty feeling; a cavity carved deep from the love of a family I was traveling away from, while leaving in its void the distant image of a young son I might know so many, many miles from there.

I was in between things, somewhere at a national park in Kentucky. My life was without context. I was past school and before a job. There was no kitchen table I would be missing from that night.

"Deer don't eat other animals," the father whispered to his son, "they just eat plants, roots, and berries."

The boy stood without moving, without breathing, staring at the animal so close. When it had had its fill, the animal gave a look in our direction and abruptly bounded deeper into the forest. The boy then turned to his father who was waiting with the smile of a shared experience.

"That sure was a sight," I called across. "I don't think I've ever seen one that close."

They turned toward the stranger who they had forgotten was there. The boy stood in front of his father in the same way he had viewed the last unexpected event.

"We saw a couple by the laundry the other day," the father said, "but they weren't that close."

He looked to the boy to finish the description.

"One was a buck, and the other two were does," he said.

The father was a strong man who possessed a gentle character. He had seemed genuinely excited about the deer the two had seen together—if only for the wonder it caused in his son's eyes.

We talked and talked, because I wouldn't stop. From wildlife in the park, to their home in Gary, Indiana, to Big Ten basketball, I would not let the conversation end.

"Have you ever seen *The Music Man?*"

When the father mentioned that his family would be leaving for home in two days, the most fascinating dimension of my chosen mode of travel became apparent: I was a hitchhiker—capable of falling into people's lives for as long as they needed a highway to get somewhere. Just a little extra room in their back seat could save me from having to hear the ranger's talk on the etymology of the Kentucky word for French fries—or something like that. They could give me a place to go for a while.

The trick was in letting them know how I needed a ride without seeming too forward. You've got to let people know your needs without sounding pushy. You've got to make it their idea. That was Hitchhiker Rule Number 3.

"Well, I don't have any way of getting out of here," I began.

"What do you mean?"

"I'm hitchhiking, I depend on people to give me rides."

"You're hitchhiking by yourself?"

"Uh-huh."

"Where are you hitchhiking from?"

"North Carolina—I just graduated from college there."

"Oh."

"I used to be in Boy Scouts too."

"Where is it you want to go?"

"Just anywhere, really. I was thinking I might want to go north after this—somewhere in the Midwest, maybe see some of the factories up there along the lakes."

There was a pause. I continued, "Guess there's a lot of factories in Gary, aren't there?"

I sat listening intently to the ranger talk about the etymology of the Kentucky words for fried fish—or something like that—hoping to at least get caught up.

"Now the reason this word comes from . . . "

There wasn't any room in the car, and after the refusal I didn't feel like asking any more, even with my thumb. I tried to concentrate on what the ranger had to say.

"And you know, the thing that's really unusual about this word here is that . . . "

In between college and life; in between Tennessee and Missouri; in between Ed and a steadfast look; in between a designated campsite and the side of the road; in between knowing and believing.

"Some people just don't even think that could be a word. . . . "

Something else: nobody had asked what my name was during any of these rides. Nobody wanted to know the name of a hitchhiker. Not one single person could go home to his wife/husband/family/friends and tell them who they had met that day on the road—except that he was a hitchhiker.

"Well, that's our program for tonight, folks. We hope you've . . ."

There are lonelinesses that know themselves. They cry out for someone they have lost or for someplace that they cannot be. They have an object. They have substance that can be defined. Then there are moments between places that have no clarity. They simply sneak in a chill that doesn't even sting—it just numbs.

Back at 26-A, there was a large American automobile with New York tags. An unexpected development. There wasn't anybody in the car, but the possibilities were enough to lift that fog in which I had somehow become enshrouded.

I stood alone for a few moments, unsure of what to do. Afraid, in a way, to find out that these people were only looking for the occupants of the next campsite.

A set of flashlights eventually found me up against their car. I could not see any faces as the lights got brighter, then metamorphosed into two men and a woman. One of the men was smoking a cigar. He was wearing wire-framed glasses and had not shaved recently. He was the spokesman.

"Excuse me, sir, but perhaps you can tell us where it is that we can find a place for this night?"

I recognized the accent accompanying his broken English. It was foreign and foreign was the type of far off and distant thing I needed. But it was a foreign that I recognized, as well—it was the foreign of my ancestry.

"Yes—*parli italiano?*"

I guess I'm Italian. When people ask, "What kind of name is that?" I always say, "It's Italian." My grandfather would have said, "It's American," because his father couldn't speak English. My father, who was the first to graduate from an American university, would also say, "It's American." They all worked hard proving it was an American name so I could spend a semester studying in Italy, and learn to say "It's Italian" in Italian. I was the first generation afforded the luxury of being American enough to be Italian again, and I was about to exercise that luxury in the midst of a Kentucky campground that offered no place else to go.

Their English did not extend far enough to understand the "No Vacancy" sign at the entrance to the campground.

"Perhaps you can show us where there is a place to stay?" they reiterated. "We have only one small tent, but without a place to put it."

"*Mio cognome e' DeTitta,*" I said.

"Oh, then you are Italian?"

"*Si, mio sangue e' italiano.*" (My blood is Italian. I said this pointing to a vein in my arm.)

"That is good. We are Italian too."

They kept speaking English.

"Perhaps you know where it is we can stay?"

"Si, . . . I have only one small tent too. E possibly per . . . you to spend la night here."

"Ahh, thank you very much; that is very kind—*grazie tanto!*"

"Sure—non 'e un problem."

The guy with the glasses was named Mario. The other two were Luciano and Maria, a couple, of sorts, but more traveling companions than anything else. They exuded a kind of carefree recklessness that was balanced by the more traditional outlook of Mario, who had left his wife and children back in Italy because he believed that traveling across America was something a man did without his family.

With his tent up and sleeping bag spread, Mario sat out on the picnic bench with me as we waited in silence for the other two to set up their tent. We couldn't help but hear the giggles emanating from their effort; we couldn't help but speculate as to what was taking them so long. We didn't really say anything as all this was happening. Maria was certainly a nice-enough looking woman.

When the two finally emerged, Mario broke out three monster Italian cigars. Before I had time to light mine, Luciano had asserted that religion is a crutch used by people who cannot enjoy life.

I remembered that Italians—perhaps Europeans in general—love to discuss life in a big way. There is no such thing as impolite conversation, only that which is trivial.

"There are two types of people in the world," Luciano continued, "those who worry about what happens after death, and those who live."

Mario did not wait for his friend to further explain before shooting out a cigar-soaked tirade in a rapid-fire Italian that was about 150-words-per-minute beyond my ability to understand. Luciano turned his head upon the first word, understanding the unintelligible only because he knew what was coming. His girlfriend rubbed up against him, sensing by the sheer magnitude of Mario's voice that we were having fun.

"My friend is the rear-end of a horse," Mario explained to me after catching his breath. "Two years ago, he was a devout Catholic, as I am now. But since he is divorced, he thinks the whole universe has changed. I also know that when he doesn't have a girlfriend, he goes to church."

It is not uncommon for the world perspective of an Italian male to take shape in terms of its proximity to the nearest set of breasts. If

Luciano's girl left him on Thursday, on Sunday he'd be in church gawking at the Madonna.

At the same time, Mario, who was about six thousand miles away from sex, was finding some sort of release in the force through which he was carrying the banner of the Catholic Church.

"You should enjoy what you are given," Luciano said.

"You should try and go beyond that," Mario countered.

When the smoke settled back into the cigars, the perspective also began to settle from the universe and back to earth. Still, the talk never got any smaller than a nation-state.

"Tell me, Tomas, what is America?" Luciano wanted to know.

"Yes, Tomas," his girlfriend could only echo. "What is America?"

Before I could catch myself, I made the mistake of answering their question with a question that had about twenty more centuries of history behind it: "Well, what is Italy?"

As I had known from a hundred train rides in the country of Michelangelo, the answer would consist of a guided tour of the Uffizi, then the Vatican, and all the way through to the artistic wonder of Giovanni Pisano's "Massacre of the Innocents," sculpted into the marble pulpit of the Siena Cathedral.

This historic holier-than-thou had me feeling less a part of my blood-line and more a part of my birth certificate. In between the Holy Roman Empire and the Renaissance, I wanted to have a good answer ready when the history of Western Civilization circled back to the present and the question:

"But, Tomas, what is America?"

My first reactions brought me onto the set of a John Wayne movie as the Duke stormed beachhead en route to liberating these Nazi-enslaved European elitists. If this was the first thought to come to my mind, then I clearly understood why our foreign policy toward our NATO allies was such a mess some forty years later.

"Opportunity," I managed. "There's the chance to do a lot of things."

They didn't seem to put much credence in this, and I guess neither did I. They wanted names.

"Is America Ronald Reagan?" Mario asked.

"Is America Swoosh?" the girl asked.

"Swoosh?"

Nike sneakers.

"I think America is Marilyn Monroe," Luciano countered.

"Fred Astaire and Ginger Rogers!" the girl cried out. " 'They Can't Take That Away!' "

"Hollywood!"

"Tell me, Tomas," Mario seemed serious. "How does a person become a movie star in America?"

I thought that most acting careers began on a college stage or in some local theater, where experience was gathered before making the big step to Hollywood. When translated for Maria's sudden curiosity, this became:

"Prima, il teatrale; secundo, Hollywood . . . "

(First the theater; then Hollywood)

"E' dopo, la Casa Bianca," Mario chimed in.

(Then the White House.)

"Bedtime for Bonzo!"

This would've been funnier a few minutes earlier. It would have been hilarious if I had said it.

But as the stars were getting brighter than the fire, and the cigars had reached their watermark, in another moment nobody cared about any of it anymore. All that really mattered was sleep.

"Good afternoon, ladies and gentlemen, and welcome to Mammoth Cave National Park. My name is Ed and I will be your tour guide for this three-and-one-half-hour, three-mile Echo River Boat Tour of the Mammoth Cave system."

Ed was a short man covered from head to toe in the official uniform of America's great outdoors. He was standing a particular distance from the mouth of the cave we were about to enter, addressing the tour group of forty people.

As he spoke, a tall man dressed in the same uniform led another group of forty out of the same cave. They were all wearing orange life preservers.

"Before we begin the tour, there are a few things I'd like to say. First of all, for this tour, you should have purchased a blue ticket that says: "1 P.M. Echo River Tour . . . ."

"If you do not have a blue ticket, but feel that you should be on the 1 P.M. Echo River Tour, please return to the entrance pavilion immediately, and ask the park service representative at the information booth for assistance."

Everybody took a good long look at their ticket in a sudden recognition of potential idiocy. The park service man waited in vain for someone to admit misplacement, then continued his assault.

"The tour we are about to take consists of a moderately strenuous 2.5-mile hike through very rugged and damp terrain. There are several sections in which you will be asked to squeeze through narrow openings in the rock. There will also be a section where you will be asked to climb a series of steep and very narrow steps. If you feel as though you will have a problem with any of these things, please return with your blue ticket to the entrance pavilion at the end of the concrete walkway, and a park service representative will gladly refund the full amount of your purchase."

A subdued mumble broke out in several places, resulting finally in three boat-tour flunkies: One overweight middle-aged woman kissed each of the six children that she could not convince to return to safety; a man with a cane in his hand (what was he doing there in the first place?); and a young woman who looked as though she had put in fifteen years in the dead-letter room.

Little did they know that the "strenuous" hike we were to embark on in plain English translated to "easiest," when one considered that the other hikes were rated "very strenuous," and "extremely strenuous." But nobody was taking any chances at a national park.

"I will be your guide on this trip, and Martha here to my right will be my assistant."

He pointed to a tall, stocky woman with long brown hair that had no character. She smiled. She was wearing the exact same uniform that her male cohort was.

"Now there are a few rules I'd like to outline before we begin.

"We ask that you not use a tripod or touch any of the rock formations while on this tour. We ask that you not make any loud noises or disturbing motions while on the tour. Please stay with the group at all times, and smoking is prohibited.

"As you all know, we will be taking an underground water journey toward the end of our trip through the caves. I am going to ask Martha now to distribute to each of you a life jacket which we ask that you wear for the entirety of our underground water journey. If anybody has any questions, please feel free to ask either Martha or myself by raising your hand now."

Both my hands were holding a life jacket.

There is no comfortable way to carry a life jacket. The thing is too fat in too many pieces to bundle or hold all together. The long straps that culminate in metal buckles bang against legs and arms that just cannot handle its excess. I had never had to carry a life jacket before: there was no method I could fall back on.

From what I had learned at the information booth, the "underground river" was more like a submerged puddle—a few feet deep and without any real current.

"*Ma, perche devo usare questi?*" Luciano asked Mario, pointing to the orange mass in disgust.

"*No lo so. E' possible c'e' un mare qui vincino?*" (I don't know. Perhaps there is an ocean near here?)

I felt embarrassed at my country's excess. We often live hard by rules and systems as if we didn't trust our humanity. The ramifications of this truth scared me. Which of these people carrying life preservers was going to stop for an unknown person on the side of the road? Perhaps I would remain in Mammoth Cave forever.

The group moved some exact distance inward. The tour had begun.

"Legend says that a man named Houchens stumbled upon the entrance to the caves while chasing a bear he wounded hunting. The section that we are currently in is called the Rotunda because of its massive size and circular shape. From this width, the caves will become progressively narrower until a width of three to five feet is reached toward the underground river we will be traveling on. We ask that you stay with the group at all times, and smoking is strictly prohibited."

The caves were long, dark, wide spaces of cold, hard rock. I already knew that they would get progressively narrower to the point that we would have to squeeze through a very narrow section in the rock. I also knew that there would be a section where we would be asked to climb a series of steep and very narrow steps toward an underground river we would have to venture on. The potential discoveries had been foretold.

Still, there was an unexpected cool temperature beneath the hot Kentucky day that set my mind wandering in a northern direction, far, far away from the heat I had been baking in the day before. It would be cooler in a place like Chicago, I thought, or maybe some other place near the Great Lakes.

The sudden termination of our group's progression into the caves caused me to take note.

"The caves reach a total of 310 miles through the Mammoth–Flint Cave System. They were formed by subterranean water dissolving the porous limestone rock, and then receding to leave dry passageways. The temperature here is . . . "

I tried to imagine Houchens looking for a wounded bear and discovering Mammoth Cave. Like the open door of an unknown vehicle, or the friendly clasp of a stranger's hand: the distant radio station that fades in and out of the night.

"When a light is shone from the other side of this passageway, the rock before you is said to look like a colonial woman, hence the name, 'Martha Washington.' The section we will be passing through next is called 'Dante's Gateway,' for the famous Italian. . . . "

The tour continued: stop, go, explain, and define. There were no new discoveries to be had on this guided tour through the caves, until about halfway through, we rounded a bend, and I heard Luciano laugh to Mario: *"Ecco America."*

The one unexpected thing I saw then was not a wonderful stalactite formation, or even a rock that looked like a president's wife. But instead—probably placed exactly 1.25 miles into this 2.5-mile jaunt, there were two signs nailed to the fragile rock formation that we had been forbidden to touch: the signs read "MEN" and "WOMEN."

Mario's translation? "This is America."

"You are welcomed to come with us for the rest of our journey, Tomas. First we will go south and then north again to New York. Perhaps you can show us some things that we don't know otherwise?"

For all the Winnebago fumes I'd suck up to use a bathroom inside a natural wonder, it was too soon to abandon my whole intent. I had a feeling my first few landings were the exception instead of the rule. The cold inside the cave had inspired me, and now, for some reason, I was desperately curious about what it would look like over the top of Lake Superior.

"Well, then perhaps we will see you again in our country. Here is a piece of paper with our names. Please let us return the favor you have done for us one day. We wish you luck."

"Si grazie molto, Tomas, e buona fortuna con tuo viaggio," Luciano said.

"Grazie, grazie tanto," I replied.

4

"We Found If We Squeezed Everything Over . . ."

I lingered unusually long in the discomfort of my own sweat that morning, fearing the ramifications of "hitchhiker" in a world that brought television sets into the great outdoors.

All roads led from a national campground.

As I struggled to reclaim my tent stakes from a stubborn ground packed hard from overuse, I noticed two other sets of eyes focused on the transfiguration of 26-A. One belonged to the boy who had been watching the deer the other day, and the other belonged to what seemed to be an older brother.

I waved to the two of them. They waved back.

This happened again and again, until they had walked back and forth between 25-A and 27-A more times than I cared to acknowledge. I thought it was pretty big of me to wave the first few times, considering the fact that thanks to their father's lack of space or lack of whatever, I would probably be spending the rest of my life buying firewood.

Eventually, the two lost interest, and the tent poles found their place on the other side of a zipper. There was nothing left but some peanuts, which I ate one at a time, until there was nothing left but to leave.

Hitchhiker Rule Number 4: It is difficult to get beyond a place that is designated for your use—even a place that you don't like. Nothing is harder to transcend than the immediate uncertainty you face on the way to someplace better.

A Plymouth station wagon heavy with "pop-up" trailer blocked my reestablishment with the infinite stretch of blacktop that began in a camping loop. As I waited for the car to pass, it slowed, then stopped, and finally rolled down a window. It was the family that had had no room: "We found that if we squeezed everything onto the floor of the trailer we could fit one more passenger," the father said. "Need a lift?"

There are things you notice as a hitchhiker. Like seating arrangements, for example.

In the front seat were the father and mother. At the moment, the father was driving and the mother was maintaining order, but the situation could reverse itself at the next rest area. Spots one and two were interchangeable. One held the wheel, the other held the bag of snacks and drinks. One drove, the other read the map. That was where it all began.

In a secure place between the two sat the most recent manifestation of their togetherness. Barely old enough to go to school, she was alert, attentive, and basking in big brown eyes. She liked the feeling of her mother's arm when she was sleepy, and took a great interest in her mother's sporadic searches in the food bag, even when the quest wasn't for her benefit.

Next in this chain of position was the deer watcher. He was somewhere in the middle of elementary school, waiting for the next stop to come but fascinated with the in-between. He wouldn't mind being amid the action of the front seat, but not at the cost of being unable to watch each and every move of the new person beside him. He wanted everyone to be within earshot, for he saw everything and kept it on the tip of his tongue.

Far in the back of the station wagon, flung out over the recreational equipment that wouldn't fit in the trailer and sitting in absolute discord with himself was the oldest member, beginning the road through adolescence. His place apart from the action of the rest allowed his awkwardness to proceed incognito. His was the private space behind the forward gaze where there were no hassles — apart from everyone and everything.

He was not bothered by the fact that there were really no places to sit on the hard metal surface, because he seemed committed to maintaining the most awkward positions imaginable for long periods of time. In fact, he seemed altogether opposed to the idea of being comfortable.

Bryan would feel like someone was going to find a pimple on his neck if he sat anywhere other than in the far back seat. His brother, Tim, couldn't stand to be that far removed from the Fritos, nor could he stand the possibility that he might miss something going on behind him. Teresa in the front couldn't be anywhere away from a gentle tap and quiet request, and the whole thing began with Mr. and Mrs. Harding in the two front seats.

You notice certain things when you spend a little time alone on the side of the road. There grows a certain fascination with that which may have once seemed mundane.

Once we had established our place among the convoy of north-bound Interstate traffic, Tim knew that I wasn't going to steal his baseball cap, and so he began to unleash what he could no longer hold inside.

"I play baseball," he began. "I'm on the Dodgers."

"Really?"

"Yeah, we won six games."

"That's pretty good."

"We lost eight."

"Well, that's still not too bad."

"You know about the ones we won?"

"No."

"Well, in the first game, we really shouldn't have won. We really lost it twenty-five to nothing the first time, but that didn't count because it started raining real bad before we could get up to bat. So we played it again and this time Randy Pinski played second base and we won three to two. I didn't get any hits that game because I was only up twice and the ump made a bad call two times when it wasn't even a strike. Do you want to hear about the second game we won?"

"Well, OK."

"We let Scott Holman bat first, and he's so short that nobody ever can pitch it to him, so he always gets to go to first base without even swinging the bat. Anyway, he got on first four times, but we were still losing seven to nothing because everybody else struck out. Then, our coach called a time-out, and had the umpire check the bat, and we won because they had sprayed some sticky stuff on it that you aren't sup-posed to use called . . . Dad, what's that stuff called that makes the bat all sticky when it isn't supposed to be?"

"Pine tar."

"Yeah, that's it, they sprayed pine tar all over the bat and the umpire said that we won, just like he did in the third game when only seven people from the Yankees showed up and you've got to have at least eight, but you should have nine like you're supposed to, but you can play with only eight, but they only had seven, so we won. One of their other guys showed up, but it was too late and we won. The other team had enough players in the fourth game, but one of them was too old, and . . ."

A few concerned looks popped into the rear-view mirror. It didn't matter, though; I was content to feel the motion beneath me. That was communicated somehow, and so Mr. Harding's gaze rested upon the highway before him, as he kept the straightest, steadiest fifty-five you could imagine.

Tim was up to the fifth inning of game ten, his sister had found a soft place on her mother's arm, and his brother had found an altogether new way to lay across metal, when suddenly it all went "kaflooey" with the squeal of a tire.

Mr. Harding strained to regain a steady direction after one of the tires had blown out. Slowly, patiently, he eased the vehicle down to fifty, then forty, pulling out the handle for the emergency blinkers and signaling with his arm for a long, gradual turn onto the side of the road.

Within a few moments, we were beside a cornfield staring at an extremely flat tire.

Hitchhiker Rule Number 5: You just never know. Even in the security of an Indiana family going the steadiest fifty-five you could imagine—you just never do.

"OK, Bryan, you go in the back and get my tool kit, you know where it is, and Tim, get the flares from the trailer. Teresa, stay close to your mother. Tom, you can help me change the tire."

Mr. Harding wrenched the bolts loose—one by one—with several hard twists from his muscular arms. When he was through with the last one, he asked me to crank up the jack.

Soon I was holding all four bolts and helping to place the spare onto its hold. I rolled the old tire toward the rear of the car while Mr. Harding finished off the last few turns.

Bryan ran over to open the door, and together, we placed the busted tire into the holder beside his domain.

With hands smeared with grease, I felt as though the only spot in the car for a hitchhiker was beside Tim, in front of Bryan, directly behind Teresa, and at an equal diagonal to the Mister and Mrs. in the front seat.

"Have you had any dangerous rides yet?" Mrs. Harding wanted to know.

"Nothing so far, but I haven't been at it that long."

"You hear so many terrible stories about hitchhikers these days. I thought it wasn't a safe thing to do anymore."

"I know, I've heard those same things. So far it's been all right, though."

"Do you call your parents a lot and tell them where you are?"

"I write, I called them when I got to Nashville. That was a big step, getting to that first place."

"When did you tell your mother that you were going to do this?"

"I'm not sure."

"Did she try and talk you out of it?"

"I don't think so."

"And you say she was the one who dropped you off on the side of the road?"

"Yeah, I guess once she knew I was definitely going to go through with it, she wanted to be my first ride."

Mrs. Harding took a hard look at her sons, who were still about a hundred tough situations from the one I was presenting.

"I think that was a very courageous thing for her to do."

"Yeah, it was."

"Mom, how long until we're going to eat?" Tim called out.

"I saw a sign for a Wendy's this exit. Why don't we stop there?" Mr. Harding asked.

"It's getting to be about noon."

"Did you ever see the movie *Dressed to Kill?*" Tim wanted to know the moment I sat down with my lunch.

"Is that the one with Angie Dickinson?"

"The lady with white hair."

"No, but I've always wanted to see that one."

"Did you see the ending?"

"Huh?"

"The ending is real scary."

"Well, don't tell me about it because I might want to see it one day."

Tim did not know what to do next. He began to eat a French fry and I watched his mouth with amazement as it became engaged in the first nonspeaking exercise I'd ever seen it perform.

Still, the show was brief.

"The guy who the lady thinks is the doctor tries to kill her, but the son saves her at the end."

"Tim, you better start eating. We're not waiting for you this time," his father said.

"OK, I'm going."

In the parking lot after the meal, Mr. Harding opened the back door and leaned over the seat while the rest of us waited. He emerged with a small leather case and locked the door behind him.

"Oh, no, Dad, no more pictures," Bryan wailed.

"We're just going to take one of the whole group of us together."

"No way, Dad, there's no way I'm getting in this one."

Adolescence despises permanent reminders of itself. There is a hormonal reaction to Kodachrome involved; this was the most I'd ever seen Bryan say or do.

"Bryan, just this one last picture and you won't have anything to complain about until next year," Mrs. Harding assured him.

Tim had already wiggled his way next to me and was looking in the direction of the camera.

"OK, now everybody squeeze in tight and look this way—Bryan, that means you, too!"

"OK, OK!"

Snap.

"Now everybody stand still, I want your mother to take one more."

"Oh, come on, Dad, you said we were only gonna take one!"

"Bryan, this won't kill you."

"It's not fair, Dad, you just said one more."

"Bryan, stop complaining and look this way," Mrs. Harding said.

"OK, but I'm not going to smile . . . "

Snap.

There was nothing particularly photogenic about a Wendy's parking lot somewhere in the state of Indiana. It was just a place to hold, and to frame forever, something that happened unexpectedly on the way back to Gary. Like the deer on the path behind the general store, or the rainbow you find when you were only expecting rain—the distant radio station that fades in out of the night—whose place on a screen would inspire its own unique brand of conversation for years to come.

"OK, everybody into the car."

"Jeez, Dad, I hate it when you do that."

The white lettering on green signs said Chicago 75; then Chicago 60; Chicago 45; Gary 30.

"Mom, how long till we get home?" Tim asked.

"Soon, Dear, less than an hour."

The Indiana cornfields just absolutely continued all around us for mile upon mile. The nearby stalks passed too quickly to discern detail, leaving my gaze far into the distance, away from the distraction of movement.

"There are two things I learned from hitchhiking," Mr. Harding began, "bright clothes and a sign, those are the two best friends a hitchhiker has."

"You used to hitchhike?" I asked.

"A long, long time ago, before I had anything to keep me anywhere."

A glance between husband and wife dissipated in the security of twenty years of marriage.

"When school ended, a friend and I decided to see if there really was anything past Wisconsin. We had about ten dollars each, but that seemed like all we could ever need. We hadn't learned to worry about things yet.

"I'll never forget that ride we got the first night. We had started out late in the afternoon and managed to get a few short rides that only got us to where we couldn't call our parents anymore. When it started getting dark, we started getting scared."

"A pickup truck finally stopped, and we jumped in the cab and had shut the door behind us before we could smell the whiskey on the driver's breath.

"He drove like a madman for about a hundred miles across Minnesota. The two of us were so scared we didn't say a word. Finally he pulled over and told one of us to drive so he could go to sleep in the back.

"We took turns driving and keeping each other awake, while he snored right through all our stops for gas. The sunrise woke him at a place called Spearfish, South Dakota. We stopped at a little diner and watched him drink ten cups of coffee and eat a piece of toast. Then he left, said he had to meet somebody in Montana, and there we were at dawn in Spearfish, South Dakota, with about two dollars each after gas and breakfast.

"We found a spot in a field outside of town and fell asleep until the afternoon sun got the best of us. We managed to find a job that night washing dishes at a hotel in town. They gave us room and board for our trouble, and that was all we needed for about three months.

"I'll never forget that trip. It was a special place, a special time."

Far, far off into the cornfields, away from the distraction of motion, it seemed as though nothing moved at all. It seemed as though everything would stay the same out there forever.

"Dad, do we have to clean the porch when we get home?"

"I'm hungry, Mom. How long till we get there?"

"I call I get the bathroom before Bryan."

I sensed a transition. Try as I might to ignore it, the sign outside the window said "Gary 15."

"Tom, I think the best place to drop you off is up ahead where 65 meets 94. You can go west to Chicago or keep going north to Michigan. That's right near where we get off."

I wasn't going to have to stand outside, again, was I?

But the car gradually worked its way to the shoulder. It stopped and no one moved. They were waiting for me to leave and I didn't want to.

"Why don't you give me your address so I can write to you?" I asked.

Six lanes of traffic were passing at high speeds to our left. Mrs.

Harding quickly ripped a piece of paper out of her pocketbook and scribbled three lines across it. In a moment it was in my hand.

"Well, thanks for everything," I said. "I hope to see you all again sometime."

Were they really going to just up and leave me there?

"It was a really fun ride. . . . "

A cool stiff Great-Lakes breeze exploding in my face reminded me that I was someplace new and different, with lots of new and different people who weren't sweating as badly. It would only be a matter of time before I'd be running toward a set of brakelights to start the whole thing all over again.

Hitchhiker Rule Number 6: No matter how comfortable you may feel at any given time, every ride has always got to end — as a Plymouth heavy with pop-up inched its way back into oncoming midwestern America.

Again, there were all those faces that seemed to know where they were going — four lanes of faces blowing east as Interstate 65 merged with Interstate 94 on the way out of Chicago.

Some wore blue suits, and some had ruffles on their shirts; some looked pensive, others relaxed. Some were trying to get in the left lane, while others were content to stay to the right.

Alone on the side of road, I felt like a sailor standing on the bow of his ship, staring into the wind that is both his vehicle and his nemesis. Like an asphalt sailor I stood searching an unpredictable gale of humanity — wondering what form of passage it would offer this time.

Sounds of a nearby stirring crept through the drone. Behind me were several low-lying and substantial homes separated from the highway by an abundance of tall grass and heavily overgrown thicket — a messy attempt at privacy from the four lanes of midwestern America merging in their back yard.

"Hey, hey you, come on over here!"

About two back yards down, in a bright red flannel shirt, an old man stood propped above the privacy brush, calling in a scratchy voice.

"You want some water? For your canteen? Do you need some water?"

I looked down to find that the clear plastic container strapped to the outside of my pack was only half-full. If asked, I wouldn't have been able to say when I had last taken a drink.

"Well, do you need some water?" the old man called again.

"I guess so," I said. "How do I get over there?"

"Just come on through, you'll find the trail. There's a bridge too — over the ditch, and steps over the fence. Just come on over."

I pulled my pack onto my back and followed the old man's enthusiasm. Sure enough, a slight trail cut through the overgrowth toward his house. There was even a small wooden bridge that crossed a swampy drainage ditch, and a stepladder that straddled the fence.

"Water ain't so easy to find when you're traveling, but it sure is something you need," the old man said, leading toward his home.

"It's hard for you to get, but I got plenty of it."

In his yard was an old Chevy up on blocks as if it had been waiting for a valve job for the last twenty years. Near it, a rusted-out washer and dryer.

Closer to the house was a long brown patch of dirt whose failed purpose was announced by three seed packets planted on a stick: "Geranium," "Chrysanthemum," and "Poppy."

"Bet you've traveled a long way," he said, "bet you worked up a good thirst today."

"I'm up from Kentucky," I said, as the man continued toward a sink in the kitchen. "That's where I'm from today. Before that I was from North Carolina."

The man turned the water on and let it run awhile as if showing off the abundance he possessed.

"You say Kentucky, huh! Well that's some ways to make in a day. I don't know if I'd have gone all that way in a day. Maybe two or three if my luck was right, but one day's an awfully short time."

A sudden gust of wind rattled an old and peeling window that faced the sound of the highway. Although the heavy overgrowth obscured the view of the road, the constant drone of movement permeated every inch of this homestead.

The old man carefully handed me the glass that held the very amount it was capable of. Then he beckoned for my canteen. I tried to get a sip off the top before the water spilled, but several drops splattered on the floor despite my best effort.

"I sure know what it means to be thirsty on the road. One thing I've got is water. I've got just plenty of it."

My glass had long been empty by the time my canteen was full. I hadn't realized how thirsty I'd been. The old man took the glass and began filling it again before I stopped him.

"That's plenty for me," I said. "I really don't think I could drink any more."

This seemed to have a disorienting effect on the old man. He began rinsing my glass excessively under the full force of tap water, nervously turning it every which way before finally setting it down on the drain board. He then took a few steps toward a table that held the dishes from the last meal.

"Don't you know, it was my birthday yesterday," he said with his back turned toward me.

"That's great. Which one was it?"

"Got a call at 11:03 from my daughter in Cleveland. Then at 11:08, my son called who lives in Chicago. They both wanted to wish their dad a happy birthday."

The old man motioned for me to take a seat behind a half-eaten sandwich.

"My wife and I separated a ways back and I'm really not too sure what happened to her except that she's somewhere here in the Midwest. I've got a young fella that lives with me now to help me keep things up around here, like the garden, the car, and stuff. Can't ask him for much rent; he's been unemployed now for more than a year. But he helps me with things, gives me a little company too when I need it. . . . Is it hot in Kentucky these days?"

As he spoke, a young man wearing a leather jacket and carrying a motorcycle helmet stepped into our conversation. I rose to greet him, but he looked angry. He turned away from me and looked to the old man for an explanation.

"This fella here's been hitchhiking, Mike. I asked him if he wanted to come by and get a drink of water."

The guy didn't acknowledge what the man had said. He didn't look as though he was going to say anything himself. There was a scar running from the end of his mouth toward his neck.

A voice called from outside: "Hey Mike, come on, we gotta get going."

"Yeah, just a minute I'll be right there."

He looked at me as if I were trying to pull something. It was time for me to leave.

"Yeah, it'll be getting dark soon," the old man seemed to agree, as he got up from the table. "How much further do you think you'll be going today?"

We walked outside to the same opening in the brush. I noticed a chair was placed in front of that space, offering a slight view of all the people going somewhere else.

"Be careful going over," he said. "You've gotta watch, there's a little hook on top of the fence that people sometimes catch their pants or shoelaces on. You see it there?"

There was a small blemish in the metal work.

"Seems most of the folks do best if they walk down a little ways past the overpass. You could get a ride in about fifteen minutes if you waited there."

I thanked him for the water and walked along the path, occasionally looking back and waving to the old man still visible from a clearing in the hedge.

Though the man could no longer travel, the ageless drone of movement behind him remained the same. It was there to greet him each morning when he woke up, and again each night as he went to bed, beckoning toward a place where memories never grow tired the way arms, legs, and feet do.

At the point that the old man had suggested, I dropped my pack off my shoulders and set it gently upon the ground. I looked back and noticed that the curve of the road had taken me just beyond the sight of the old man's house.

I turned once again to face the swell of humanity in motion that offers the greatest fascination for those who try to understand it once. I wondered how many other hitchhikers had stood in that exact same spot with a full canteen of water.

A cool, Great-Lakes wind gained intensity toward an everlasting twilight, and swept me up in a wave of optimism that couldn't imagine what it would be like to feel any other way. Standing safely several hundred miles and twenty degrees cooler than I had been when I awoke that morning, the cars blowing toward me seemed like opportunities waiting to offer another drink of water.

This hitchhiking was the event of a lifetime for all those who took a chance, I decided, while patiently anticipating the next wonderful experience that would present itself with the opening of a car door. A pretty young lady would do just fine, I thought. Perhaps I would refuse all other rides.

When a car finally did pull off the highway, I bounded toward it, opened the door, and threw my pack into a burgundy Impala, without the least bit of concern as to who was behind the wheel or where he was going.

The door locked shut as I closed it—kerplunk. The car had push-button everything. I looked across to find a conservatively dressed man easing back into the flow of traffic without saying a word.

Five miles into the ride and the man beside me had said nothing but "uh-huh" to whatever I happened to have mentioned.

"You work in Chicago then?" I asked.

"Uh-huh."

"Chicago a pretty nice city?"

"Uh-huh."

He seemed preoccupied: conversation was a distraction he only vaguely acknowledged. It was very likely that in fact he hated Chicago and didn't even work there.

"You married?" I asked.

"Nope."

The car was traveling over sixty miles per hour. My driver was awkwardly scratching his shoulder with an unusual intensity.

"Boy, am I ever tired," I said, straining for innocuous conversation. "Boy, am I tired."

The man turned toward me for the first time since I had gotten in the car.

"Oh yeah, well, do you want to take a nap?"

He was waiting for an answer.

"A nap??"

"Yeah, at my place. You can take a nap just as long as you'd like. I might just take one with you. I'm kinda tired myself."

He was smiling at me.

Hitchhiker Rule Number 7: Always talk to your driver before getting in the car so you know something of what he is about before the locks of his burgundy Impala go "kerplunk."

"No, I'm really not that tired. I've got to get where I'm going tonight, you know ' . . . and miles to go before I sleep,'—ha ha."

The words coming out of my mouth were completely distant from the fear and anger swelling inside with no place to exit within the locked doors.

"You just said a minute ago that you were tired."

"Yeah, well, I guess it's just one of those things."

My words were smooth, cool, without bite. Beneath every huge wave that looks like it is about to knock you over, there is a still pool of water that remains unaffected. That was where I needed to be. That was Hitchhiker Rule Number 8. Nobody was going to change anybody else's sexual preferences. This would be something I would chalk off to experience and he could chalk it off to whatever the hell he wanted to chalk it off to. The emphasis was on "chalking it off."

"Are you sure you don't want to stop for just a few minutes? You might feel a lot better afterwards."

"Yeah, no, I appreciate it though, but I've just got to keep on going. ' . . . and miles to go before I sleep. . . . ' You know how it is."

"No, I don't really."

"Why don't you let me out here?"

"Here, all by yourself?"

"Yes, please, now."

As he sped away, I found myself staring into that gust of humanity another ten miles down the same road. The gales had shifted though, and I felt vulnerable to any possibility that was human. A continuous barbed-wire fence that separated me from houses meant that I had to continue. In my pack I found a book called *American Youth Hostels* with a triangle over a place called Coloma, Michigan.

Hitchhiker Rule Number 9: Sometimes you can't look the way you feel. With all of midwestern America looking hard, I had to suck it up somehow and appear completely in control. There are things you can do that make a difference. Most weirdos won't mess with a good strong look.

A rusted Volvo station wagon pulled across two lanes of traffic and came to rest about fifty yards beyond me. I took my time getting to the passenger window, trying to figure out whether it meant something to have a muffler held up with copper wiring.

A young woman unlocked the back door. There was a man of about the same age behind the wheel. While traffic buzzed at a feverish pace beside us, the two of them waited for me to open the door. But I waited for them to open the window.

"Hi," I began.

"Hello," the girl continued.

"Where are you heading?" I asked.

"North along 94 on into Michigan."

That seemed coherent. I couldn't smell any alcohol.

"Seeing relatives?" I asked stupidly.

"No, . . . in fact we're going to a pottery festival near Detroit."

The man looked behind him at all the cars that were passing so close, so fast.

"I think there's a youth hostel at a place called Coloma. Are you going near there?"

"Yes," the man called across the woman, "right by it."

On the other side of this door was a sober couple going to a pottery festival north of Detroit. The vehicle had been established; all that was left were the miles.

Hitchhiker Rule Number 1: There are things you can do.

There was a fruit stand at the end of this ride, set on a hill beside the highway. I held the whiskery coarseness of a peach so fresh it sprayed juice into the back of my throat upon first bite. My ride bought a basket's worth, then headed on without any real good-bye. I surveyed the land from still another vantage point and ate four more peaches.

The first hints of night were appearing in pink streaks across the sky. Page thirty-five of the book I carried on American youth hostels pointed out that the hostel listed under "Coloma" was in fact about nine miles west of the town I hadn't even gotten to yet.

"About how far is it to Coloma?" I asked a guy stacking apples.

"Where you want to go to?"

"Just into town."

"Well, it's about a mile to the traffic light; mile, mile and a half, maybe."

"How do I get there?"

"Just follow the road over the Interstate, take a right at the Quick Mart."

It felt good to be walking alone in the cool air approaching dusk. Potential rides sneaked up behind me and twitched at my thumb, but there was a kind of certainty in my steps—one in front of the other, on and on—that I did not want to give up near the end of that long day.

The Quick Mart countergirl quickly calculated the roll, banana, and can of tuna fish I had offered for appraisal.

"That's $1.07."

Another countergirl who was without customers came by to view the transaction. They were about high-school age, and both looked like they had made one too many trips to the bakery section. They stared while I dug deep for correct change. My backpack remained against the red, white, and blue bags of charcoal stacked at the entrance of the store.

"You're not from around here?" the one finally let out while the other bagged my dinner.

"I live in North Carolina, but today I'm from Kentucky. I'm hitchhiking around the country."

They looked at each other.

"See, I told you," she said.

"What?" I asked.

"Oh, it's nothing."

Past a stately old house with a long row of privacy hedge, past a park that had no benches, around a corner where I thought I heard people, and suddenly there appeared the one-traffic-light spectacle of small-town America.

Teenagers with no place to go crammed into late-model cars and cruised up and down the street called Main. They screamed, they called out, they were mad at their parents.

The older men grouped in front of the fire station to talk about life—real life, not the ramifications of the ranger's talk on the etymology of the Kentucky word for fishing. Perhaps they even talked about the women who were bunched in front of the drugstore across the street.

They stood about and they shifted positions; they waved to other people passing by; they shook their heads at the blaring music.

They were all looking at me.

Had I forgotten about the large hump on my backside? That was probably something they were not used to seeing around there on a Tuesday night. Who was I, anyway, and what was I doing in Coloma, Michigan?

Slowly, cautiously, with an artificial smile that I tried to keep from being too imposing, I found a place along the westward road out of town.

The cars packed with teenagers were suddenly quiet as they passed by me a first time. The second time through, they giggled. They discovered new sounds to make with their mouths the third time, until they'd finally worked their way up to their original raucousness in acceptance of this new thing they had found on the side of the road.

The groups of adults on either side of the street did not have a similar method for accommodating my presence. Each member in each group took his turn to look, while the others talked. They all talked, while I waited in the western shadow of their only stoplight for ten, twenty, thirty, then forty minutes.

As illumination began to spread from the street lights and the storefronts, I began to search the places left dark for a possible home for the night. Behind the drugstore there was a spot beneath the fire escape; beside the fire station there was a wooded area.

As I scanned the dark slivers of Coloma, Michigan, a flash of perspective intruded heavily into my reality. Six months ago, I had been sipping champagne at a graduation party. Every day of my life before this trip, I had known where I would be sleeping that night. At the moment, I was trying to figure out which bed would have the fewest rats. And this caused me to wonder: Why leave?

Then, without my immediate notice, a Toyota hatchback stopped, facing the all-important westward direction. Some guy popped out wearing steel-rimmed glasses and a moderate case of acne.

"You need a ride or something?" he asked.

"Boy, do I."

"My name is Andy," he said.

I had to shake his hand the moment I closed the door.

"I live in Benton Harbor, but my job takes me all over: Grand Rapids, Gary, Kalamazoo. I've got a northern-Indiana, western- and central-Michigan territory that really keeps me hopping. Wouldn't have it any other way, though. I just love to keep moving."

I could see what he meant. He seemed to find his seat amazingly confining, sliding back and forth and over and back in an endless search for comfort.

"I need to go to a youth hostel near the end of this road," I said.

"At least I think there's a youth hostel there. The map I have is kind of old. Have you ever heard of one?"

"Uh-huh, sell Culligan Water Products as a matter of fact. Have been for about a year now."

Salesmen have this way of saying what they want to say — regardless. It seemed there was to be one topic of conversation between Andy and me that night.

"What are Culligan Water Products?"

Within a moment there were six descriptive leaflets and three free samples of Culligan Water Softener laying on my lap.

"It is by far the best product on the market. It will make your washing and drinking water . . . "

I tried to explain to him that I didn't even have a house.

"Well, you can't live on the road forever, now can you? Someday you'll be settling into the good ole nine-to-five just like the rest of us."

I tried to explain to him that I didn't think I would be settling into the "good-ole nine-to-five" in northern Indiana or western Michigan.

"Culligan will ship anywhere in the U.S. except Alaska and Hawaii, and we'll guarantee satisfaction on the product for as long as you are using Culligan."

I said that there was a good chance that I might live in Alaska. He laughed and gave me another pamphlet along with his card, then pulled over when the road we were on didn't go any further.

"Remember, Andy and Culligan. You'll be needing us when you're a little older," he said.

"Thanks," I said, "I'll keep you two in mind."

I guess I was one of those long-shot prospects that salesmen harbor just in case.

5

A Wendy Night Along the Shore

The tall, thick maple trees that lined the road bent like twigs in the hard-driving gales off the lake. Somewhere above swinging branches, a light secured to a telephone pole bounced just enough illumination onto my map to inform me that a home for the night was still a mile north—at least in theory.

The highway that had begun behind a set of brake lights in North Carolina now made a long, northern curve in the direction of the wind before fading into the roaring trees. There were no homes visible from the road, only an occasional unmarked driveway bound for darkness.

Was there really a youth hostel nine miles outside of Coloma, Michigan? I listened to the slow, deafening creak of bending wood along the path of an unsure destination and followed the only direction I had known—forward.

In this dark and stormy emptiness, a mind that had been forced to adapt from one car to the next was now taking a stance. In a place nestled deep beneath layers of reality, a slow, steady snowfall softened a mountain range, until I could almost feel my lonely steps tracking through the new snow—one step in front of the other, on and on.

I vaguely recognized the image as one that had been just beyond my grasp each morning since I had been on the road. It burst forth now, a subconscious wave that was about to drown a weary reality:

It was very cold and I was wearing only a light pair of pants and a spring coat. I was in a hurry to get back to somewhere—a place away from the terrible cold.

Especially clear were my footsteps through the snow, one ahead of the other, on and on, leading me in their own particular direction, on and on. I concentrated on that feeling through the cold. I held it tightly.

Then somehow I was on a train, an old, noisy train that was going somewhere.

But where?

An old conductor was scurrying up and down the vacant aisle. He asked for my ticket, and when I told him that I did not have one, he would look terribly hurt, then rush off to find another passenger, only to return for the same ordeal again and again. For I was the only passenger on the train.

I remember looking out the window as we approached, although I didn't know what we were approaching. The land was flat and open. I noticed that the tracks went in a circle, pushing ahead a bit through the open space, then returning back toward where they started—although I wasn't sure where that was either. We seemed to have been on a plateau the whole time, and although I couldn't see it, I knew we were moving toward an ocean.

Nearer to the shoreline, all that stood upon the rocks and the grass was a row of burnt-out houses, all about the same distance apart.

The old man stood before me once again. He was very excited this time. It appeared as though we had come to my exit. I got off the train, though I don't ever remember its stopping.

The rumble of the train's engine soon grew distant. There was a large, burnt-out house between me and the sea. I thought I heard the sound of children playing behind it, so I walked past the house and off the end of the land, where a narrow, sandy beach stretched forever beside the ocean.

I searched all about for the children, but I couldn't find any. There was no one anywhere. The train had long gone.

I remained motionless for several hours as the wind grew and the temperature dropped. I remained there listening to the gentle pounding of the surf and the distant laughter of children playing.

Then, slowly, I made my way up a flight of ragged wooden steps toward the house. As I carefully walked to avoid the nails and splinters, the sea rose behind me, covering each step that I had just taken.

The charred door broke in my hand as I tried to open it. I had to step over and under the two-by-fours strewn about the rooms as I made my way through the rubble to what seemed like the back of the house.

The ocean winds grew stronger through the badly damaged walls. It had become terribly cold. On I walked, through the burnt-out house, toward a room in the very back. . . .

A flash of southbound headlights focused my attention onto a rusted sign that read "American Youth Hostel."

The sign was nailed to a fat oak tree on the lake side of the road. Its direction pointed down a dirt path that was made darker still by an awning of trees.

Several cottages began to appear, offering either dim light or none at all. Finally, I saw one that seemed more brightly lit than the others.

There were no signs or other markings to distinguish it. Just a light on the porch that shone through the darkness better than anything I had seen that night. Without resolution, I walked toward it, and though it must have been well past ten o'clock, I knocked, and waited in the broken light filtering through the venetian blinds.

An older woman appeared. She was wearing a robe and slippers. Her hair was in some sort of net that barely concealed the curlers beneath it.

"We usually don't get people here this late," she said, opening the door for me. "Actually, we usually don't get people here at all."

"I was afraid this youth hostel didn't exist. I've been hitchhiking all the way from North Carolina."

The woman pulled a register out of an antique walnut chest and flipped a few pages as the dates beside varied signatures quickly changed in leaps and bounds up to the present: The blank space awaiting my signature was only a half-page away from a year ago.

The gusting wind outside was but a dull drone through the crack beneath the door. I watched in wonder as the woman made arrangements for me to lay a head that was weary from so many miles.

"I hope you don't mind being by yourself," she said. "We had a person here the other day, but he's gone now."

"That's OK, I'm getting kind of used to it."

She called her husband, who had been watching television. As soon as he found his shoes, he loaded me on the back of a pickup. We drove enthusiastically beside cottages and baseball diamonds; volleyball nets and picnic benches. The look of a summer camp was all around. In the end, we came upon an old majestic rock house that stood directly on a cliff overlooking the lake.

"This is it," he called to me, shouting to be heard through the wind. "This is where you're gonna be staying."

The surrounding trees bent further toward the ground than any I had ever seen before. Their branches grew only in a leeward direction in acquiescence to that which had battered them so.

The old man unlocked the door to a faint musty smell, then turned on a light that revealed a world of couches and kitchen appliances — symbols of comfort I had never dreamed would be my own that night.

"Just holler if you need anything," he said. "They'll be serving breakfast tomorrow at 8, lunch at 12:30. You're welcome to join in. Just holler if you need anything."

The old man was talking to himself as I had become absorbed in the switches and buttons that turned on and off — amazed at the shelter I had come upon, while somewhere close, and getting closer, severe thunderstorms raged.

"Yeah, if you need anything at all, just holler," he said once more before I heard the door shut.

Small bugs and petals of dirt detached themselves from my skin and floated gently to the bottom of the white porcelain tub I had discovered upstairs.

There are no greater pleasures in life than those that are unexpected.

My skin cleansed, my body and soul refreshed, I went down to the edge of the cliff to face the storm I had been heading toward. Its violent swells lit up the sky in many different directions, casting flashes of light on a churning and turbulent Lake Michigan.

The wild gusts battered and bathed my face in a celebration of life, leaving me ecstatic in the impression it made on my skin—still damp from the hot bath. Slowly, I unbuttoned my shirt to let the wind into the moist canyons of my cleanliness. Each part of me that still held clothes yearned in anticipation.

Back inside, the windows in the upstairs bedroom had large wooden boards fixed in them to shut out the tremendous force they had become accustomed to. In another moment of complete optimism, I removed all shelter and allowed the gales to explode into the room I had chosen.

In a few moments, however, the storm that had been just a distant vision came hard upon the land, pouring painful pellets of rain through the passages I had left unsecured. The wind had grown frightening; the thunder was in the same room.

I slipped on the wooden floor on my way to the window. A lightning bolt cracked nearby and sent me reeling out of fear to a place in the hall, then back toward the openings that needed to be closed.

My movements were automatic, continuing without my notice, almost as though I didn't exist at all. I pulled one of the heavy wooden window boards into place, but it slipped out of my hand and landed its sharp corner directly on the arch of my naked foot. A spurt of blood shot up from a vein, then a flow oozed onto the wooden floor. I watched; I didn't notice any pain.

Several more attempts finally yielded success, and soon I had done all I could do to protect myself from the surrounding intensity. I lay in bed, wet and exhausted, while a towel absorbed the blood that poured from my foot. The lightning continued to jolt me from different directions, while the wind pounded upon the old rock house I had somehow come upon that night.

My exhaustion began to tear at the magnitude of the stimuli around me with an equal force, trying to quiet a mind that was exploding in thought.

There, somewhere between a deep sleep and a frightening reality, I found myself again in the burnt-out house, walking over and under the charred two-by-fours, walking toward a room in the back. In the background the ocean swelled as the thunder cracked, leaving in its lull that same sound of children playing on the beach.

The woman sat amidst the rubble in the corner of the room. Her light-colored robe was stained with charcoal and dirt. She was not ugly, and she was not pretty. She was someone I had never seen before.

She looked at me and smiled. I smiled back. I went to her and she opened her robe and wrapped my shivering body in it. She held me closely and never said a word. The only sounds left were of children far off in the distance somewhere, and the gentle pounding of the surf.

I kissed her ice-cold face, and I felt safe.

Then, there was a man lying face down in snow that was beginning to cover him.

The next morning I was held captive by the security of an immobile mattress. I had no interest in the new day; I wanted only to linger. The dream had embellished itself delightfully on the initial feminine theme — as the lightning struck and the thunder pounded — leaving me twisting and turning between awake and asleep, trying to recover faces that had already passed me by.

Had it not been for several long, continuous screams coming from the other side of my windows, I would have stayed in bed right through till night justified it again. I rose to find scores of children being helped by counselors toward a red building in the center of the grounds. Some were being rolled in wheelchairs, some were being carried. Some refused to move, and stood screaming in one single place as if nothing in the world could make it better.

My alarm clock said 12:20, but what was it that man had said about meals the night before? I found some clothes and the way out the door. It's awfully difficult to lie in bed when the world is moaning outside your window. That was Hitchhiker Rule Number 10.

"Didn't see you at breakfast," the man called out as I walked through the dining hall door. He seemed to be implying something. "Guess the storm kept you up most of the night."

He laughed and patted me on the shoulder. People over fifty get a real kick out of people who sleep past eight.

Far across the room, my attention became centered on a woman who was helping a student into a chair. She had long brown hair and a kind look. She seemed to be about my age. I watched as she placed herself gently upon a chair at the table. She never noticed my gaze, but I continued to watch — still far, far away.

The man introduced me to Frieda and Jane and Matt: the kitchen staff. He said something about how I might give them a hand with a dish or two in exchange for some lunch. The group didn't acknowledge his attempt at an inside joke, while through the window from the kitchen, another female counselor was helping to pour ketchup on a young girl's hamburger.

In another moment, a hot dog lay before me, along with a glass of red punch.

I stood in the middle of the kitchen holding an empty, yellow dish rack and watching the clean-up activity. In the few short minutes since lunch was over, I had already learned that the relishes didn't come off the tables until after dinner; the floor didn't need to be mopped; the cups weren't washed by hand, but instead went in the rack; the racks were in the closet in the back of the room; the green rack didn't fit in the machine they had just gotten; the yellow rack didn't go on the wooden counter; and a few bucks isn't much to pay for a meal.

"Just set it against the wall, and I'll load the cups as soon as I get done with this," Matt said.

"No really, I'd like to help."

"OK, why don't you go out and check to see if all the doors are shut?"

Matt was a bottom-line sort of a sixteen-year-old. While Frieda and Jane incessantly criticized my attempts to help in their kitchen, Matt had the problem solved: "Why don't you go out and check to see if all the doors are shut?" Case closed. I'd shut the door on the way out.

Then, through the passageway that led to a bed and the comforting thoughts of the morning, another woman with soft facial features appeared with a clipboard in her hand. She smiled at me as she passed too close, on her way to get a bag she had forgotten. She smiled again on her way out, and suddenly there was no particular place that I had to be.

Matt came through the swinging doors carrying a dish towel and began wiping off the tables. Without much thought to what I was saying, I called over:

"Tell me something, who works at this camp?"

"Huh?"

"I mean, are most of the counselors about my age, or are they a lot older?"

"That depends. How old are you?"

"Twenty-two."

"Yeah, well I guess some are your age and some aren't."

Matt was ready to continue his routine behind the swinging doors when I called out in the same way:

"Are there about the same amount of girls as there are guys on the staff?"

Matt thought for a second, then continued through the door he was headed for. In a moment he returned with a broom.

"Why don't you meet me by the pool at three o'clock," he said. "I'm going to have to introduce you to Wendy."

"Wendy?" I asked.

"Wendy."

"Three o'clock?"

"Three."

"Yeah, I think I can make that."

I spent the next two hours of my life reading a *National Geographic* article about either Vermont or Bangladesh; I wasn't really sure. At exactly five minutes before three, I was out the door.

At the pool, Matt was talking to a woman whose back was toward me. He waved for me to come over.

The woman had blond curly hair that fell directly onto two deep brown shoulders. She had a firm, athletic build that tended more toward field hockey than water ballet. She wore a single-piece, bright orange bathing suit that barely contained the thrust of her breasts.

"This is Wendy."

That was all Matt said before leaving.

I noticed that the pants I was wearing didn't have any pockets.

"Hi," I managed.

"Hello."

"You lifeguard here?"

"Yeah."

"Seems like a nice place to work."

If it hadn't been for some of the kids screaming, there would have been a very long silence.

"You get used to it," she said finally. "This is my third year here."

"Right."

One little boy with hardly any legs floated on an inner tube without a motion, without a sound, as if there wasn't a thing in the world that could be more engaging than the cool water and hot sun in the middle of the afternoon.

Wendy suddenly blew her whistle at another boy who was almost running. The boy paid no attention to her and jumped feet-first into the pool.

"Guess you're pretty busy," I said.

I still felt as though I wasn't completely awake.

"No, not really."

"Oh, I see."

There was a reason I had said that. If I couldn't remember, it seemed that Wendy could.

"Why don't I meet you over at the steps to the lake when I get off at four? We can talk better then," she offered.

"Yeah, sure, that sounds great."

The mud created from last night's storm oozed under the bottom of my shorts as I tried to slide down an eroded cliff to the lake. The steps that once navigated this forty-foot drop had flat-out been beaten.

Wendy managed the drop much more easily than I had, simply guiding her fall through the mud, until her momentum carried her several paces across the beach without so much as a single brown streak on the back of her legs.

Wendy flung her muscular body upon the lake in four splashing leaps, and then a dive headfirst. I waded in step by step, allowing each inch of skin a chance to become accustomed to the cold Michigan water.

"You chicken!" Wendy yelled, letting out a splash that totally destroyed my gradual transition.

Instinctively, I leaped forward and grabbed her leg, ready to dunk her into the murky depths around me. Then suddenly I noticed the soft, firm skin I was holding in my hand. Wendy's curly blond hair was batched in wet strands that gently clung to the upper parts of her body. Her skin was so taut it beaded the lake's water like a car that had just been waxed.

She began to notice that I was holding her leg without knowing what to do with it. She giggled. I finally let it drop and threw myself deep into the change I had been hesitant to make, remaining underwater until it felt as though I had been there all along.

We walked along the shore with an awkward space between us that demanded several more formalities before it would disappear.

"Are you the only kid?" I asked.

"No, I've got two older brothers."

"What do they do?"

"Play football."

"For a living?"

"They've got college scholarships."

"Have you decided where you're going to college next year? . . ."

I shifted my conversation into automatic pilot, working through all that was necessary, while a tremendous, nondiscriminating desire flooded through me.

In a patch of low grass near the top of the hill, Wendy suddenly grabbed my leg.

"Will you look at that," she said, pointing down.

Beneath us, two large insects that looked like dragonflies were on top of each other in a position that suggested sex. The male was holding the female beneath him, while the female wiggled and squirmed.

"Well, what do they think they're doing?" Wendy asked.

In a complete and utter blow to my perception of the world at that moment, she then picked up a stick and tore the two apart, sending the male off in a frantic circular path, around and around, and then away.

"Why should they have fun when the rest of us have to work our butts off at this camp?"

The female remained motionless for a few moments, assessing what had happened. She then ran off in the direction of the male.

"Sorry about that, baby," Wendy said. "I guess he must've been pretty good."

Wendy and I agreed to meet for supper at "my place" directly at eight.

There was spaghetti waiting on the table, and there was anticipation. There was the hope that the girl would bring the sauce, and there were sore legs from the quick jog to the nearest grocery store. There was a bottle of wine on the table, in violation of all youth hostel regulations. There was another one in the refrigerator.

At 8:01 there was the girl, and there was meat sauce along with the sausage she had promised to bring.

She broke the wad of noodles in half and set a hunk on each plate before indiscriminately pouring the sauce over the two batches. We each guzzled about two glasses of wine in the course of a few bites of spaghetti.

In a moment, we were on the floor where the hard-packed rug began to burn my knees.

"Why don't we go over to my cottage?" Wendy offered suddenly.

"Yeah, that sounds like a good idea."

There was an overwhelming comfort in Wendy's smooth skin and firm touch that the confusion and disorientation of my essence rushed into, and became lost in. For a moment, the movement stopped. There was no place else to go. There were only warm hands in warm places and soft whispers that led further and further into the night.

Well into the comfort of caresses, I suddenly wanted the moans and sighs between us to become audible. There was so much I still did not know; so many things that I was searching for, and it seemed the answer was there somewhere.

"You know," I said finally, "I'm not really sure where I'm going."

"You mean tonight?"

Giggling, she rubbed up against me and began to kiss. She did not want to venture where I was leading.

"No, I mean on this trip, and after it, too. I just don't know where I'll be, or where it is that I'm going."

She looked up without knowing what to say: she kissed again. She felt a wall suddenly grow strong around me, but she kissed again.

It was the best she could have done. Why hadn't I seen that? The wave she had set in motion was out of place. I had to stop its force somehow before it bruised.

Suddenly, I saw myself running through a field—just running—in search of a horizon; reaching for a place that was waiting just beyond my grasp. Motion, for no other reason except itself—running simply because it had to run.

Again there was comfort. The wave of self that had been misdirected was back on course in the only place it should have ever been. The image held the energy I had stifled, and allowed my hand to reach back toward the soft moment I was next to.

I think often a woman's embrace lures a man into believing he can deposit his soul at the base of her being. When he finds that he cannot, however familiar the supple contours, he becomes angry and hates her for what she cannot do, instead of loving her for what she can. But in fact, there is a part of every person that is never understood; that runs through a field in search of a horizon that can never be reached, and whose only peace is motion.

6

THIRD-PERSON SINGULAR: CINDY, RANDY, AND TOM

Randy Zasman was out driving a beat-up Fiat toward a job in Green Bay that he didn't like, when he spotted a guy with a sign that read "G–Bay," and skidded to a halt. A sense of obligation overcame him from all the times he'd been in the same situation. He brushed the empty beer cans off the passenger seat and got out to open the door that simply wouldn't work any other way.

"I gotta stop and fill out a job application on the way into town," Randy said. "That OK?"

"That's fine with me. I've got nowhere I've got to be."

Randy watched as the hitchhiker picked out a couple of bottle caps he had sat down on. Randy almost said something but then decided not to. He couldn't remember anybody apologizing to him when he had been on the road.

"Where you getting a job at?"

"There's this bar down the road, place called the Maple Inn," Randy said.

That was all he said.

"What kind of work will you be doing there?"

"I don't even know if I got the job, yet."

"Well, if you get it what kind of work will you be doing?"

Guy had a lot of questions, Randy thought.

"Bartending; I tend bar. That's what I'm doing now, too."

"No kidding, I've always wanted to be a bartender."

"It's lousy work, it just *seems* good to people."

"Oh yeah? That's what it used to be like for me working on the beer truck. All my friends thought I had it made—drink all the beer I

wanted and all. But that just wasn't the way it was. Worked my ass off is
all I did."

"That's the same way with bartending. That's the exact same
thing."

Randy usually spent too much of his time trying to explain to
people that life on the other side of the bar was a whole different world.
It was good that this guy understood that right off.

"You ever hitch?"

"Hell, yeah, used to do it all the time," Randy replied.

"You like it?"

"It was pretty good most of the time. Sometimes it wasn't though.
Sometimes it really stunk bad."

"It hasn't been too bad for me. I've been at it for about two months
now and I've only gotten one bad ride."

"Yeah? That's pretty good."

"I'm just lucky, I guess."

"Where is it you're going in Green Bay?"

"Nowhere really. It's just along the way."

"To where?"

"Wherever."

"That's how I used to do it too," Randy said, "just whatever and
wherever the fuck."

"Yeah, whatever and wherever the fuck. I guess that's all there is to
it."

Randy laughed and felt good. It'd been a long time since he had
talked that way.

"We'll give you a call in a couple weeks if we want ya," the bald guy
smoking a cigar told Randy.

He'd heard it before.

The hitchhiker was waiting at the bar with two beers in front of
him.

"I'll finish them both if you don't want one," he told him.

"No, I want one, OK. I sure do want one."

"How'd it go?"

"Well, he told me they've been taking applications since a week ago,
and they're cutting off today. They've gotta have about four thousand
fuckin' applications by now. It's a shot in the dark, but what the hell."

"What's wrong with your other job?"

"Nothin' really, 'cept I'm sick of it."

"How long you been working there?"

"Just five months. Ever since I moved down here from Manitowoc
to live with my girlfriend."

"Five months isn't that long."

"I know, I guess I'm just sick of it."

"Packers' game tonight," Randy said.

"Really! Who are they playing?"

"Minnesota. It's just exhibition, but everyone gets pretty worked up about it anyway. The fuckin' bar will be a disaster after the game."

"Sounds like something worth hanging around for."

Randy thought about what his girlfriend would say if he brought a hitchhiker home. The guy seemed OK. He couldn't see why she wouldn't like him. But she just might decide to not like him for the hell of it, and it began to bother him that he had to think about these things.

"There's places at the Y you can stay for cheap. I could come down and give you a lift to the bar and you can hang out there for a while."

"Yeah, that sounds real good. Let's do that then."

Randy hesitated, thought for a minute, then went ahead anyway: "Hell," he said, "you might even be able to stay at my place."

Randy quietly entered his girlfriend's house while the hitchhiker waited in the car. Cindy would be going to the game that night because of the tickets Randy had gotten her. She would probably be in as good a mood as could be expected.

In more than a little while, Randy came back out the door with a smile that he hadn't gone in with.

"Go ahead and bring your stuff with you. You got a roof to keep it under tonight."

He felt proud saying that, until he realized he really shouldn't have. He watched as the hitchhiker carried his backpack into his girlfriend's house.

Six Scotch and waters needed to get over to the far end of the bar, and three Miller's had to be deposited along the way. Who gave him the twenty? Green Bay lost, as they had been doing these past few years, and Randy couldn't remember who had given him the twenty.

He popped open the cap on the beers and dropped them off. There was a bottle of Scotch waiting at the far end. The guy he changed the twenty for didn't seem surprised. He must have guessed right.

Two more hours and he'd be pushing them out the door. Three more hours and he'd get to go himself. Usually, it'd be straight home and to bed. But the hitchhiker at the end of the bar didn't look tired. They might even go out and get some breakfast.

"The thing about hitchhiking is you just never know," Randy said. "I mean, there you are, out on the road stickin' your thumb out to anything, and anything can happen in just a minute. Pass the salt, OK?"

The eggs were barely cooked; the toast looked as old as his grandmother. It'd been a while since his last battle with early morning food, but Randy remembered that any egg could go down with salt and heavily buttered toast. A couple of cups of coffee, and it tasted even better.

Cindy might be mad, he thought. Right at that very minute, she might be sitting in the living room chair waiting for the door to open. He didn't know for sure. He had never been away from her like that.

"I ain't had nothing like that happen in a long time. Nowadays, I pretty much know what to expect."

"That'd be nice; know where you're going to sleep each night. That'd be something I wouldn't mind, at least not for a few days. I haven't known where I was going to sleep for the last couple months."

"Well, you get kinda used to it after a while. It's not so much that you get used to it as it is you just don't notice things anymore. You kinda forget about sleeping—it's just something you do."

"How'd you wind up out here?"

"Cindy. I was dating her twin sister for a while and Cindy came in one day and took control. It messed me up for a long time 'cause I didn't know who was who. When I had it figured out, she told me I could move in with her. I had been out of work for about half a year. Before that I had been bummin' around. It seemed like a good thing then."

"She seems like a nice girl."

"She listens to what you've got to say. I keep her up half the night trying to get all the stuff that happened sorted out. She listens to most of it."

"Like what?"

Randy hesitated. He hadn't told those things to anyone but the girl. She was the only one around to listen.

"I was hitchhiking in South Carolina a little while back," he began. "One day a cop picked me up and found this bag of pot in my pack. It was a real small bag; I forgot I even had it.

"There wasn't even anybody I could call. I didn't know no one down there. I didn't have nothin'—just my backpack. They really screw you around in a place like that. They fuck you around bad, real bad."

Randy slashed his toast across an unbroken yolk, and yellow just oozed.

"I seen some things inside there that just kind of stayed with me. Guys would come in from out of state for some stupid ticket about something, and there were these two guys that used to get a hold of 'em, hold the guy down, and a bunch of his buddies would take turns with the guy. You'd hear screaming like you never heard in your life. Nobody would come to help. The two guys would just beat the shit out of him. Right there, in front of me, some guy getting raped. . . .

"You see stuff like that, you just can't forget about it. It stays with ya, you know? Now, every once in a while, if some guy pisses me off, I get these shakes. My arms and legs and everything just start shaking, and then I go nuts. I just start beating on anybody around me. I'm blank the whole time it happens—I don't know nothing."

Randy could feel the sting of tension accumulating at the table, like the scent of the ammonia-based cleaning product being mopped onto the floor beside them. Stuff like that is pretty tough to hear about, Randy thought. But not as tough as it is to live through.

It felt good to let somebody else know.

Randy called for the waitress to bring another cup of coffee, even though it was probably five in the morning.

Randy wasn't sure what his girlfriend was thinking that next day when he awoke around noon. There had been a few drowsy words between them as he crawled into bed close to dawn. ("Where were you all this time?" "We got something to eat after closing.") He thought he could smell bacon cooking in the kitchen: at least things weren't in a crisis.

Cindy barely talked to him as she moved her utensils in preparation of a meal she wouldn't ordinarily have been making for two. The hitchhiker was still asleep on the couch. Randy spoke softly.

"You sure you don't mind him staying here?" he asked.

"No," she said. "You have a right to have your friends, too. We both live here."

She didn't really mean that. It was more a point of law. She looked as though she were putting up with an intolerable situation.

Randy hated to ask the next question—every bit of him hated it.

"You mad that we got in late last night?"

She stirred the scrambled eggs, then turned down the heat beneath the bacon. Randy heard a movement in the next room.

"I thought we could show him a little bit of the town today," Randy said. "This is his first time to Green Bay. Maybe we could all three go to the zoo and places like that."

"That sounds fine. I haven't been to the zoo in ten years. I'd like to see if they've still got animals there."

Randy turned away from the woman and went in the other room to wake up the hitchhiker.

Cindy was short and had long frizzy hair that she combed as if it were straight. She spent most of her days writing tickets so people could leave Green Bay on a Trailways bus. She had a huge doll collection that was spread all over the house. She made sure she was cordial to the hitchhiker that morning, offering him eggs and bacon until he couldn't eat anymore.

"That was really good. It's not every day I wake up to a big breakfast."

"Well, it's not every day that Randy brings home a hitchhiker," Cindy replied.

When everyone was finished, Cindy announced that she thought it would be a good idea if the hitchhiker got to see a little of the city. Did he want to stay another night, she asked? Good — then she thought the first place they should go to was the zoo. The hitchhiker agreed to that willingly. Randy did too.

At the zoo, Cindy told Randy that they should see the wolverines because that was the state animal of Wisconsin and she thought their visitor should see the state animal.

That seemed to make sense, and Randy agreed. They saw the wolverines.

Then Cindy told Randy that they should see the ducks, because there were so many of them that time of year, and maybe Randy could find some bread in the car to feed them.

That seemed to make sense, and Randy agreed. They fed the ducks.

After a little bit, Cindy told Randy she thought they'd seen all they needed to see at the zoo and that they should go down to the park and show their friend the lake.

Randy didn't have anything to say to that. He didn't know what there was and wasn't at the zoo. He couldn't give a reason for staying even if he wanted to. He had just wanted to go to the zoo.

They headed back to the car and drove in the direction of a park along the lake that Cindy knew about. On the way, Randy stopped at the beer store and bought a cold six-pack of Miller's. He offered one to his friend Tom, who refused so early in the day. And so Randy popped off the cap and reached for something he had begun to feel late last night.

About halfway through his purchase, Randy began paying less and less attention to what Cindy said, and began noticing the pretty college girls clustered on blankets near the water.

He decided to turn it all into a friendly gesture.

"I bet you ain't had many broads with all that moving about," he said to his friend. "I bet you'd like the one in the red swim trunks for a quick stopover, huh?"

Cindy couldn't get mad at him for being sympathetic to his friend's needs, Randy thought.

"Or how about the one with the sunglasses against the car," he said. "I bet she'd make your tent a little more crowded. . . . "

And so he continued, even after Cindy was ready to go.

Randy didn't pay attention to his girlfriend's request to go to the museum. He was out of beer, and he didn't think they sold any there. A bar seemed like a lot nicer place to be.

For a moment, he was unsure of which bar to go to. He didn't know what Cindy thought because she wasn't saying anything. He decided to make a right turn on Union Street.

Sitting at the bar, Randy decided he would try to help his friend out in terms of the cute bartender who had caught his eye.

" . . . and this is my friend Tom who wanted to talk with you."

The bartender turned toward Randy's friend and said hello. Then she waited.

Randy waited too.

So did Cindy; so did the guy at the other end of the bar waving a five-dollar bill in the air.

Randy couldn't understand why his friend didn't just ask her out that night. Imagine being free and able to ask out anyone you felt like? Randy couldn't understand his friend's hesitancy at all.

Then Randy whispered something to the bartender that nobody else would ever hear, and she gave him a funny look and walked off.

"She's not your type," Randy offered.

In less than two hours, Randy had tried to set up his friend with two bartenders and six other women, despite the fact that his friend didn't seem to know what was good for him.

"He's a little shy right now," Randy confided to one. "Maybe he'll come around a little later."

Cindy was utterly silent through all the goings on. Randy knew that later that night, when he and his girlfriend were alone, she would unleash a fierce tirade at him for some reason. But at the moment, Randy wasn't thinking about what that reason would be. As far as he was concerned, all that mattered was the here and now, and there were about a hundred more women left in the bar that still hadn't met his friend.

When the band took a break, Randy captured the band's lead singer and led him to the table.

"This is my friend Tom, and my girlfriend Cindy. This is Bud. He's the guy you've all been watching all this time," Randy said proudly.

"It's nice to meet you all," Bud returned.

With a large black cowboy hat, and turquoise studs all over his belt, Bud looked as though he'd played "Good-Hearted Woman" more than once. He also looked like he wanted a beer, and wanted to spend his few moments between sets away from the people he'd been standing in front of all that time.

He began to head on, but Randy grabbed his elbow.

"Cindy here sings a lot of country music," he told him. "She's real good too."

Cindy's look held a warning.

"Is that so? Well, we're always looking for people to come join us on stage for a number or two," Bud said.

"Well, really, I don't think I'd . . . ," Cindy began.

"Tom here plays the drums! Didn't you tell me you played the drums, Tom?"

"Yes, but . . . "

"How about having both of them come up and do a number!" Randy exclaimed. "Wouldn't that be great? Both of my friends go up and do a number? You want to do that, Tom?"

"Well, I've never really played country music, but . . . "

"It'd be easy," Randy assured him. "You could do it easy."

"Well, if Cindy wants to do something, I'll back her up."

"Great! How about it, Cindy?"

What Randy saw in his girlfriend's eyes penetrated his drunkenness—though just for a moment—and brought him back to thinking about things: a late-night conversation, the time she had told him about the way her mother used to make Cindy and her sister play in front of people, and how much she hated it.

But Randy thought about how incredible it would be to have his two friends on stage. He would have gotten on stage himself if he could play an instrument or sing. He'd give anything to know how to play an instrument or to sing, so he could—right then and there—get up in front of all those people. How could they say no to this? How could anybody say no?

"Come on, Cindy," Randy argued, "why don't you get up and sing one?"

"Sure, Cindy," the stranger in the black hat added, "We'd love to have you."

Cindy took in a deep, deep breath. Without looking at Randy at all, she looked directly at the man in the cowboy hat.

"No. Thank you, but I definitely don't want to."

She only had to say it once as far as the musician was concerned. Her boyfriend, however, was a different matter.

"Oh, come on, Cindy, just do one song!" he insisted.

Again Cindy said no. Nothing else—just no.

Randy felt as though she had never done anything he had ever wanted her to do. He couldn't remember a time when she had ever made him happy. He felt himself on the top of the world, being pulled down by this woman.

"Cindy, just do one song," he demanded. "Just do one song."

The singer excused himself. It was nice meeting all of you, he said, but he had to go get a drink.

Randy watched his big chance to have a special place among all those people leave in a trail of rhinestone and turquoise sparkle.

"Randy, take me home." Cindy said.

Take her home? Randy couldn't understand.

"Right now!"

The people at the next table looked over at Randy and his girlfriend.

On the car ride back, Cindy sat in silence, waiting for her boyfriend to say something so she could explode. But Randy never did. He just dropped her off and went back to meet his hitchhiker friend, whom he had told to wait for him at the bar.

The two of them found a place that stayed open till three. There was a band there, and people dancing. They talked to a couple of pretty girls who had been standing alone all night. Then Tom asked one to dance, and he went off with her. Randy stood facing the other girl. He couldn't remember the last time he had danced. He wondered if he ever had. Still he asked her anyway, and she agreed to it.

He looked around on the dance floor and tried to imitate some of the people nearby, but he couldn't seem to keep up with all they were doing. Finally, he decided to just listen to the music.

Out of the corner of his eye, he could see a couple of people laughing at his herky-jerky movements. That didn't matter, he thought. He just listened hard to the music and kept on moving—wishing he had tried this before.

There was no smell of bacon in the air the next afternoon when he woke up. With a mind full of the memories from the night before, Randy walked into the kitchen and found Cindy, alone, with the remains of a dish of cold cereal before her.

While the hitchhiker slept, they talked. He talked and she talked, and then it was decided.

Randy went in the room to wake up the hitchhiker.

"You gotta go now," Randy said. "We've both gotta go. She's getting you a bus ticket from her work. We gotta go pick it up. You got a free ride."

Cindy had told him she did not want to see the hitchhiker. She left the house while the two cleared out. Randy was not sure why.

The bus didn't leave until three that afternoon. It was going north through the Upper Peninsula of Michigan. In the meantime, Randy needed to pick up applications for full-time work at four different paper companies and at a factory at the end of town. Randy didn't want to work at a bar anymore. He wanted something that would last.

They were left with about forty-five minutes before the bus departed. Randy decided to take his friend to a place for lunch. They each had a hamburger and a glass of water.

"Hey, look, I'm sorry if I messed things up for you. I didn't mean to cause you any problems with your girl."

"No, you didn't cause any problems that weren't there already. You just helped me see things, that's all. It'll be better this way; it just might take a while."

After lunch Randy dropped his friend at the bus station, and watched as the Trailways heading north inched its way along the city streets toward some other place.

When it was gone, Randy felt a sudden panic run through him as he turned to face a town that suddenly didn't have a place for him to sleep. He sat for a moment to remember what that had felt like. Then he headed out the door, one step ahead of the other, on and on, to the public library to fill out job applications.

7

Jesus on the Road

Once again the cars paraded by in single-laned arrogance. Chevy, Plymouth, Ford, and Toyota had each sponsored its own Impala, Fury, Mustang, Corona float. Finally, a GM van with "Lankell's Refrigerator Repair" decorating its broad side stepped out of formation for a spectator who wanted once again to join the parade.

The driver, who was probably Lankell himself, wore a Frigidaire cap. He seemed to possess a great deal of random energy, as he bobbed back and forth at the edge of his seat while driving a lowly forty-five in a fifty-five zone.

"You're twenty-two, huh? Well, that's a great age! Do you know why it's a great age? There're twenty-two books in the Bible that have more than twenty-two chapters! Did you know that? I bet you didn't. Do you read the Bible? I bet you don't."

Lankell was a self-proclaimed minister who fixed refrigerators for a living. His van contained only his seat and a whole shitload of refrigerator parts. I sat on a box where the passenger seat should have been and gazed up to watch him rattle off Bible trivia.

"Do you know how many books there are in the Bible? Can you tell me how many books there are? There are sixty-six. Did you know that? I'll bet you didn't know that. Do you read the Bible? I bet you don't."

That was his method—he'd ask a question then answer it himself. Everything he said had to do with amounts of things in the Bible. This was the first quantitative approach to that book I'd ever encountered.

"Do you know how many times Mary is mentioned in the Old Testament?"

He could've gone through his whole life making all that stuff up and nobody ever would have known.

"How about Joseph? Do you know how many times . . . "

Fortunately he was going only as far as the next town, so the show ended before we had a chance to get to the twelve apostles. As I jumped out of the van with my pack, he called out to me, "Read your Bible, then you'd know these things."

He never asked my name.

After a few brief moments on the side of the road, I was back in church again, this time with a couple of high-school sweethearts from Norway, Michigan.

"We were going to spend a few of the Lord's hours at the fair in Escanaba," the guy whose name was Peter said. "You're welcome to join us."

"Thanks, I was hoping I'd get to see some of it."

His girlfriend, Maria, scooted over next to her boyfriend so that I didn't have to sit by myself in the back seat. Her hand closest to me clasped a black Bible, while the other one rested somewhere on the inside of her boyfriend's thigh.

"We usually always try to make it to the fair for at least two or three days, but this year we've been so filled with the Lord's work that we were lucky to be able to get away for an afternoon," Peter said, and his girlfriend seemed to agree.

He spoke in an unusually soft and conscientious manner that contrasted sharply with the war that hormones were raging on his adolescent complexion.

"We should be there in about twenty minutes if the Lord wills it," Peter said.

There was really nothing I could add to a conversation that was predestined.

Under a big yellow tent stood row upon row of exhibitions, the type that county fairs all over the world tend to attract. While my two companions were drawn to a man selling leashes that made it look like you were walking an invisible dog, I came to rest in front of a man who was dicing up celery sticks with a knife that had just cut through a pine log—just in case you wanted to cut down a tree before preparing dinner. Across from him a little bald guy was doing a "hands-on" demonstration of a portable electric back massager to anyone who passed within five feet of his booth. An old lady with a cane joined the knife demonstrator on stage to further illustrate his points of ease and manageability.

An "Excuse me sir" crept up from behind me.

"Who me?"

A frail woman was manning the next booth in excruciating black-rimmed-glasses sincerity.

"Excuse me sir, but would you like a road map on how to get from Michigan to heaven?"

I stood silent for a moment.

"What? . . . "

"I said, would you like a road map on how to get from Michigan to heaven?" she repeated.

"Have you found the Lord Jesus in your life, yet?"

She handed me a stack of pamphlets, one of which was entitled "How to Get From Michigan to Heaven."

About that time, her next-door neighbor began mauling another pine tree with a kitchen knife. Somehow, this just didn't seem like the right place to find religion.

I backed away from the woman, thanking her for the offer, when suddenly my attention was abruptly redirected to what felt like a snake crawling down my back. I turned quickly to find the little bald demonstrator holding an "Electro-Massage" in his hand.

"Just $39.95 and you can feel great the rest of your life."

Further down the rows, a disturbance was growing as the people in the Pro-Life booth began calling the ones in the Pro-Choice booth a bunch of murderers, while the "murderers" responded by singing "God Bless America."

It was time to head outside and see the livestock exhibitions, where the animals were decent enough to leave their shit in little piles on the ground.

"Remember, Jesus loves you and he's always with you," Peter said as they dropped me off in front of a Kentucky Fried Chicken in town.

After devouring three pieces of chicken and a biscuit, I wiped about a half a ton of "Extra Crispy" onto the floor and reached for my pack. The waitress, who had offered the $2.39 special for sacrifice less than three minutes earlier, looked on in disgust.

The sun was setting somewhere behind the mass of tall, scrappy pines that framed Michigan Route 2. Somewhere else, "a little ways down the road," the countergirl had claimed there was a campground.

"It's not a religious campground, is it?" I had asked.

She didn't understand.

The heat lingered along with the humidity of a day that had forgotten its afternoon thunderstorm. My goose-down sleeping bag would be exceptionally uncomfortable tonight, I thought, as I continued along the slight path that left only a few feet between myself and four-wheeled death.

The campground couldn't appear too soon. The road was wearing me down. Light-headedness overcame me at forty-yard intervals, leaving me searching for strength on rocks, stumps, and old tires that sporadically appeared beside the highway.

In between the constant flow of vehicles beside me, I spotted the image of a man approaching along the other side of the highway. Despite the evening's heat, he was wearing a full-length, green army jacket. He held a blanket in one arm. He seemed to be very big. He was walking extremely close to the traffic, which came up from behind him. He was walking on the wrong side of the road.

His sparse hair flew up in random directions from the cars that came dangerously close, but like a dazed madman, he never even acknowledged the horn blasts of those that swerved to avoid him. He then crossed the busy highway as though it were a parking lot. The cars and trucks honked and swerved, but he never noticed.

Then he was on my side of the road. The sixty or so yards between us was becoming fifty. Quickly, I mustered some energy and continued my search for the campground.

He reminded me of someone I had seen once in Central Park sleeping in a cardboard box. Another day he might have been an interesting experience. At the moment I wanted only to go to bed.

I picked up my pace, but so did he. When I walked he trotted, when I trotted he ran. I was tired. I couldn't see continuing much longer. After about a quarter mile of his gaining on me, there was still no campground in sight, and I had to stop to get some air.

"Hey, hey, are you going north, man? Are you hitchin' north?"

He was much bigger standing two feet away than he had been at two hundred feet—about six and a half feet worth. His continuous smile revealed a general lack of teeth. The few rotting and crooked ones he had were partially obscured by an unruly mustache that fell to two different lengths on his chin. His heavy army-surplus jacket was zipped three-quarters of the way up, despite the unusual evening heat.

"Right now I'm heading north," I said. "What about you?"

"Yeah, I'm heading wherever, I guess. Anywhere away from the sewage and slop that's all over."

I didn't know what to say to that.

"Like Chicago, man," he continued. "Chicago, New York, Milwaukee—they're all the same. Nobody likes me there because I know their sins. I preach the word of God in those sewers and they throw me out—lock me up."

Oh.

"We gotta watch for Satan around here, man. He'll mess with you like he messes with me. Man, when Lucifer messes with you, you're in lots of trouble."

He stuck his finger into the far reaches of his mouth and began scraping.

"Maybe we should hang out together for a while, I'll get you straight on the whole thing."

If I tried to run, I wouldn't have gotten very far with the pack on my shoulders. If I tried to stick out my thumb he could've just jumped in the back seat with me. I couldn't just belt the guy, and if I did, he probably could've belted me back with a lot more power than I possessed at the moment.

It looked as though I was about to get straightened out.

This man saw Satan on the highway and in the forests; above us, beneath us, and all around. His world was nothing but a constant struggle to keep Satan on the outside. The urgency was apparent: if he stopped for a moment, Lucifer and all the fallen angels would march right in and set up camp. I had a feeling they knew just where to pitch their tent.

In this manic devotion, he was not unlike the wave of screaming zealots I had encountered earlier. Equipped with road maps to heaven and easy phrases that sounded like religion, they frantically put up walls against an evil they had known intimately.

How can the devil get to you if you're selling road maps to heaven all day? How can he find that place in you when you spend every free moment counting names in the Bible?

The god of state-fair religion was more a therapist for evil. Instead of being loved, he was being used. Instead of inspiring wonder, he was a quick sale beneath the big yellow tent.

A flash of sunlight reflected off something the lunatic held in his pocket—something metallic. A knife? A gun, perhaps?

"Let's see if we can find someplace to eat around here," I said, quickening our pace.

"Where are you thinking you're gonna go?" I asked.

I wanted to be the one asking the questions.

"Wherever God tells me, that's where."

"Well, where's God telling you now?"

"North away from all the sewage and rats and shit. Over the lake into Canada. I gotta meet him there. That's what I heard."

The same place I was going, and his eyes were absolutely glazed.

Nightfall quickened its pace. The darkness that overcame the forests framed a constant barrage of headlights that blinded me to all else. Ahead, the light seemed to curve around the darkness. Perhaps there was a place on the other side.

"Nice car, man," I said. "Dig the car."

Adopt the native tongue.

"What car, man?"

"The one with the wheels, man, the weird-looking wheels."

Adopt the native logic.

"Oh yeah, far out."

Adapt completely to the circumstances. Feel yourself a part of what you are afraid of. Keep close contact; never let there be any distance. That was Hitchhiker Rule Number 11.

Maintain a conversation—your conversation in his language—to keep from hearing what he would have to say on his own.

"Man, that's a nice jacket you got. You like that jacket?" I asked.

"Used to be Lucifer's till God took it away from him and gave it to me."

Maybe I was wrong.

The bend in the road led to a gas station where squeegees immersed in soapy water and cans of motor oil stacked according to viscosity welcomed me in their typicalness. I was drawn to the neon lights like the many bugs seeking radiance from the darkness between the trees.

A freckled, red-haired boy was collecting money from a green Chevy as we approached. He looked about fifteen years old. His face lit up when he saw the backpack I was carrying: something new was about to enter the routine of his life at the filling station.

"Are you two hitchhikers?" he called out.

"I am," I said. "I think he is."

"Where are you from? I mean, where did you start hitchhiking from?"

"North Carolina," I said for the both of us.

He followed us to a counter inside, where a somewhat older-looking co-worker collected the Chevy's exact change.

"North Carolina, that's sure a long ways from Escanaba!"

There was a brief moment of smooth living under their neon as I bought a pack of cigarettes and some Starburst candy.

"Be $1.37," the counter boy informed me.

"Hey man, you got the devil in this place or what?"

I watched a moment of deep concern pass over the two boys' faces until it looked as though they had decided the big guy in the green jacket was just kidding around.

"I think you got Lucifer himself in here somewhere and you're not telling."

This time they caught the glazed look and the crooked, rotting teeth. Fear took a more permanent stance through the nervous silence that followed as they realized that it was too hot to be wearing an army jacket.

"Hey man, I'll let you use the bathroom first," I said handing my companion a Starburst. "Just don't take all day."

The kid nervously pointed to the "Men's" sign along the back wall, and we all watched as the man began laughing hysterically on his way to the bathroom.

"What's wrong with that guy?" the kid asked when the door snapped shut.

The two of them closed in on me as I leaned on the counter to talk softly.

"Listen, this guy's been following me for about a mile, and I think he's nuts, but I can't get rid of him because of all the stuff I'm carrying. Can you drive me to the campsite real quick so I can ditch him? Then you can call the cops if he doesn't leave."

"I can't go," the counter boy said. "I gotta stay here and he ain't old enough to drive."

"There's Roy!" the freckle-faced kid said pointing to a new motion at the self-service island. "Roy'll get you out of here!"

"Will you ask him for me? And don't tell him anything about the other guy. Just tell him I need a ride to the campground."

Tuning right in to the urgency of my tone, the two sprang into action.

"How much do you want, Roy?" the younger asked, while already pumping the gas.

"Just two dollars."

Roy sat back down in his seat. He had been on his way to pump his own gas.

"Hey, Roy, you wouldn't mind taking a friend of ours up the road to the campground, would ya?" the older one asked.

"No, I don't mind. Throw your stuff in and let's go."

"Two dollars and a little bit extra," the kid hovered around Roy, then grabbed two bills from him. "Thanks, Roy."

I dumped my pack in the back seat then jumped in the front. Roy started the engine and threw it into drive. Then a thought caught him, and he knocked it back into park.

"Ahh, hell, I hate to put anybody out."

He rolled down the window and called out to the freckle-faced kid, "Hey Billie, how much 'extra' do I owe you?"

"Nothing, you don't owe me a thing. I was just giving it to ya."

"Sure?"

"Yeah!"

"OK, if you say so."

He rolled up his window and would have started off, but the back door popped open, and in fell the seer of Lucifer.

"I got us a ride to a campground. Want another Starburst?" I said.

Roy didn't seem bothered by the extra passenger. He waited for the door to close, then drove off, waving to his two friends who stood motionless, staring beneath the light at the self-service pump.

The campsite finally appeared in another three miles. (So much for the countergirl's sense of distance.) It was kind of a primitive campsite, consisting of only an oblong loop of gravel and the most basic facilities.

Roy dropped us off at a little shack where a couple of signs hung off the door saying "Attendant Not On Duty" and "Camping Fee, $3 a Night."

It seemed the type of place that provided an overnight stop-off for an occasional midwestern hunter or fisherman on his way to Canada. Because of the fair, however, it was filled with a gamut of recreational vehicles set up in various stages of an extended stay.

Most important, there were lights, and with those lights, people. Nice sane people from Illinois and Wisconsin who had friends to write postcards to that said nice sane things like "Greetings from the Upper Peninsula State Fair."

Several strings of multicolored porch lights greeted my fear and made me feel ashamed of my earlier cynicism. That night they represented nothing but safety.

"Thanks for the ride, Roy," I said. "You sure you don't want to stay around here for a while, maybe eat some Starbursts?"

"No, thanks anyway. I gotta get back home. You two have a good night and don't let the bears get ya."

My companion had not said a word during the entire car trip, but continued to smile the way he always had.

His good behavior was short-lived, however. Once out of the car, he began loudly pointing out swooping demons, ducking as they supposedly jumped at him, and all too often screaming out the name of Lucifer.

The families from the Midwest who were supposed to be my protection began eyeing me with suspicion. Fathers stood up from their places at the campfire and stepped between us and their families.

The lights of the campground offered no safety at all, but instead presented another danger. Who was I to walk beneath the illumination and explain my predicament? Who was I to stop the campers from calling the police? I was, after all, a hitchhiker alone with a man who was seeing satanic images in the middle of a campground.

I needed to get us both out of there before my companion caused the campers to act on their fear. There was a grass field at the end of the loop that extended about a half-mile away from the campground. An idea came to me that required taking a big chance, but taking a big chance is the only way to escape a big problem. That was Hitchhiker Rule Number 12.

I found the nearest open site and dropped my pack there to claim it.

"Man, I gotta leave this here because it hurts and I just don't want it no more," I said.

That didn't make any sense, but how would he know? He was nuts. (Hitchhiker Rule Number 11).

"Hey, man, let's go here," I continued. "Come on."

I handed him a cigarette and he followed. Behind me, unprotected, lay everything that I needed in the world.

As the lights from the campground grew distant, so did any sense of sanity in my companion.

"I think the devil's on you, man," he turned and said to me. "I think he's on you."

"No, he ain't on me. Quit preachin' would ya? You want cherry or orange?"

"I think he's on you."

The hand that had remained in his pocket all that time began to shake.

"Cherry or orange?"

We came to a river and found a log to sit on. The air rising up from the water was cool and moist, and the log damp. I had one Starburst left, and somehow he held the pack of cigarettes. My companion stretched out upon the log and looked over the water. A few distant lights flickered from the campground behind us.

"You know," he said, "if a bullet goes through you, it doesn't matter if it's a bullet or a fly, it's still Lucifer."

I pretended not to hear. Beneath every huge ocean wave that looks as though it is about to drown you, there is a safe place where the water remains calm and unaffected.

A car passed through the campground. Its distant flicker of head-lights opened the door just enough for me to see out.

"Holy shit, I don't believe it! They're taking my stuff! Those jerks are taking my stuff!"

I was up, jumping, screaming, banking on Hitchhiker Rule Number 11. The lunatic barely turned to look.

"Listen, stay here, man, stay here and wait for me! I'll be back in a couple of minutes. Don't go anywhere and don't let them catch you! I'm getting my stuff from those jerks and I'll be right back."

Toss him the last Starburst and move quickly. Don't give it a chance not to work. Just run with everything you've got across that open field, and don't look back.

Quickly, my pack, and then search for a hiding place in the woods—only to realize at the edge of the campground that I was too shaken to leave the security of multicolored porch lights.

I set up my tent on a site between two big trailers, pulled my pack inside with me, and listened for sounds outside my thin blue nylon protection.

The slight patter of a few errant raindrops brought me back into the world well past noon. Sleep had been scarce through a night that would not silence every unanswered movement outside from asking, "Who?"

It was dawn when my mind's exhaustion bore through its fear.

The tent came down in record time. There was a piece of cardboard in the trash can beneath a pile of stained newspaper. Soon it said, "S. Ste. Marie." The clouds were drawing space between them. It looked as though it might not rain.

My thumb was facing traffic once again. I had to really work to keep from looking the way I felt. People can sense when you're desperate to get a ride. Then you're bait for all those idiots who wouldn't dare mess with a good strong look. That was a hitchhiker rule from somewhere.

In less than five minutes, a pickup with a camper top came to a slow stop about fifty yards ahead of me. I hooked my arm through one of my pack's straps and hoped like hell they were atheists.

The driver had tufts of grey hair that he combed as though it were blond. He spoke across a younger guy and girl who rolled down their window on the passenger side.

"We can take you as far as Saint Ignace. After that we're headed south to work a fair in the Lower Peninsula. You'll have to hitch north from there to get to the Soo."

"That'd be fine with me."

"Thing is, you're gonna have to set in the back with the dog cause three's all we can fit up front. That OK, too?"

The driver hopped out to open the back of the truck. A Labrador-ish mutt met him with a wet tongue across the face.

"Damm you dog, how'd you like to make Escanaba your home?"

The "damm you dog" didn't fit with the way he almost caressed the animal aside. It seemed the two of them had done a few miles together.

My pack slid easily into the back of the old pickup, while my body fit nicely between a sack of dog food and some old tires.

"I'm sure he'll enjoy your company. Dog's name is Rimshot. That's what you call it when the ball bounces out of the hoop in the carnival game—Rimshot. Bad luck, just like that dog's been, nothing but bad luck—ain't that so, mutt?"

Rimshot licked my face a couple times before I managed to convince him otherwise.

"Go to sleep, dog."

"Go to sleep, dog."

"Go to sleep, dog."

"Cut the shit, mutt!"

I was not in the mood for a playful pup. Soon Rimshot heeded my advice, and there was peace and quiet against a sack of dog food. With tired and bloodshot eyes that barely worked, I sat back and enjoyed the glimpses of Lake Michigan that began to appear through the back window of the camper top.

A moment before sleep, the back window framed the green army coat and lopsided mustache of the night before. He was walking along the road—just walking. He looked tired and hot and mad—not even turning to face the cars that passed him.

The last of the fear my mind was capable of producing shot through my fatigue and made me start.

"North away from all the sewage and rats and shit," he had said. "Over the lake into Canada . . . "

There was nobody there to help me last night, I thought. Not one single person was there to give me a hand.

But the man was getting smaller and smaller. Soon it was impossible to tell which side of the mustache was longer, and shortly thereafter he disappeared behind a curve in the road.

A wave of calm that had grown huge behind a wall of fear drowned me in its release and offered a hard temporary sleep against the dog food, while the hitchhiker's lullaby droned through eight cylinders pushing in my direction.

The quick squeal of the truck's brakes interrupted my slumber. We were stopping in the middle of nowhere for a hitchhiker who happened to be there too. Reluctantly, I sat up and watched him running toward the truck with a small case in his hand, a dufflebag slung over his shoulder, and a funky-looking hat hanging down over one eye.

"No man, you gotta understand something right off. There's some cats they 'play the trumpet.' Then there's dudes like me, we 'blow the horn.' That's what I do, man, I blow the horn."

I thought I'd asked a pretty straightforward question after recognizing the trumpet case he was holding. I guess it wasn't that simple.

"I been doing it now for 'bout fifteen years. If I can get some cats to go in with me, I jam. But most of the time it's me and this case on the street for change. That's cool, too. Has been for fifteen years."

If there was ever a person that deserved the title of "cat," it was this guy sitting across from me with a scraggly goatee and sideburns, black vest, a-little-too-short blue jeans, and of course, the cap buttoned down over one eye.

Jack DePhillips was on his way back to his very first wife, whom he had married four months ago, and whom he had left in South Carolina three months ago to find a home for them in Montana.

"I thought I had the deal sewn up," he said. "A nice little cabin in the hills overlooking a valley, well water—the whole bit. Then things started happening, and the next thing I know, I'm nursing four broken ribs and on my way back to Carolina."

I had noticed a slight limp when he walked up to the truck. He had seemed to be favoring one side as well.

"Couple guys, one day they're my best friends, next day they got me down on the ground, kicking my ribs in with steel-toed boots."

He said he didn't know why they had done that to him.

"They got money, too. About three hundred bucks worth. Now I'm completely broke. I pick up a couple dollars here and there with the horn, but that's gone for food or beer as soon as I get it."

Jack squatted the whole time he talked, facing me as if he were giving a pep talk. There were plenty of places for him to sit, but he squatted anyway. He seemed to be on edge.

I tried to put his pieces together, but the guy didn't make sense. On the one hand, he had abandoned a new bride and done something that in someone's eyes warranted four broken ribs. Yet, the floppy get-up on his head certainly made him look harmless enough—almost entertaining. Plus, he had a certain sparkle about him, especially when he talked about the trumpet.

The sun fought to squeeze itself through a thickening afternoon cloud cover. The moisture off the lake responded by giving substance to the long vertical rays that cascaded into a tremendous pool of glitter floating on the water.

The worried look Jack had held began to give way to an expression that indicated happier thoughts, as he stared out over the spectacle.

"This morning was great, though," he began. "I hadn't eaten in two or three days and I decided to give it a shot at a diner about fifty miles west of here. I didn't have a cent in my pocket.

"I went inside, sat down at one of the tables, and watched as the waitress brought over a menu and a glass of water. I put the menu down and didn't touch the water, and in a few minutes the waitress was back again, asking me what I wanted.

" 'Ma'am,' I said to her, 'I don't have any money, but I haven't ate in a couple of days, so if you've got some dishes that need cleaning or some floors that need to be swept, maybe I could do that in exchange for some food?'

"She stood there for a couple minutes looking like she was trying to figure me out. I told her that if they didn't have any work for me, I'd just go ahead and leave. Then she went off into the kitchen, and came back after a little bit.

" 'The owner says you can have whatever you want, and not to worry about no floors,' she said with this big grin on her face. Man, I couldn't believe it! Let me tell you something, people will always come through for you when you need them. I mean, there I was so bummed out about those bad acts in Montana, when just like that, those dudes in the restaurant got their hand out to pull me right back up again."

"What did you order?" I asked.

"Stack of pancakes and a medium orange juice. And coffee, lots and lots of coffee. I guess I could've ordered the steak and eggs if I wanted to, and they were probably expecting that I would. It's just that when somebody does you a good turn like that, you don't want to put them out, you know what I mean?"

"Yeah, I know exactly what you mean."

For the first time since he'd gotten in the truck, Jack found himself a seat on one of the tires, then gradually fell into a reclining position that led to sleep.

His calm offered a more restful sleep for me, too; a sleep that lasted longer through the reminder that there are people out there ready to help a hitchhiker, or how else could I be where I was?

Again, sleep ended with the long gradual squeal of the truck's brakes, as we awoke to find ourselves pulling into one of those "non-facility" rest areas.

Once parked, the older guy came around back and stuck his head conspicuously through the window of the camper top.

"You boys wanna smoke some grass?" he asked.

I'd never seen a man smile quite the way he did just then. If he was a cat, you could've seen the feathers sticking out of his mouth. To him it was a rhetorical question at best: he was offering two hitchhikers free grass.

The whole day for me had been a fight to keep my eyes open. Mellow was not where I needed to be. For some reason, Jack didn't seem too keen on the idea, either.

Yet from what we both saw in the expression of our driver, if both of us hitchhiker types refused free grass, we'd completely demolish his sense of reality. There'd be nothing left for him to do except throw himself in front of an oncoming tourist vehicle.

"Hey, let's go for it," Jack said.

Hitchhiker Rule Number 13: Don't destroy your driver's sense of reality before he drops you off.

We were a real ratty-looking group, traipsing through the woods in search of privacy from all the scattered males who had thought there'd be a rest room at the rest stop. The old guy who led the way was carnival through and through. His pointy-toed cowboy boots and his faded blue jeans looked as though they had been about three sizes too small when he bought them ten years back. But relentless use and material durability had made them a part of his skin.

I thought that I might have won a rabbit from this guy at a fair in '67.

The young guy and girl said they had just started running carnivals with the old-timer. The guy's boots were stiff and bulky-looking, and his jeans still a deep blue. The three of them were making a living from one town to the next, collecting tickets, dipping apples, manning the booths — whatever work was available at the time.

They had left the Upper Peninsula Fair early for some undisclosed reason and were on their way to a county fair in central Michigan someone had told them about. No phone calls to confirm the thing existed, no setting up employment interviews; they just followed a rumor in the wind, and if it brought them to a fair and that fair needed workers, then the three of them had jobs for a while. If not, they moved on.

Finally, we found a place near the bottom of a hill where there didn't appear to be anyone going to the bathroom. The old guy pulled a real fat joint out of a plastic bag in his wallet and handed it to Jack.

"How do you like that stuff?" he asked.

"Fine, fine weed," the jazzman responded.

When the little bit that was left started burning people's hands instead of their taste buds, Joe Carnival snuffed out the last bit of flame with his fingers and placed the remains into the plastic bag.

He searched around real slow to make sure there had been no witnesses to the crime, then placed the bag back into his wallet and placed his wallet back alongside his hip. Then he perched his right knee on a log and faced Jack and me at a forty-five-degree angle, resting his right elbow on that knee and scratching his chin with the same hand. The carnival man had something to say.

"Well, boys, 'bout ten miles down the road, me and my partners here have got to be heading south. That's where this younger fella here's gonna be getting off to go to the Soo.

"Now, you're wantin' to get south to the Carolinas, right?" he asked Jack.

"South Carolina."

"Well, we can take you another forty miles along your way before we've got to head east to where we're going."

The carnival man had it all figured out and he loved telling it. Occasionally he looked at us when he spoke, but most of the time his glance was off in the distance to our left, as if he were on stage doing his very best performance of himself.

When he finished, he ran an old black comb through his hair a few times before heading off to the pickup and points south.

"Did you like that grass?" I asked Jack back in the cab.

"No, man, that stuff tasted like soap or something. I just kept blowing it through my mouth."

The ten miles left for traveling with John were passing too quickly at a rate of sixty miles per hour. There was more that I wanted to know.

"Hey, did I tell you that I've got a pair of drumsticks in my pack?"

"All right, man! You play the skins?"

"For about twelve or fourteen years."

"Well, holy shit, there's only one thing to do when two musicians get the same ride . . . "

That was to buy some beers and jam.

Jack gave up that extra forty miles of a ride and I gave up $2.75 for a six-pack at a convenience store. I still had a couple of sandwiches from someplace, and so we found a spot on the side of a hill overlooking the lake and got some refreshment.

Shortly thereafter, Jack started cranking it up.

"Oh, Mistra Armstrong, please, please sir, don't play dem blues again. You know how sad theys makes me. Please sir, don't play dem blues."

With that intro, he burst into "Do You Know What It Means to Miss New Orleans?" sending long, clean notes across the wide-open sparkle, in the direction of his home.

When the trumpet touched his lips, it was as though he had been reunited with a part of him that he had missed terribly. The joy of that reunion blistered through the dented valves of his instrument, as every muscle in his face, neck, and arms, strained toward the meeting of flesh and steel that made it all worthwhile.

You can never understand a musician until you hear him play. The music wasn't just a piece of Jack's puzzle, it was the glue that held together all of the other pieces. It was the unity that allowed him into so many disjointed corners, knowing that each night, no matter what he'd been through during the rest of the day, the horn would be waiting to let a little "Mistra Armstrong" seep through.

Jack played on without even breaking between songs: into "Misty," then "Stardust," . . . "Do Nothing Till You Hear from Me."

I tried to keep a beat on his trumpet case, but he was well into his own time. The best I could do was listen to his music through the rushing swell of leaves from the wind off the lake.

"One O'Clock Jump" . . . "Two O'Clock Jump" . . . "Up on the Roof."

"That last one I found at a Salvation Army Store in Missoula," he said, taking time to down another beer. "Piece of sheet music buried under a bunch of foreign-language books. The guy let me have it for a nickel. I kinda like the tune.

"There was another song I got turned on to while I was out there that I'd give anything to get the music to. You ever hear a song once that comes outta nowhere and just moves you all around?

"It happened to me when I was sitting at a bar there in Missoula, a song came through the jukebox that I wasn't even listening for, and bam—hit me right between the eyes, right on target.

"I listened to it for a while and just got caught up. Before I knew it, the song was just about over, so I had to run across to the jukebox to quick get the number before it was gone forever. I got out a couple quarters and spent most of the night playing it over and over till I could get all the words down. You see, I wanted to keep it with me. I got it here somewhere, man."

He opened a crushed velvet flap in his trumpet case and unfolded a shred of brown paper bag.

"No, that's a letter to my wife."

After discarding three other scraps for the same reason, Jack finally found what he was looking for.

"Here, man, this is it. When I'm down, that's where I've been, man, right in that song—right on target."

The song was called "Sunday Mornin' Comin' Down."

"Johnny Cash is the one that sings it, but I don't know if he's the one that wrote it."

The song was about a guy who falls hungover into a Sunday only to find "the smell of someone fryin' chicken," "a daddy with his little girl that he was swingin'," and a Sunday school, "with songs that they were singin'."

Chorus:

"On a Sunday mornin' sidewalk, I'm wishin' Lord that I was

stoned; cause there's somethin' in a Sunday, that makes a body feel alone.

"And there's nothin' short of dyin', that's half as lonesome as the sound, of a sleepin' city sidewalk, and Sunday mornin' comin' down."

A Sunday mornin' comin' down. When the wonder and excitement of it all become only a far off and distant longing—a distant sadness—in a life so many miles away from anything certain.

"That's it, right there, man. When I hit bottom, I get that out and read it. Lets me know that someone else has been there too. Helps me get by."

"Mind if I write it down?"

There were words to songs that had followed me into so many different places along the road. Lines I'd play over and over in my head, like those few from Tom Waits' "Ole 55" every time I was saying good-bye to someone: "Just a wishin I'd stayed a little longer. Oh Lord, let me tell ya the feelin's gettin' stronger." Over and over again, time after time.

Good company, that. Anytime you needed it to smooth out the reality, it's always there for you.

"But man, when it comes to jammin' music, there ain't never gonna be anyone like Mr. Louis."

With that he stood up and began wailing "When the Saints Go Marchin' In" with such intensity that it brought a group of nearby convenience-store employees out their back door to witness the blistering rendition of a song they recognized with applause.

After the music had been played, the two of us took some time to talk. Jack was the first person I'd come across who was finding his way along the road the same way that I was. I'd come to respect him as more experienced at traveling by thumb.

I told him about this strange urge I had to get over the top of Lake Superior, in the hope that he could explain to me the nature of my desire. Was it divine?

Instead, he just sat back and laughed a bit.

"When I was young like you I was always thinking that I had to get here or there, but when I got there, it seemed like it was never any big deal. Then one day I realized, it's not where you're going, it's how you get there that matters! It's how you get there, and that's here and now, drinking beer and playing music."

We talked and played a little more until all the beers were finished and the sky began to glow in anticipation of the sunset.

The Interstate before us crossed north in the direction of Sault Sainte Marie, and south toward the Carolinas. A chilly evening fog rolled in off the lake as we made our way toward the sign "Mackinaw Bridge and points South." Jack took an old green blanket out of his bag and wrapped it around him. I found a sweatshirt.

"Hey man, it was great jamming with you," Jack said, shaking my hand at the foot of his entrance ramp. "Just keep hoping the Lord's staying on your side, and you'll make it all right."

Jack sensed my discomfort over what he had just said. I took a couple of minutes to explain to him that I'd seen the Lord work in some mysterious ways recently.

He looked down at the ground and hopped a few times to fight off the chill that was creeping through the stillness. He tightened his blanket around him, looked up, and reached deep into my eyes with a firm, kind look.

"Don't let anybody get you down about God," he said. "No matter what you hear about him, or what type of guy says it, God is still a good dude!

"I mean right this minute he's looking out after me. The little nobody who I am, and God's looking out after me! He's looking out after you too, man—he really is."

We shook hands and headed toward the highway in our own directions. I carried Jack's words with me down the long and gently sloped entrance ramp that led to the four-lane. It was like a dozen others I'd walked in search of a ride, and probably like hundreds Jack had struggled along, hoping there'd be someone at the end to take him somewhere.

There was a religion to what we were doing, I realized. Like members of a congregation, we hitchhikers knelt at our asphalt altar and handed our fate to something greater than ourselves, with the hope that we would be delivered safely to a destination yet unknown.

God was not found in a church or at the end of road maps. He wasn't in the memorization of Bible trivia, but he was in Lankell's brakelights and his safe transportation a little further down the line.

He was in the waitress that fried up those pancakes for Jack, asking him in return to play another song or tell another story to someone who needed it. God was in the things people did for one another, not in the things they said about him. The wonder of a Sunday morning—the feeling that there was something greater than what you knew—was alive each day through the mysterious destination the passenger seat offered. It was not caught up in a vision of a world yet to come, but bound to a fascination with the here and now.

I needed to hear that "God was a good dude" from a guy who blew the horn with so much feeling and so much joy: I needed to hear it from that guy wrapped in a blanket and heading south. There was another guy once who went around spreading good news to people. He never seemed to have a whole lot of money either.

Me, I had an ear to lend to people who needed to tell a story, and excitement to offer people who had gotten pretty used to their lives. That was my communion.

At the end of the ramp, I leaned my pack against a metal reflector pole and pointed my thumb in a northerly direction. I couldn't see the cars approach because the fog had blanketed the highway. But the sound of their engines getting closer filled me with a happy sense of wonder, as I waited for one to break through the emptiness and see me waiting to go wherever.

8

"Dear Jessica..."

The fog settled onto the fields in thick, still batches beneath the bumpy ride of an eighteen-wheel flatbed on its way to Canada to pick up logs. A line of deep red broke through a grey western sky as if trying to squeeze a whole magnificent sunset through one tiny unstitched seam in the cloud cover. Seagulls dropped and soared in and out of the ground fog, above and below the thin line of color that would become orange on its way to yellow.

Because the long trailer was still empty, it grabbed each imperfection in the highway and magnified it a hundred times, leaving the contents of the cab bucking up and down as if riding a blacktop stallion longing to rid itself of passengers.

Joe was the head rider in this Interstate rodeo. He rested both hands and both elbows firmly on the steering wheel and smiled upon Interstate 75's reach toward Canada.

"I seen it like this a few times in Arkansas," he said. "Few times like this in Kentucky, few times out along here. Near these big lakes it's just fog rolling in that rolled too far. I'm not sure what causes it down there."

"I've never seen it red like that," I said, "not through fog anyhow."

I wasn't sure if he heard me or not. There was something in the soft, pastel shades of the day's end that projected his interest far off into the distance.

"Want a mint?" he offered.

"Thanks. I'm fine."

He reached into his pocket where a half-opened pack of Lifesavers had been waiting. With one hand, he popped one into his mouth and stuffed the excess paper back over the rest.

"I got a boy at home I go driving with sometimes. He gets real excited over fog, especially if it's laying low at night and we're busting through it with my bright yellows. He gets all worked up over it."

"How many children do you have at home?"

"Just the boy. I try to take him whenever I can, but he can't afford to be away from his studies too much. He's like his dad, never could understand anything when it came out of a book. Sure you don't want one?"

"Thanks anyway."

Joe leaned forward in his seat. He stretched his neck toward his rear-view mirror and studied it up and down, even though ours was clearly the only vehicle along that stretch of highway. He tossed about some in his chair until he found a more comfortable place to talk from.

"His mother's been gone for a while now," he began. "She came down with some sort of something. Took us all by surprise. I've got a sister that looks after the boy when I'm gone, but I try to take him with me as much as I can."

"The company doesn't mind your taking people along for the ride?"

"There's no company. I'm an independent, see, I can take whoever I want to."

"Do you pick up a lot of hitchhikers?"

"No, hardly ever."

"Why'd you pick me up?"

"I don't know that there's a reason. I guess I just felt like it."

Joe pushed a lever on the dashboard, and I felt a sudden burst of dry warmth accumulate around my feet.

"It's tough leaving things behind, sometimes," he said. "Best you can do is hope it'll all stay the same when you get back to it."

"Yeah, I suppose you're right."

"You got folks waiting for you somewhere?" he asked.

"I've got my parents. I don't know if they're waiting for me the way you're saying it. I guess I got a girlfriend back in New York."

"You're not sure?"

"I don't know. It's been such a long time, I hadn't really thought about it. It gets a little crazy out there on the road sometimes. Kinda keeps you from thinking about things, I guess."

Outside, the sliver of sunset held a moment of dim yellow after-glow before finally surrendering to the soft purples and blues of the night, while an empty flatbed stole ahead through fog-shrouded darkness toward its destination somewhere in Canada.

"What do you think's in the chef's special casserole?" I asked.

"At a truck stop? You're not serious, are ya?"

"It's got a good price to it."

"Why don't you just get the hamburger plate, and I'll spot you the difference."

"No, you don't have to do that."

"For a buck and a half, I can feel like I'm saving a life."

"No, you see I've got this deal with my stomach to forgive and digest for a while."

"Living on a pretty tight budget, huh?"

"I can't afford any hotels."

"Well, where was you planning on spending the night tonight?"

"Wherever I can. I've got a tent in my pack just in case, but usually something comes up."

"I bet you've slept in some pretty unusual places."

"Yeah, I guess you just have to figure that it really doesn't matter where you wind up, because you're just going to be sleeping through it anyway."

At a rest area on the American side of the bridge, Joe hung a canopy of thick green plastic over the wooden bed of a truck that was supposed to rest lumber, not a hitchhiker.

"I got some newspaper and a couple cloths in the back to make it a little softer," he explained. "Be just like a hotel except that it's green all over."

After dinner, Joe decided that he'd just as soon remain in his native country till morning. I think he really wanted to see whether someone would actually sleep in the back of his flatbed.

"I don't mind the green," I said. "It's light blue I'm getting sick of."

"Huh?"

"That's the color of my tent."

"Gotcha."

From the open sides of my makeshift dwelling, I watched the seagulls mill about under the lights for the public rest room, then scatter whenever a car brought patrons. Through the trees in back of the modest facility, the lights of the bridge to Canada twinkled in the wind. Around it flowed the rhythmic metallic clanging and low moans of large engines, as ships slipped from one Great Lake to the next through the locks that this city of Sault Sainte Marie was famous for.

Along the bridge, crossing and crossing back again, the fragmented flow of headlights moving closer toward, and further away from, a place on the other side that was waiting for me: Superior.

"It's tough leaving things behind," Joe had said. "Best you can do is just hope they're waiting for you just like they were before you left 'em."

I hadn't really thought about it till then. I'd never really looked behind me. But in the shadows of a bridge to someplace else, I began to remember all that had been before the Interstate began.

There was a woman somewhere back there whose face lit up over the word *love,* and whose eyes sparkled when I said it to her. She had remained in New York City, where she had wanted me to stay.

"I'll be a better person for you when I get back," I had said.

Joe was wrong; I didn't want it to be the same. Maybe I wanted the people to be the same, but I wanted my life to be different—even if it was the same. That was the whole idea.

The cool Great-Lakes breeze found more openings than I could defend against, and so I allowed it to bathe my face in a soft, continual flow toward sleep.

"Rise and shine! We've got some miles to go before half the day is gone."

The sun was up around six, and so was Joe, banging around under the hood of his truck. Eventually, I could no longer ignore the brilliant sunshine filtering through the dew-soaked discombobulation of a misused tarp.

Children at the rest area pointed with both hands at the movement that was beginning to take place beneath all that green, while I tried to figure out how I was going to get my pants on without turning it into an R-rated feature attraction.

Most of the time you can just close the door.

The few moments I had spent in the bathroom had been more than enough time for Joe to have disassembled my transient hotel. He was waiting in the cab with the engine running when I came out.

"Well, you coming along or not?"

The bridge glistened in clear morning sunlight just a single word away. But the seagulls' caw and the smell of the wind before 7 A.M. demanded I be a part of someone's town that morning. A hot cup of coffee and a morning newspaper in Sault Sainte Marie was in the air.

"I think I'll hang around here for a little bit," I yelled through the engine's drone.

"OK, I wish I could stay and have some breakfast with you, but I gotta make a two-hour trip in an hour and forty-five minutes."

With that he hopped down the short row of metal steps and shook my hand.

"Wish you luck the rest of the way," he said. "Stay away from those chef's casseroles, and you're halfway there."

"Got it," I said. "You too."

"The Place" hung tightly to the corner of Main and something. On the counter next to the cash register were a couple of disheveled copies of the *Sault Sainte Marie Herald* waiting for the next patron to spill coffee on the sports page or tea on Ann Landers.

I sat at a booth behind a grey-haired man addressing a young couple across from him. The two seemed very interested in what the man had to say. I sat with my back to them so that I didn't have to pretend I wasn't listening.

"Would you like coffee?" the waitress asked.

"Sure. Do you have tea also?"

"Yes."

"I think I'll have tea instead then."

Waffles, French toast, eggs, oatmeal, pancakes . . .

"Ready to order?"

The old man spoke louder than anything my newspaper and French toast could muster.

"I think the thing you'll find most attractive about the area is that there are so many things to do. The college, as you will soon see, offers its staff excellent academic opportunities, while there are more than enough bars and restaurants to satisfy . . . "

The couple from someplace else listened to the man's every word. They looked like they were about to embark on an unfamiliar stage of their life together.

"Why, I remember when I accepted my position after graduating from Chicago twenty years ago; my wife had seen the town only on several childhood visits to the locks. As far as she could tell there was only a rest room at the Gulf station and visitors information center. But when we got here . . . "

Why hadn't I written? There were plenty of post offices along the way.

"It's like any place, there are advantages and disadvantages, and it's just up to the people . . . "

Perhaps I had believed it would all stop where I left it, the way a child believes an object no longer exists when it is hidden from his sight.

"You simply have to say, 'This is my life and this is where I am going to live it,' and then . . . "

My contribution to the disruption of type on the *Sault Sainte Marie Herald* was a line of syrup across the front page. I left three dollars for a lunch worth half that much, and hurried out the front door to buy stationery.

Dear Jessica,
   I'm sorry I haven't written in so long but . . .

Dear Jessica,
   How are things in . . .

   There's this bridge sitting in the shadows of where I am right now, and on the other side is some place I've really wanted to get to for a long time now. I'm not really sure why I want to go there, but I know I do, and it got me to thinking about you for some reason last night and today.
   How are you?
   You'll have to forgive me not writing, it's just that I wanted to make real sure that I got away without thinking I'd have been better off not going. I'm not sure what that means, but I thought I did last night.
   Sometimes you just have to say fuck it, you know? Fuck it, fuck all of it, fuck every little bit of it because I've got no use for it at the moment. I'm not sure how I got there, and I don't know why I wanted to be there. Like college, how was it we went to college and studied the things we did?
   Does that make sense?
   It's just that life has this way of sucking you up in different directions, like there's this momentum pushing from the minute you're born. All these people telling you things; all these choices that keep popping up from somewhere, and it would be so easy to just try and keep up with it all without ever trying to make sense of it.
   It's just that I wanted so terribly to break from that momentum and get the ball in my court. The only way I knew how to do that was to say "Fuck it." Fuck it to you, and everyone else who had some claim to me. I know that was not fair to you.
   This is a very roundabout way of saying "Sorry I didn't write," isn't it? It's just that I want to know if you're OK and I wanted to tell you that I really don't not love you or anything, even though I hadn't written in a while.
   Can you see that? Are you going to stay the same? Are you going to be there when this is all said and done???

Dear Jessica,
   I'm sorry I haven't written in so long. It's just that it was very difficult leaving you, and I had to get some distance before I could feel comfortable writing.
   I'm just very curious to know how you are. Why don't you send

me a letter c.o. general delivery in Minneapolis. I should be there
in a few weeks. I'd really love to hear from you. I hope all is well.
    Love,
        Tom

I walked my stamped envelope two and a half miles past six
mailboxes to the inside "Out of Town" slot at the main post office.

My American youth hostel book said that the facilities at the
college were no longer being used as a youth hostel as of last year. I don't
know why they bothered saying that.
    "You see, I was thinking of going to this college next year, and I
wanted to spend the night so I could look around more tomorrow
because it's so late already," I told the lady at the information desk at
Lake Superior State College.
    "Well, we used to leave some of the dorm rooms open for a youth
hostel, but we stopped doing that last year. . . . Hang on just a second,
let me find out something."
    The school sat on a hill overlooking the town. It looked about
empty. It must have been vacation time. The lady at information sent
me to housing, and housing was off checking with someone else.
    "We decided that if you're a potential student and you want to see
the school it's OK. There's hardly anyone here right now anyway. Here's
the key to room nine, it's in the dorm across the street. To get there,
you've got to go . . . "
    Hitchhiker Rule Number 14 in the general sense: You've always
got to be on the lookout for the potential because the actual doesn't
always present itself.
    Hitchhiker Rule Number 14 in the specific sense: Where there are
students, there are beds.

On the other side of the sliding glass door to suite nine I found
something absolutely amazing:
    There was no one there.
    It was just me.
    I shut the door. . . .
    I didn't hear anybody threatening satanic images.
    I checked under the bed just in case.
    There were no stories to be told, no advice to be given. There
weren't any lives to become involved in; there was no need to watch
what I said.
    I checked behind the curtains.
    I didn't feel obligated to anyone; I had paid my four dollars for the

room. People wouldn't laugh at the place where I was sleeping that night. Nobody was going to drive my bed away if I didn't wake up in time.

I laid my body across a totally unoccupied mattress.

Alone. A word that described the state in which I was traveling. It described my situation along the roadside as cars passed, as well as the state that I was in walking down a dark road at night. It was this very same word that was the reason for the absolute joy I felt at that moment, as well as the word used to describe my situation while listening for the sounds outside my tent.

Alone. A word whose preponderance of definitions on the road rendered it meaningless.

There was a man knocking at the entrance to the only peace I'd known in weeks. He was holding a bicycle and wearing a backpack while I was stirring a can of Spaghetti-Os on the stove in the kitchen all by myself.

He must have been lost.

"I read my youth hostel book wrong, but they said that there was someone staying here tonight anyway, so they said I could, too."

He pulled his bicycle into the room just far enough for the back wheel to get caught on the sliding glass door. He opened the door a little bit more, but slammed his wheel against it anyway. Finally, he managed to get the bike inside, but when he went to close the door, the bike fell down. I would've helped, but I was afraid to. He set the bike against the wall, and walked carefully back to the door and closed it gently, giving the bike a watchful glance—and me just standing there stirring noodles that came from a can.

The man had a long beard and looked in his mid-thirties. He dumped his things onto the bed I had been laying on.

"It was really funny, the book said NO youth hostel after this year, and I thought they meant there was going to be one."

He laughed.

Hitchhiker Rule Number 15: For all the time you spend alone in this world, it's really difficult to get some privacy.

Jim was a janitor from Grand Rapids who had studied philosophy at the University of Michigan. But before I could ask him about this apparent contradiction, he had four maps sprawled across an empty bed and was studying a pocket watch.

"Let's see, I started in Strongs at 7 A.M. this morning and traveled twenty-three miles before stopping in Brimley for forty-five minutes, then arrived at Sault Sainte Marie exactly fourteen minutes ago, that's

6:23, which means my traveling rate is about 4.6 miles per hour not including stops."

Guilt began to creep in as I watched the little red bubbles accumulate in greater number along the top of my dinner. There was just about enough of it for me, but there were two people in the room. Had I forgotten so soon how I had gotten here?

"You want some Spaghetti-Os?" I asked.

"You got enough?"

"Yeah, I guess."

"Sure, OK, I'll have some."

Hitchhiker Rule Number 16: If you ever do happen to come upon a private type of alone, lock it up and hide it.

"What are you gonna do tonight?" Jim asked.

"I don't know. I was going to hang around here, but now I think I'm going to go downtown and see what's there."

"Well, I'd really like to go, but I've got to get all the way to Cheboygan tomorrow in about five and a half hours."

"Well, what's the point of going to Sault Sainte Marie if all you see is a dorm room and a bowl of Spaghetti-Os?"

Suddenly, I found myself arguing directly against my own interest. It was an academic point I was making, inspired by some words said along the lake the day before. However, I had failed to foresee the immediate, practical ramifications of that philosophy at the time.

"Well, I guess I could go with you if we don't stay out too late."

Walking down the hill into town, Jim explained to me that the one time in his life that he had been hitchhiking, his girlfriend took everything but the clothes on his back and left with a truck driver.

"It's really hard when someone does that to you, especially if it's your girlfriend."

"Yeah, I can imagine."

"So ever since then, I've been traveling by bike. I figured I've gone 7,550 miles in the last eight years."

For some reason I knew he would know that.

"Haven't you ever had trouble on the bike?"

"Sure, the last trip I took, I ditched my bike about a half mile into the woods to take a walk, and when I got back fifteen minutes later, it was gone."

"That's been your only bad experience, huh?"

"No way. I've lost three bikes and have been driven off the road twelve times. I even broke my arm twice."

"And all you lost hitchhiking was a girlfriend?"

"What do you mean?"

"Why are you working as a janitor when you studied philosophy at Michigan?"

"It's a good job. There aren't any hassles, it's very peaceful at night in an empty building. . . . "

Most of his words were mumbled into his beard while his eyes studied the ground as if searching for a contact lens. However, as we approached the lights of a drugstore, something drew his gaze upward and held it there while a smile lodged itself permanently across his face.

I followed his line of vision through the front window displays and to a row of magazine literature with titles like *Cunt* and *Beaver*. The pace of our walk slowed to a standstill as we approached.

"You like that stuff?" I asked.

No reply. Just a distant grin of acknowledgment.

After three beers, Jim was very obviously undressing every woman he could see at the country-and-western bar we had stopped at on Main Street.

"I better quit drinking these," he said after ordering another round of Miller Lites. "I've got to get to Cheboygan tomorrow. But holy geez, would you look at that one in the cowboy boots!"

"Hey look, I'm going to go out and get some air for a minute. See what you can do with the empty seat, OK?"

"Got ya, Chief."

Chief?

Saturday night, the streets of the Soo were lined with all those people who had discovered the opposite sex, but were too young to pursue their discovery indoors.

I began to walk.

"Hey, Janie," some guy called from a car called beside me. "Billy says he loves you."

A girl walking with a group turned away. Silly boys.

Love.

Again, there was the woman, waiting somewhere where the road had begun. I thought about the time we had pulled off the road on the bridge to Manhattan and watched the lights of the city through all of the cars.

"Hey Charlie, get fucked."

A man ran at the car, which screeched off.

I continued to walk. Between the longing to hold, and the longing to continue somewhere else, I walked, one step ahead of the other, trying to get back into a bar where loud music and forced conversation would keep me from having to think.

In the few moments I had been gone, Jim had managed to surround himself with four women who were barely female. Before I could make my way back out the door, he spotted me.

"Hey, Tom, over here!"

I had no choice. I pulled up next to a woman with a rose tattoo on her left forearm.

"Guess I got it like you said, Chief," Jim hit me on the shoulder. "Let's get another round for all of us."

When the liquor was running low, a finger would too, somewhere across my suite-mate's thigh, leading to an inevitable: "Waitress, another round for all of us!" as Jim was being milked for every cent he was worth.

"Boy, let me tell you something," he yelled across the table, "right now, I could care less about Cheboygan!"

When he got up to dance with one of the women, I excused myself and went to buy my own drink.

"I'll have a Scotch and soda," the woman with the tattoo called out to me.

I stood waiting and she began a half-hearted search through her pocketbook. Then she stopped.

"Oh," she said, putting her purse away.

"Oh, what?"

"Well, you looked like you weren't expecting me to pay for my drink."

"Yes, I was."

This was not something she had made any provision for.

"Well . . . I'm collecting welfare!"

"Well, I'm unemployed and I'm not collecting anything."

"But I've got three kids to support!"

This actually continued all the way up to the number of days her mortgage payment was overdue.

"Why don't we split it fifty-fifty?" I offered finally.

"OK, that sounds fair."

After the purchase, I exited quickly before the woman with the rose tattoo was wearing half my shirt.

To bed; a slight buzz. I tried not to think of anything at all.

I heard the crumpling of Jim's maps far too early the next morning. He entered my room wearing plastic pants, plastic coat, a plastic hat, and even socks covered with plastic bags.

"There's a forty-five percent chance of rain for today," he said. "If it rains, I'll probably only make it to Mackinaw City. That's ten miles less than I had planned."

"How'd things go with the women last night?"

"Well, it was the funniest thing. After that place closed, we went next door to another club till very late. I thought for sure they'd ask me to go home with them, but all they said was good-night."

"You were thinking of going home with all of them?"

"At least one. I just can't figure it out."

On his way out, Jim left me with the name of a "great friend" of his who lived in the Black Hills of South Dakota.

"If you get out there, he'd be a fantastic person for you to stay with."

My first impulse was to leave "Bobby Davis, Deadwood, South Dakota 555-4562" in the nearest waste paper basket. But an instinct developed through weeks of dependence on strangers guided the small slip of paper into the compartment on the top of my pack.

Hitchhiker Rule Number 17: When you never know, you just never do.

9

T-Bay

The little girl smudged her face against the window of the bus. Her mother pointed to the ship that was passing beneath the bridge to Canada. The mother grasped the child's waist tightly, just in case.

The bus cost fifty cents and was the only way for me to cross a bridge that restricted the use of both feet and thumbs.

The customs officer wanted to know where this trip had started twenty-two years ago.

"Teaneck, New Jersey," which was about an hour or so from New York City.

How long was it by mail from Michigan to that city, I wondered?

Probably about three months too long.

Apart, with a green hump, at a place called "INFORMATION." Mothers cupped their children away from my unusual massiveness for fear I might contain a sharp edge.

"Yes, ma'am, I need to get to the Trans-Canadian Highway toward Thunder Bay, and I was wondering if there were any . . . "

"Turn to your right out the door, cross the street, you'll see the sign for the stop, take Bus 17 to the end of the line," she snapped out automatically.

"That will get me to Route 1 to Thunder Bay?"

"Right to it."

"And I can hitchh . . . "

"You certainly can."

"Well, thank you."

I lost a dime on the exchange rate for Bus 17.

"Will you tell me when it's the end of the line?" I had asked the driver.

"Don't worry, you'll know."

There was no room for my pack except in the aisles. Every time someone needed to pass, I had to squeeze it onto my lap, with a little excess falling onto the lap of the gentleman next to me, who appeared not to have a neck.

"You should get a smaller one if you're going to be traveling on buses," he scolded.

"Thanks, I'll remember that."

"A person has to be able to say, 'All right, I did a bad thing. That does not mean that I am a bad person! That does not mean I am bad for doing that.'"

The only other person left after twelve stops of Bus 17 was one woman possessing both a child and a shopping bag. She had hair that wanted to be blond. For the past three stops, she had been loudly addressing an uninterested bus driver so that all the rest of us could be enlightened by the wisdom she had stolen from her last counseling session.

"You see our behavior and our selves are two different things. When we start judging ourselves by our behavior, that's when we start getting into trouble."

She continued. . . .

"I mean, how can we be considered bad just because our actions are?"

She looked back at the one remaining member of her congregation as if waiting for an ovation, but I continued staring toward roads that contained fewer and fewer signs of life.

To my surprise, I noticed a hitchhiker standing out there with a sign that read "T-Bay."

"Are you a hitchhiker?" the woman called back to me.

Yes I'm a hitchhiker I graduated from college and I'm going to see the country those certainly are lovely children – child – I left from North Carolina no I haven't had any real bad experiences yet and yes my mother does know that I'm doing this.

"How did you know I was a hitchhiker?"

"Well," she giggled, "we get a hitchhiker or two on Bus 17 every once in a while."

Before she could explain, the bus pulled to a long, slow stop, which was – as the driver had said it would be – obviously the end of the line.

"This is Route 1 to Thunder Bay?"

"This is the one."

"Thanks."

The moment my feet hit the ground, the bus's engine accelerated away. I could hear music being played somewhere near where I had been deposited, and I turned toward it.

About fifty yards away, on the same side of the road I had intended, there was a small commune of tie-dye-looking people playing guitar and singing. One member held a cardboard sign out to a deserted two-lane. His request: "The Mighty Thunder."

A bit beyond, on the same side of the road—the same side that I would be standing on—there stood a man who looked like he had once been a member of the same group. He held a similar sign with a similar message: "Thunder Bay."

Beyond him, another man.

Beyond him, another still.

In fact, it seemed the whole of this section of Trans-Canadian Highway was lined with people who looked like they were waiting to stare God in the face, or something.

I passed by six signs before staking my claim at the entrance to a gas station. A guy who looked a little less Woodstock stood at the exit. He looked kind of worn out, but he didn't look Woodstock.

I could see eight signs in front of me and eight behind me, all asking an anemic flow of traffic for the same thing. I could not see a lake anywhere, only a forest in the direction where it should have been.

The worn-out-looking guy wandered over in sheer boredom.

"I've been in this exact same place since six this morning," he said, "and if I don't get to Thunder Bay by morning, the shit's gonna be flying everywhere."

"Why's that?"

"They said I hit my wife, and they said that she didn't deserve to get hit. They didn't say nothing about that she hit me first. Anyway, they said I had to be in court tomorrow or they said I was gonna get fined two thousand dollars, and that's when I started listening."

A car would pass about every ten minutes—would pass and keep on going. The music was growing softer as the day grew colder and cars less and less frequent.

I watched a look of complete disgust grow permanently across the face of the man beside me. Unlike the others who could at least strum or sing, there was no music to this man's failing purpose. His sign simply read "T. B."

Standing at first.

Just standing for a while.

There was a little bit of color in a maple tree across the road.

Three hours ago, it looked like the red of fall.
At the moment, it looked more like the brown of winter.
The guitar strumming had stopped.
The wind whistled in the cold.
Off a lake that was somewhere.
Where?
I reached into the very bottom of my pack for a sweater.
The guy who hit his wife quit bothering to hop up and down.
Alone.
It was different from closing the sliding glass door.
Because there was someplace else to go.
And the only place I was going . . .
Was nowhere.
Was that a California license plate?
I added "Please" above my request for Thunder Bay.
I tried standing with my left foot closer to the road.
I tilted my sign a bit more to the right.
I thought I should try smiling with this combination.
I could not.
Another car.
Was that a New York license plate?
The guy who hit his wife broke off a piece of something in his mouth.
He began chewing.
There was a hell of a lot of grass along the highway.
The white line was badly worn and needed a new paint job.
How many feet was it across the highway?
Tilt the sign a little more to the left this time.
Try with all your might to smile
—SMILE!
No way.
Another car.
The man who hit his wife was still chewing.
I leaned my pack against the telephone pole.
I gave up standing.
The ground was cold and hard.
The color in the tree across the street was clearly brown.

"Look's like I'm gonna be two thousand dollars down come noon tomorrow," the guy next to me said. "That damn woman."

Another car, blue—maybe green—worked its way toward us, then slowly away.

"Damn woman. . . . My brother was right all along."

A pickup pulled into the station for gas.

I saw only the space in the back end of the truck. All that potential for movement just going to waste. If it had been filled with stolen property my mind would've made peace with it sooner.

When the man came out and started his truck, I walked over, indignant.

"You don't mind if I hop in the back of your truck, do you?"

"You mean, you want a ride?"

"How far you going?"

"Only ten miles or so up the road."

"That's fine. I just need to go."

The ten miles would probably just put me somewhere further from food and shelter. It was not a smart ride to take, but I had become hooked on the idea of movement and needed a fix right then more than anything in the world.

I waved to my companion with the "T.B." sign. This ride wouldn't have done him any good at all. He didn't know that, though. He didn't wave back.

There wasn't a whole lot to this other place.
A red room behind me said "Labatt's."
It also said "Pabst."
With lips of orange curtains.
A few pickup trucks in front.
Including the one that had carried me there.
It had been nearly forty-five minutes.
And the dust still hadn't settled.
The red room had a motel sort of tacked onto it.
Like an accessory.
Like an afterthought.
I thought I heard a jukebox inside.
It all just sort of held a spot.
Between rocks and trees.
And still, no lake.
The long string of hitchhikers hadn't disappeared.
They just grew more lonely.
There were two ahead of me.
One behind.
How far did this line go?
I found a bag of peanuts in my pack and tried to keep busy.
The cars came less often.
They passed without interest.
They'd seen it all before.
Not even a swerve of avoidance.

They slapped the ever-chilling Canadian air against my face.
Stranded.
Hope drew lower and lower into the horizon behind the trees.
No one built anything there, except for the owner of the red bar.
The land was brutish.
A car. A single, solitary Volkswagen camper.
Moving on.
This was not a place for people.
Too far in to get out.
A trap for all those who chose to travel by thumb?
A land, north of Superior, using pictures and continuous red lines
to lure restless spirits into an intriguing rocky, rugged wilderness.
Isolation looks so beautiful from a room filled with people.
Or a book whose page you can turn.
Or a map whose information you can fold up.
Or a commercial whose channel you can change.
A land luring hitchhikers to it by day, then freezing them by night
in drastically cold temperatures the pictures never mentioned.
Route 1 from Sault Sainte Marie to Thunder Bay:
The world's only
freeze-dried
hitchhiker
disposal
unit.

A large man appeared outside of the bright red. He must have
weighed at least three hundred pounds. A third of which were un-
necessary.
He rolled up his sleeves. He squatted up and down. He almost fell
on the third squat. He had had something to drink.
A younger, but equally excessive, man appeared and began the
same ritual.
Both took off their shoes.
They were twenty yards away from me, but neither noticed.
They began hopping up and down. They began circling each
other, two grizzly bears fighting in the wilderness.
One stepped up and the other stepped back; one kicked, the other
one swung.
The one who came out first reached in hard, hoping to injure
severely.
The other stepped into the advance.
There was a sharp crack.
The older man's head snapped back.

The rest of the man's body followed the head onto the gravel of the parking lot.

There was no longer any motion in that man whatsoever.

The other quietly put on his boots, let his sleeves down, and went back inside.

Nobody else had witnessed the fight. There was no one there to break it up and get them to come to their senses. No one was around to keep the younger man from killing his opponent when he was down.

Just two grizzly bears obeying the laws of nature, in some godforsaken Canadian wilderness that I was absolutely stuck in.

Another car.

Driving slowly.

A man cocked his head back and stuck his thumb deep into his throat.

A homosexual invitation.

The car pulled over about fifty yards from me and waited.

Still.

The flattened grizzly bear got up, shook his head, and went back inside.

What would he do there?

The car circled back.

There were no civilized people around there anywhere.

Again, he passed slowly, opening his mouth as wide as it would go, and thrusting his thumb in and out between his teeth.

He stopped down the road again, waited, then circled back.

Where could I go?

Again, the thumb down his throat, up and down, in and out, until it began to upset me.

"Screw you you asshole; why don't you go blow yourself, dick-breath!!!"

Over and over I screamed this, jumping up and down, flipping him off with both hands like an insane grizzly bear.

He stopped again in the same spot.

He waited.

He moved on.

The winning grizzly bear came out of the bright red bar with a woman around his arm. They were with the man who had driven me there, and they looked as though they might be heading north.

"Nice fight," I called over.

I am an opportunistic grizzly bear.

"You guys wouldn't be heading north by any chance, would you?"

*   *   *

Another ride, another ten miles, passing another ten hitchhikers soon to become freeze-dried grizzly bears.

"I didn't mean to hurt him, ehh? I just thought he said some things to my girl that he shouldn't have."

That girl was on his lap smiling. She held her hero around the neck.

There was still no sign of the lake.

A road appeared at the bottom of the hill and that was where they needed to go.

Thanks for the ride and all.

There were no buildings anymore, just rugged hills surrounding an empty road.

I had to start walking.

Like those men you see walking with their backs to traffic and you wonder why it is that they are walking when they need a ride?

Nashville, Tennessee.

A steadfast and enduring look.

Somewhere in Canada.

A rocky crevice loomed at the edge of a long field beside me. The passage of yet another car destroyed the last of my interest in forward and behind. I hid my pack in a ditch that offered weeds and thistle and wandered off to the side.

The forest was packed tightly at the edge of the hill, leaving only a slight crack in the rows of pine trees that survived upon rocks. It continued on to a path carved by rain determined to find the quickest way down. The path may have ended without warning. It was not man-made; it didn't have to go anywhere.

I began to climb.

The forest began to thin out and grow short, leaving an ever-increasing sky. When there was no place higher, the land leveled into a coat of moss and fern.

I turned to see a lake glistening with a red source of light that was almost upon it. There, somewhere along the side of the road, this place called Superior.

I sat and watched as the lake tossed wind upon the mighty land, shaking batches of green here and there. This type of alone felt wonderful. There is no desolation without direction, I thought; only whatever you come upon.

"That's here and now, man. . . . That's here and now . . . "

I sat a good long while atop that field in the air, looking wherever my mind had an interest, until, somewhere in the valley and getting closer, the all-too-familiar drone shattered my contentment. Suddenly, there was fear. Where was I going? The area that I had been sitting upon seemed absolutely small and I began pacing its parameters in search of a trail that led somewhere.

A vehicle approached. I faced it with my sign and tried to find the position that would make this person stop and deliver me somewhere.

The pickup truck with Ontario tags pulled off fifty feet past my astonishment. I grabbed my pack and ran. There was a short man behind the wheel with plenty of room beside him.

"I'm planning on getting all the way back to Alberta," he said. "How far are you going?"

My sign said Thunder Bay.

"Well, good, we can keep each other company through this godforsaken drive."

Derrick Johnson was a pert man from eastern Ontario who sounded British. He was on his way to Saskatchewan to build a barn and would be gone for three months. Apparently, his wife and two daughters had gotten used to his being away because he had been a carpenter his entire life and there wasn't always something to be built in eastern Ontario.

"We send tapes back and forth, and write long letters to each other. It isn't so bad, really. It could be a lot worse."

He wore tight, wire-framed glasses and a down vest. He kept a plain blue coat neatly folded beside him for trips to restaurants and lavatories. His cab teetered in an exact balance of warmth and fresh air with the side window slightly opened and the heater on slightly more.

"I was hoping you'd be going all the way to Saskatchewan," he said. "I think it's great if I can get someone to travel the whole way with me. It makes the trip go by that much quicker."

"Did you come through The Soo?" I asked.

"Yes."

"Why didn't you pick up someone there?"

"Well, two reasons, Tom. First, most of them were so close together that I didn't want to offend anyone else or start a riot by stopping for just one. And second, most of them looked rather unkempt, and I didn't want to have to smell anything I wasn't used to all this way. You see, once you pick up someone out here there's really no way of getting around that decision until Thunder Bay. I think that's why a lot of people here are wary of hitchhikers."

"How far is it to Thunder Bay?"

"It will take about eight to ten hours."

"Ten hours, tonight?"

"No, I've planned on stopping for the night after about another three hours of driving. We'll have to finish the rest in the morning. If we get going about six tomorrow, we should get there just in time for lunch. Is that soon enough for you?"

"Actually, I was thinking of getting out and seeing some of the country before Thunder Bay."

"Out here, in the middle of nowhere?"

"I was thinking of it."

"Well, there's really not much out there between The Soo and Thunder Bay. Wawa is the next real town, but there's a prison there and I doubt you'll ever get a ride out if you make that a stop. The country-side doesn't change at all either, and unless you have a particular affinity for pine trees, there's really not much else to see. You'll like Thunder Bay, though. It's sort of the Hollywood of Canada—they teach a lot of motion picture courses at the college. No, I wouldn't get off before Thunder Bay; you just may never get there if you do."

That made absolutely perfect sense. What I wanted to do didn't make any. Yet, as we drove steadily by, my eyes wandered over the striking Canadian wilderness, watching places pass along the side of the road.

At a restaurant named Husky, I spotted the man with the court date in Thunder Bay. He was ahead of me in the cafeteria line helping himself to three different types of dessert. When I caught up with him at the condiment table, he was pouring sugar into his coffee.

"That no-good woman ain't gonna cost me no two thousand dollars," he exclaimed, still pouring the sugar. "She'd a-liked it that way, but I got me a good ride all the way into town tonight. Yeah, she'd of liked it that way, but it ain't gonna happen.

"I can't wait to see the look on her face tomorrow when I show up in that courtroom. She'd a-thought I'd never show up, and there I will come. The judge will understand why she deserved to be hit. I'll tell the judge my story, and he'll understand. I won't have to pay a thing.

"Another thing too," he added before sitting with some trucker, "there's some faggot around there's got hisself a broken nose that he didn't have before he tried putting his hand on my lap. Ain't nobody ought to do that, less he wants a broken nose. I guess he just wanted a broken nose. Drove by me three times making some weird signs before picking me up. I guess he just wanted a broken nose."

Derrick snuck up from behind with beef stew and a shake.

"You want to grab that booth over against the wall?" he asked.

"Yeah, that sounds like a good idea."

*   *   *

There was a boat launch off an unmarked road that Derrick had used as a resting point for his voyages through the area.

"We'll just park it along the side here and call it home," he said. "I'll get out the air mattresses. You can have the back of the truck, while I'll sleep in the cab."

The temperature was moving well into the lower end of thirty that night. It would've been real cold on top of that hill by myself, I thought. But that first view of the lake lingered and made me feel as though I were somehow off course.

Moving toward a frosted sleep, I once again became a passenger on that familiar train, heading toward the ocean, then the burnt-out house. This time, as I made my way through the rubble and into the room in the back, the woman was not there. Search as I might throughout the house, the woman was simply nowhere to be found.

"I know you'll never believe it, but it's 6:30 already!"

As far as I could tell through chilly eyeballs, it hadn't even become the next day yet. But the way Derrick was hustling about, you'd have thought we'd just slept through an afternoon wedding. I think it was the first time in my life that my eyes had ever felt cold.

"I can't figure out what happened. I guess we must have just overslept."

I thought he was just kidding until he pulled the plug on the air mattress beneath me. This man was seriously on a schedule; Thunder Bay was going to disappear if we didn't get there by noon.

But when your ride says go, you must, especially if you're in grizzly-bear country north of Superior. That's hitchhiker rule number something or other. I was too tired to figure out which one.

"Husky," who had served us dinner the night before, was serving us breakfast another sixty miles down the road. This outfit seemed to be Canada's own national food service.

"Are you ready to order?"

Derrick let me go first. I wondered on my own lack of decisiveness, until I realized I hadn't been given a menu.

"I don't know what you've got."

"Do you need a menu?" the waitress asked.

"Yes."

"I'll have a number seven, with both eggs sunnyside-up," Derrick said before she put away her notepad.

The waitress smiled. This was one of their regular Husky-ites, she thought. A good nationalist.

She came back, dropped a menu in front of me, stood there and waited.

"Coffee . . . toast . . . two scrambled eggs . . . forget the eggs — French toast."

I handed her back the menu.

"Do you want the French toast?"

"Yes."

"Do you want toast *and* French toast?"

"Yes."

"Toast, French toast, coffee . . . how about some English muffins?"

"Thanks, just water,"

"Water . . . anything else?"

"Ice."

And a bed.

"That's what I like so much about America," Derrick began, "the paid help are so much more friendly. Here they think they're doing you a favor."

I thought of all the times I had wanted to throw up when the cashier at McDonald's told me to make sure I had a nice day and to come back soon.

"A number seven, and this one without a number — toast — French toast, coffee and water — with ice."

And then I decided a little cheerful anonymity wasn't such a bad thing after all.

A few hours of driving and it was all gone. The tall majestic pines and rugged countryside gave way to poplar trees and scrubby vegetation after the signs started reading "Thunder Bay 20."

Billboards.

Places to eat in Thunder Bay; places to stay in Thunder Bay; places to spend money, which meant they were of absolutely no interest to me.

"Do you know where you want to go in town?"

"No. No idea."

"Are you sure you don't want to go on to Saskatchewan?"

"No, this is fine."

On the map, Thunder Bay appeared to be a big town. But as we drove into the city limits, I didn't see any big buildings. Just a lot of grey, beat-up-looking houses and cars jammed all over four lanes decorated in traffic lights.

"Why don't we get something to eat?" Derrick asked.

The houses looked like they were just waiting for winter to beat the hell out of them again; the people walking along the streets looked like they lived in those houses.

How had everywhere I had ever gone brought me now to Thunder Bay?

We found a McDonald's. I found two hamburgers and a glass of water. Together Derrick and I found a booth across from a lady scolding her young son, and I guess we found nutrition.

"It really is a wonderful town if you get to see the right sides of it."

There was no ketchup on my hamburger.

"If you want we could look in the phone book for hotels."

He was talking as if there was something wrong with me. I couldn't understand what? Why worry about places to stay at night? Why worry there in T–Bay?

"I think you'll be impressed with the waterfront area . . . "

To relieve his persistence, I recalled that there was a youth hostel in Thunder Bay. I even called to find out exactly where.

It was somehow determined that I needed to take a bus to get out to it—Bus 27 in fact. Derrick asked some unnamed person where the bus station was, and soon I was sitting at that very same bus station waiting for a bus that left in two hours.

In the bus station, people sat in chairs and ate candy from the candy machine. Sometimes, they read magazines from the magazine rack. All this after buying their tickets, and in between using the toilet.

I sat absolutely and completely still in my chair as I waited at a bus station in Thunder Bay to go somewhere else.

Two hours later, someone somewhere said a particular bus was leaving. An old man asked me for my ticket at the door. He looked worried, I found a ticket in my pocket and gave it to him.

For some reason, the bus began to back up, then head in a particular direction—as if it knew something the rest of us didn't. I offered no resistance.

Later, a man at the very front left-hand side of the bus called toward me. He seemed upset.

"You wanted to go to the youth hostel, right?"

That seemed to make sense.

"Well, this is it, Bud—this is your stop."

I thanked him and got off the bus, watching as it continued on.

There stood a house and a barn and several people and a dog. I walked up to the place, and a man greeted me at the door.

"You look like you need a place to stay," he said.

I followed him inside. I signed a book of his. He hugged me for some reason, and I just stood there.

The next day, his family dropped me off in town, and I walked up and down the aisles of a Woolworth's store for a very long time. Then I sat on the curb at the edge of a parking lot eating a glazed doughnut, until that same family found me and brought me back to the place where I was supposed to sleep—which I did—immediately.

The next day I found myself at breakfast, then lunch, then dinner, then back to bed where I slept.

The sparkle of a woman's eyes was the first thing to shine through the fog, while I was sitting on the edge of the same parking lot outside Woolworth's.
I needed paper, and a pencil, both in the store. I then returned to be near the empty cars. The blank paper seemed safe. For a long while I did not want to disturb it. But there was a girl somewhere else.
Write.

Dear, . . .

Dear Jessica, . . .

Dear Jessica,
I am thinking of a song that I am going to write down. This is how it goes: "Don't turn me home again, I just can't face myself alone again."
I am in the parking lot at Woolworth's that I like . . .

Dear Jessica,
I keep thinking I'm missing something, and when I get to it, I'm missing something else. . . . Can you understand??

Dear Jessica, . . .

I threw the letter away. It didn't make sense.

Back at the youth hostel, I asked where the lake was.
"About a mile through the trees. Just take that road and you'll be headed in the right direction."
I walked because I walked, and could not—would not—stop for even a moment, through trees and yards, and even along a railroad track, on and on, until I came before water that stretched on without end.
There was a flat stone lying before me on the shore of Lake Superior outside of Thunder Bay. I threw it out onto the still, clear

water, watching it skip from one spot to another before finally coming to rest in an altogether different place.

I reached down and took a handful of water from the lake, brought it to my mouth and drank. Maybe there was something symbolic in doing that. It made me very happy. Unreasonably happy as a matter of fact, while I felt the heavy hand of deep depression waiting just a moment away from this strange gladness.

There was no defense. I was no longer traveling in my life, but travel had become my life. There was no place to go. I was in Thunder Bay, Canada.

I had to move, just move.

At breakfast the next day, I found a pair of New Zealanders who were heading to the western end of town to see some fort out there.

"Do you think you could give me a lift to the highway out of town?" I asked.

"I don't see how that will be any problem."

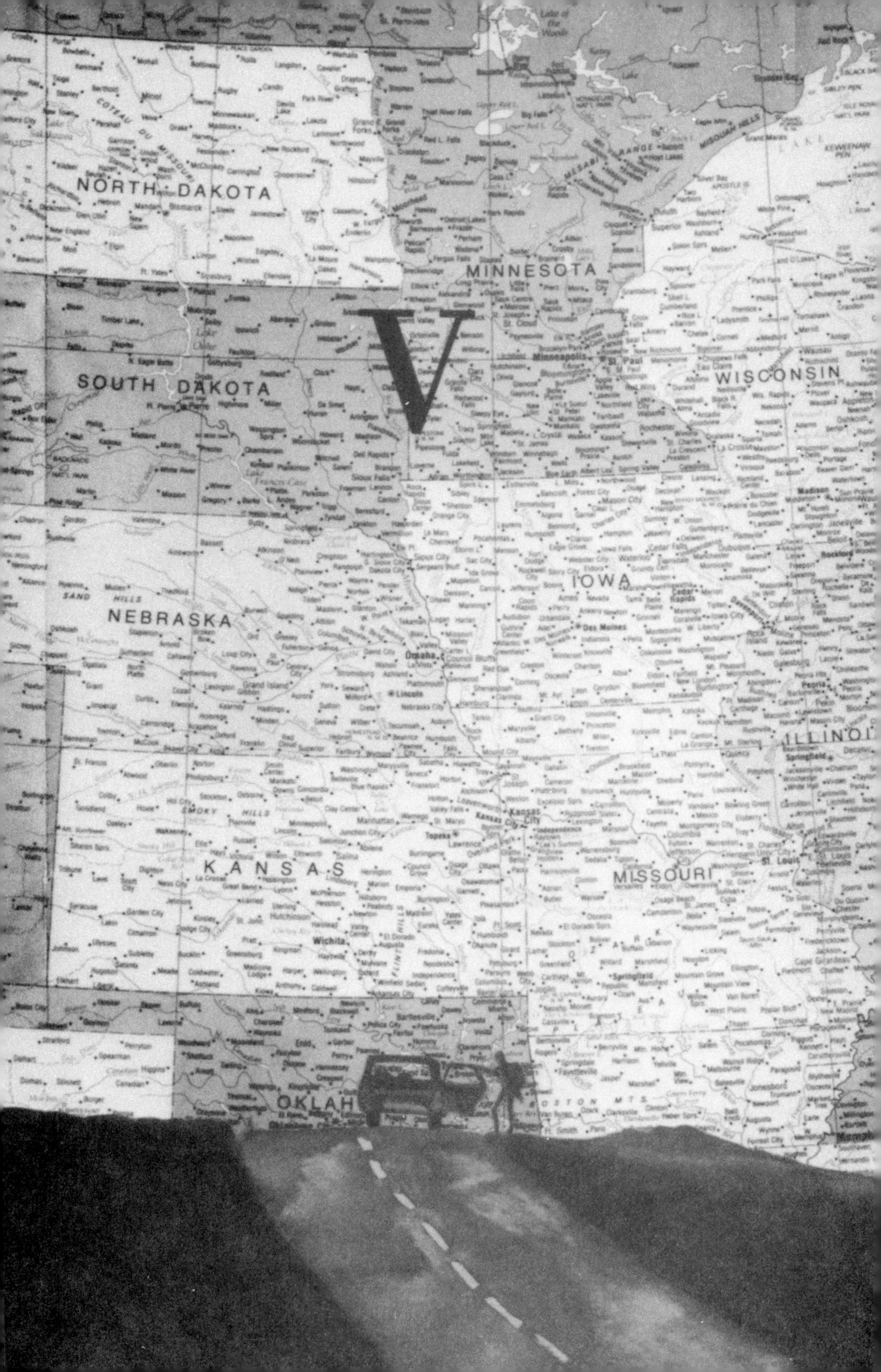
V
NORTH DAKOTA
MINNESOTA
SOUTH DAKOTA
WISCONSIN
NEBRASKA
IOWA
KANSAS
MISSOURI
ILLINOI
OKLAH

10

"THE LORD HELPS THOSE
WHO HELP THEMSELVES..."

"Some people think it's in Arizona, but it's really only in Colorado."

"Look, my parents took me there when I was a little kid and I know it's in Arizona because I was in Arizona when I saw it," I said.

"You only thought it was Arizona."

My ride out of Thunder Bay was in the back of a pickup truck loaded with a family named Spencer, who were leaving the town of perpetual greyness for their summer vacation into the American Midwest.

The cab was completely occupied by father and mother and daughter, leaving me in the back with sixteen-year-old son Eddie, who was trying to convince me that the Grand Canyon was not in Arizona.

"I don't even think the Grand Canyon goes much into Colorado," I said.

"Man, are you stupid."

Eddie had one of those Rod Stewart haircuts that every teenager in Canada has been wearing for the past ten years. He had a slight build, but rolled his T-shirt sleeves up to his shoulders as if he didn't. I guessed that he had a seventy-five-pound weight set in his room at home, and I was certain that he got beat up a lot by his friends.

"Maybe you're thinking of the Colorado *River*," I said. "The Colorado River goes through the Grand Canyon."

"And what state do you think the *Colorado* river is in—Mexico?"

I didn't know what else to say. I was tired. I sat back into the deflated rubber raft and propped my legs onto a case of Labatt's beer.

How did this get started?

I seemed to have remembered Eddie saying something about how his dad liked to pick up hitchhikers, which led to the story about the

one they picked up in Omaha who Eddie thought was a real jerk
because he kept telling Eddie to shut up and let him enjoy the scenery,
which led to Eddie saying how happy he was when they finally dropped
him off, at the Grand Canyon—in Colorado.

"You should try and figure out who told you that one about the
Grand Canyon being in Arizona—I'd beat him up if I were you."

"Why don't we look at the scenery for a while?"

On the other side of a sliding Plexiglas window, mother and
daughter laughed and kidded and ate from an ever-present bag of
potato chips with both hands, while Mr. Spencer held the steering
wheel with large calloused hands and concentrated on the road.

For a moment through yet another ride somewhere, poplar trees
gave way to cornfields that offered impressive grain silos to empty steel
rails. For a moment, there was an unexpected view of the sun sparkling
on the lake—unexpected and totally engaging.

For a moment, though, only for a moment.

"Do you want to hear about the fishing trip me and my dad took in
the north country?"

No response.

"That's where we met the people we are going to see now," Eddie
continued. "We showed them the right place to fish, so they invited us
down to their farm."

"Where do they live?" I asked.

Eddie thought for a moment, then reached back and banged on
the window.

The sliding Plexiglas door opened.

"What do you want, Eddie?" his mother asked.

"Where do the Kozels live?"

Mrs. Spencer leaned toward her husband, then leaned back.

"Foley," she said.

"When are we gonna eat?" Eddie continued.

His sister slammed the window shut.

I got out my map.

"We're only going to stay a few days, then we're going camping in
South Dakota. The last time we went camping in South Dakota, my fat
sister . . ."

Foley was about fifty miles northwest of Minneapolis. I knew
somebody who lived in Minneapolis. She wasn't exactly an old friend,
but I suddenly had this longing to see her. Unlike everyone else I'd
known the last few months, she knew me from before the moment I met
her and there was an extraordinary comfort in that.

In her company, my hitchhiker's title could rest in the closet for a while. I could even step outside of the trip's relentless narrative and tell a few stories of my own.

She had been in either my intro-psych class or freshman English. We might have even sat next to each other once. I was sure that if I talked with her long enough on the phone, she would remember who I was.

In the meantime, there was Eddie—well into a monologue about outdoor life in "the Great White North"—throwing around foreign-sounding words like "Bombaday," and "Water Skidder," which could have been the trade names of laxatives for all I knew.

My curiosity stopped him on "Rousgard."

"You don't know what a 'Rousgard' is?" he asked.

"Never heard of it."

Eddie slapped the side of the camper so hard in his pursuant fit of laughter that even his father turned around to see what was wrong.

The sliding Plexiglas door opened, again.

"Everything all right back there, Eddie?" Mrs. Spencer asked.

"This guy doesn't know what a Rousgard is."

His mother rolled her eyes and looked at me with an expression that said, "Yeah, well we would've rather had a German shepherd, but . . . ," then closed the window and turned to explain it to her husband, who kept his eyes on the road, and drove straight ahead toward the U.S. border.

Along the border between the U.S. and Canada, there are a bunch of border patrolmen whose job it is to remind everyone trying to enter their country that they are travelers and therefore suspect, and that one is particularly suspect if he does not possess his own means of transportation.

"Where were you born?" the man in the uniform asked me.

"Teaneck, New Jersey."

That did not match with three "Thunder Bay, Ontarios."

"Are you with this family?" he asked.

"Yeah, they picked me up hitchhiking outside of Thunder Bay."

I was asked to get out of the car and to take my backpack with me.

In a moment, all that I had was sprawled out across the border patrolman's table. The Spencers looked on patiently, but with a renewed interest now that the question had been brought up. Eddie even opened a side window of the camper top to get a better look.

"Open that flap," the patrolman ordered, pointing to the one flap whose contents had not been exposed.

The zipper was jammed.

"Open that flap or you're not going anywhere."

I asked him to try.

Together we stripped it open about a half-inch, whereupon he began probing its unknown contents with his finger. It was a flap that I hardly ever used. I had no idea what was in it, but I hoped it was dirty underwear.

As the patrolman hissed, grunted, and strained to get into my sealed compartment, I looked across at my possessions sprawled about on the table.

The threads were starting to wear thin on my jeans. There were little fuzzy patches on the knees and the thighs.

The fifteen or so bags of peanuts I had bought as emergency food before starting out were seeing the sun for the first time, as was a khaki shirt purchased for three dollars from a pretty saleslady in Kalamazoo. It was about three sizes too big, but she had the most beautiful eyes...

The mess kit I had bought in Nashville still hadn't held any food, and those same stale cigarettes I had offered to the thin, black wanderer on a Kentucky back road were now about to fall off the table from the slight breeze.

The search of my secret compartment revealed a few more bags of peanuts.

"Yeah, you can go," he said.

After the final OK, I slowly rerolled each shirt, each sock, and each pair of pants with a deliberateness that afforded me the fewest wrinkles for the smallest space. If my ride had to wait for that to become undone, it was going to have to wait for me to put it back together again.

Sometimes you wish for stuff.

The central Minnesota farm country we had come upon offered long, straight rows of cornstalks that reached into my heart and pulled its confusion into their orderliness, their stability.

Eddie was giving me a living demonstration of all that had been for too long. Soon after our passage into America, he began sneaking his father's warm beers at an approximate rate of one every ten miles. Once he realized that the folks up front knew what he was doing but weren't going to do anything about it, he began loudly stamping the aluminum cans into the floor.

Several times his sister reached through the little window and tried to grab her brother, but she succeeded only in spilling the bag of potato chips.

From this, appeared "FOLEY, MINN," written on a water tower, and tinted in pastel orange from the setting sun. Beneath it, high-school football players sprinted in waves before packing it in for the day.

The purple light of television was beginning to glow from homes that exuded toys and swing sets up to where the grass began to grow tall.

Beyond, cows grazed in fields marked by carefully laid and mended fences, while the crops shimmered in the breeze that brought the night's cooler temperatures.

For the first time, I could see where the road led, as it lay before me and continued in a single direction as far as the eye could follow it.

At a gas station a few miles back, Dale had asked me where I wanted to go, and all I could say was Minneapolis. He told me that they were running late for dinner at their friend's house, and that he wanted to stop there before dropping me off on the highway that led to the city.

But I looked at the peace and order of this central Minnesota farm country, and wished otherwise.

One long straight gravel road led to another, then another, and still another, until finally coming to rest at Gene Kozel's dairy farm, where a white house, a barn, a silo, and several pristine sheds were surrounded by cows, pasture, and row upon row of cornfields.

The Kozels' three boys bounded out of the house to greet our arrival. In the kitchen, Mrs. Kozel and her two daughters were maneuvering through mounds of fried chicken draining on paper towels.

"Well, you must be the Spencers," Mrs. Kozel said while wiping her hands on her apron. "Gene's still cutting hay in the field next to his brother's. He should be back any minute now."

We talked while we waited. First the introductions: The Kozels were Dave, fifteen; William, thirteen; Bradley, five; Pat, sixteen; Jane, fourteen; and Frances, the mother.

The introductions were necessary because only Gene and Dave had gone on the fishing trip where Eddie and his father, Dale, had shown the two farmers their secret fishing spot. That meant that to all Kozels concerned, I temporarily assumed the status of "Spencers not seen before."

Within a few minutes, the head of the household arrived from his work in the field. Before entering his wife's clean house, Gene Kozel beat the dust off his worn overall blue jeans, and tucked in his flannel shirt with the cutoff sleeves.

Gene reached out a friendly hand to Dale, then a pat on the shoulder to Eddie, and finally a courteous "Hello, it's my pleasure to meet you" to both of the Spencer women, the whole time grinning from ear to ear beneath the brim of his green International Harvester hat.

"And Gene," Dale said, "this is a fella we picked up hitchhiking whose name is Tom . . ."

"DeTitta."

" . . . DeTitta. I was gonna drop him off near Saint Cloud so he could get to Minneapolis, but I wanted to check in here first."

The word *hitchhiker* sent Bradley a few steps back into his mother's apron. The girls tried not to look up from their work while the other two boys just flat-out stared.

Again, I was before the inspector, wondering if I would pass or not.

"DeTitta, huh.... That Italian?" Gene asked.

"Uh-huh."

He was a solid man who moved slowly and deliberately. His forearms and the part of his face that wasn't shaded by the brim of his hat had a deep workingman's tan.

"Well, I can't see sending a man out once he's smelled my wife's chicken—especially if he hasn't been eating well as I imagine this fella hasn't. Why don't you stay for dinner there, Mr. DeTitta?"

Perhaps our faces always reveal our deepest desires. Perhaps it's impossible for a hitchhiker to be restrained in a room full of fried chicken. Whatever the case, sometimes you wish for stuff, and sometimes it turns out for you—but wishing is the first thing you gotta do.

Suddenly in front of me was fresh corn on the cob, fried chicken, mashed potatoes and gravy, two types of Jell-O mold, rolls, and something with beans in it.

There was no menu between me and it; there was no need for the usual "Well, let's see, if I get the hamburger plate I get cole slaw and French fries with it, and maybe they'll give me crackers as well for $2.85, but if I just get the hamburger, I can get two side orders of French fries for almost as much, and maybe I can scrape the pickles from the hamburger, moosh them up with the fries, add lots of ketchup, and make a sort of casserole..."

All I had to do here was reach across the table and dump food on my plate, which I was at first hesitant to do for fear of losing control.

Gene noticed my inhibition.

"The Lord helps those who help themselves around here, Tom," he said. "Go ahead and dig in."

Eddie, who had been in a stupor since arriving on the farm seven beers to the wind, began to gain strength through the meal, along with two glasses of wine. By dessert he was telling off-color jokes that the others were pretending to laugh at.

"That's enough, Eddie!" his father had warned several times.

Not to be silenced, however, Eddie announced that "however-you-say-his-name" thought the Grand Canyon was in Arizona.

The room was silent except for Eddie's laughter.

"It *is* in Arizona," his father said.

Eddie demanded an atlas, which Dave soon provided. He opened it to the map of Colorado and paused. Then he turned to the map of Arizona, and paused. Then he flipped to the general map of the U.S. in the front of the book, turned back to Colorado, back to Arizona, Colorado again, Arizona, then closed the book and said, "It's not in here."

After the meal, the kids went either upstairs or outside, while the elders assembled around a pot of coffee in the living room. A couple of neighbors stopped in then, as seemed to be customary, with stories of the day's work and talk of the weather.

"So what makes a young fella like you decide to pack it up one day and hitchhike around the country?" Gene asked, as several conversations went on around us.

"Well, I just got done going to college for four years, and after four years of reading about things, I figured I'd better go out and see stuff for myself."

Gene seemed satisfied with that response. He sat back, in what was definitely his chair, to ponder it awhile. He was not the type of guy that would run through the usual "bad experience—what does your mother think—when were you most scared" barrage. Instead he asked one question, got an answer, and thought it over.

In the silence, I basked in the newfound after-dinner comfort and thought about how nice it would be to feel that way again tomorrow. Just then I heard a cymbal crash from upstairs, followed by the beat of a bass drum, followed by a whole lot of noise. I quickly ran up the steps to find Eddie mauling a beautiful old set of Pearl drums.

"Get him out of there," William beseeched me, as Eddie knocked over a floor tom-tom.

All the kids had gathered in the room to listen to records, when Eddie spied the drum set and decided to do his Keith Moon imitation.

Eddie's sister, who at that point had been nicknamed "Screech," had found that she couldn't fit behind the drum set to dethrone her brother, and so instead she was throwing miscellaneous bedroom items at him.

But an inebriated teenager behind a drum set never notices mere projectiles—the band played on.

I grabbed an extra pair of sticks I found lying around, and thought about the type of people the Lord helped around there. I began beating "Wipe-Out" loudly on an unoccupied tom-tom. People think you know what you're doing if you can play "Wipe-Out."

That shut Eddie up enough to allow me his place behind the set under the condition that I play his favorite song, "Back in Black," by AC/DC. William and Dave scrambled to find the album, then watched in amazement as drums that had made noise suddenly made music.

"How did you learn to do that song?" William asked.

"That's so easy, I could teach you how to play it in two weeks," I said.

The bedroom door opened and in popped Gene, curious to find out who had made his son's drums work.

"Daddy, he said he could teach me to play like that in a week," William said, running to his father.

"Let's see you play a few more tunes there, Tom," Gene asked.

How do you play a tune on the drums? Embarrassed, I hit the things a few times and tapped out a couple of beats. I felt like a trained seal. If it would've gotten me a place at their farm, I would've rolled over and clapped. Instead, I played a little bit of "Wipe-Out" again.

Sensing that he might hear more by leaving, Gene went back downstairs, and William and Dave immediately began fighting over what song I would play next. Most of their selections came from their three AC/DC albums, with a couple from Kiss thrown in for good measure. Eventually, Dave pulled out an electric guitar and began adding noise. Eddie found another stick to keep loud, inconsistent time on one of the cymbals, while William stood perfectly still and watched my hands keep time with the music.

About halfway through what had been destined to be a late-night concert, Gene came upstairs and told everyone to turn the record player off, that it was time to go to bed.

It was decided that both William's and Dave's double beds would each share an out-of-town guest that night. We all washed up, because people get clean before going to bed there in Minnesota, and soon the lights had been shut on another day.

It took Eddie about three warning shouts from Gene to "knock it off up there and get to sleep" before he stopped pulling Dave off the bed to wrestle. But eventually even Eddie burnt out the last drops of the day's energy and fell into a slumber shared with the rest of Foley, Minnesota, at 11 P.M. on a Thursday night.

There was a moment of panic on my side of William's bed as the momentum of the day's events dissipated into the snores and stillness that surrounded me, and questions that had been waiting by the side of the road began to creep into my consciousness.

Just moments ago everything made sense: A ride took me to a home where dinner was already on the table, and so I stayed. Their boy wanted to learn how to play the drums, which I already knew how to do, and so I played.

As night approached, it was time to go to bed, because people sleep at night. William and Dave had double beds, but they are only single people. Eddie and I are single people too, so we each shared one-half of the boys' double beds. One-half of two is one, and that was why we fit so nicely without falling off. Four spots, four people who were asleep, because it was nighttime and nighttime is the time to sleep.

Except for one, drifting out of the order of things through questions that demand answers: What am I doing here? How did I get to a farm in Minnesota?

Different forms of the same questions had thrown me out of sync and onto the road: What was I doing a college graduate? How did I get there? Where did I belong?

Now, the questions were adding up with each mile, and with each mile demanding more miles still, to escape the gut-wrenching fear that shatters a still moment to ask "What am I doing here?" But now I squeezed my pillow on a farm somewhere in Minnesota, with absolutely no place to go.

I was awakened the next morning by Bradley standing eye-level to my bed.

"Mom and Dad said if you want breakfast you gotta get up now," he said. "Everybody's waiting for you."

The clock beside my bed said 8:10. Bradley looked as though he'd been up for three hours.

"We're having sausage," he said.

"Tell them I'll be right down."

Yesterday's shirt and pants were the closest things in reach. Boom, into the bathroom—bang, cold water on the face—bing, bang, bong, down the steps and into the kitchen, then into the only empty seat, hoping no one would notice.

They all did, however; everyone except Eddie, who had his head down on the table in remembrance of last night's alcohol.

"City folks don't usually get up until ten, isn't that right there, Tom?" Gene asked.

"Noon," I said, releasing the chuckle that everyone had been waiting on.

Let's eat.

Sausage and bacon, cereal, French toast, eggs, orange juice, hash browns, rolls, and three kinds of homemade jelly.

"*WAKE UP, EDDIE!*" Screech screamed from across the table.

"Hey, that's enough of that!" Dale said.

After breakfast, I volunteered to go with Gene to the farm-supply store to get some parts for a disabled tractor. There was a matter of farm

work and three square meals that I was meaning to talk with him about
in private.

"You keep pretty busy this time of year?" I asked Gene as we drove
off in his pickup.

"Yeah, seems there's always something to keep you going on a
farm. You ever work one before?"

"No, but it's something I've always wanted to do," I said, perhaps
too eagerly.

Gene rolled down the window to let some cool morning air into
the cab, now hot from the sun through the glass.

"I used to work on a beer truck," I added.

"How's that?"

"Did a lot of lifting there."

"Oh, I see."

Soon we were at the store.

"Mornin', Bill," Gene said to the man behind the counter.

Gene fished the broken part out of his pocket and laid it on the
table. Bill put on his glasses to get a better look.

"Seems like you been runnin' that tractor of yours more than it's
used to bein' run."

"Gotta get that hay up before the rain gets it."

Bill went through the shelves in the back room and found what
Gene needed. Gene abruptly ended their conversation after Bill mentioned the forty-percent chance of rain forecast for later in the day.

"Gotta get that hay up before the rain hits, and I gotta talk with
some guy from the radio station before that."

Gene gave a moment to his watch.

"Matter of fact, the feller said he'd be over to the house about now."

"That'd be about the election I suppose," Bill said.

"That's what it'd be about."

A little bell rang above us as we passed through the door.

"What election is that?" I asked as we drove off.

"Well, the wife and I kinda decided that maybe I ought to give a
shot at running for county commissioner," Gene said.

"Boy, I sure used to go through a lot of candidates' press material
when I worked for newspapers," I said.

"Spent some time on a newspaper, did ya?"

"You sure get to see the difference between a good press release
and a bad one real quick."

Gene thought on that awhile.

"Where did you say you was heading after this?" he asked.

"I hadn't really given it much thought. I've been an awful lot of
places in the last couple months. It'd be nice to stay put for a while."

Gene was wise to me.

"Are you looking to get paid?"

"Room and board maybe."

He raised his arm slowly, took off his cap and scratched his head.

"Well, I've got a field of hay that I was hoping to have baled and stored before the rain got to it. The kids seem to like ya, and William could use all the help he can get on those drums. Heck, there's always plenty to do on a farm."

Gene turned down the last gravel road to his house and flashed a knowing grin.

"I guess it would all depend on what you thought of my wife's cooking," he said.

The weather was perfect as Gene pulled the flatbed trailer containing William, Dale, and me toward the hay that had to be baled. The temperature was somewhere in the low seventies, humidity was non-existent, and there was a comfortable breeze.

Still, Gene pointed to the high cirrus clouds accumulating in the west—the forty-percent chance of rain he'd heard about—and hurried the tractor. Rain would spoil cut hay and make it much more costly to feed his cows that winter.

I didn't know the function of the machine that was hooked to the back of the trailer until it started spitting fifty-pound bales of hay at us. Quickly, William showed Dale and me how to stack the hay, and we formed a chain. I picked up the bales and tossed them to both William and Dale, who did the stacking—three and two and two and three.

For once, I felt a part of the scenery. I was one of four people in a field in Foley, Minnesota, working hard to save a crop from Mother Nature.

The machine caught the three of us grouped together stacking the seventh layer, and spit two bales onto the ground instead of the flattop. Gene looked back to see if he should stop the tractor. I jumped off after the two errant bales, grabbed one and tossed it to William, then quickly grabbed the other and tossed it to Dale. With one hop I was back on the tractor to receive the next bale and toss it to Dale, who had already gotten his last one in place.

Gene looked back and gave us the thumbs-up sign. The tractor had continued without hesitation.

The romance of the whole thing began to fade as the job started showing its teeth. Picking bales out of the field was not nearly as difficult as stacking them in the barn. There, the hay was piled in stacks two stories high. Each bale had to be placed very tightly against the one next to it because soon it would become the floor for the next layer. The job was difficult enough without having to pull your foot out of a crack every few steps.

And so you've got to push and shove and shove and push each and every bale into its exact place because sixteen hundred bales need to fit into a space just large enough for sixteen hundred bales. That was the amount Gene said we would be stacking that day. After the first load of four hundred, I thought we were done and ready for more chicken. Imagine my surprise when I heard that we had three more trips to go.

"You're not tired there, are you, Tom?" Gene asked.

For some reason I remembered lying on the ground during a high school football game after three guys had just mauled me. I'll never forget my coach standing over my fractured state with the sympathy of a New York cab driver: "You're not going to let them get the best of you, are ya?" he had asked.

Seeds and pieces of hay burned in my eyes and blocked my nose so that I could breathe only through my mouth. I tried to find a rhythm to plug into so the work would just happen without my feeling how miserable it was. But too many bales went where they weren't supposed to, causing me to spring into a more calculated form of action, and thus destroying whatever automation I might have established.

William had left to join a baseball practice that Eddie and Dave had used as an excuse long ago. Only Dale and I were left to do all the work, and Dale was supposedly on vacation.

"Doesn't matter to me," Dale said. "I've worked hard all my life, what's another day?"

All the lifting and tossing and piling seemed to come naturally to him. He said he had never worked on a farm before, but you could tell he'd strained a few muscles to put food on the table. He was able to find the mindset I was looking for, and it stayed with him no matter where the machine tossed the next bale.

"Spent twenty-two years working for a railroad in Thunder Bay," he said. "Twenty-two years of hard work, lifting, and moving things where they wanted them. Twenty-two years, and that's it."

"What do you mean, 'that's it'?"

"I guess times are hard or something. That's what they told me anyway. This vacation is gonna last a lot longer than the kids think."

He picked up another bale and rhythmically tossed it into place while I strained to keep going.

"Just don't think about it," he said. "It's not so bad that way. Just do it and don't worry why. That's something that I learned years ago."

After dinner, Gene took all the grown-ups out on the town. All the hay was where it belonged, and that was as good a reason as any to celebrate. Sightseeing consisted of looking at the church and the town hall from the perspective of a couple of Ford headlights.

"Oh, that's very nice," Mrs. Spencer said.

Then, we hit the bar scene in central Minnesota—interrupting successive bartenders' television viewing as we went from one empty spot to the next.

The elevator music rattling through the jukebox at the fourth bar was neither loud enough nor interesting enough to keep me from falling asleep on the counter. The first couple of shoves Gene gave me weren't strong enough to wake me up either.

"What's the matter, there, Tom, had a rough one last night?"

"That was a heck of an introduction to farming," I said.

We all generally had a good time. Gene had his "city-boy-on-the-farm" jokes, but every once in a while, he'd let me take a little pride in a job well done.

"That's the most I think I ever baled in a day," Gene said.

Outside all of it was Dale. Out of work and sore from an unexpected day's labor, he sat listening to the conversations that went on around him. Finally, when it was time to go, he slapped down the last of his Bourbon and water, and said pretty much to himself, "Yup, it's only a moment of fun we remember in a lifetime of work."

The next day, the Spencers left for the rest of their vacation through the Plains and the Midwest. Dale figured it would be at least eighteen hours to the Black Hills of South Dakota—the place he said he liked the most.

The members of the front seat all seemed set and ready to go. Screech had her bag of chips, Mrs. Spencer had her sunglasses, and Dale had his steering wheel. Only Eddie in the back seemed discontented—having a big mouth but no one to talk to.

Maybe for Eddie's sake they'd find some guy along the road trying to follow their direction. Maybe Eddie would upset the guy trying to tell him that New York City was in California. But eventually the hitchhiker would get where he wanted to go—and maybe even a little bit more—as his reward for listening to a cantankerous teenager who really just needed to hear himself talk.

After four days on the farm I was no longer allowed to stumble bleary-eyed to the table an hour late for breakfast. I was up at 6 A.M. and into the barn a half-hour later, dropping hay in front of cows.

Dumb animals—eat your hay and no mooing before noon. Don't

try kicking anybody when they try to hook the electric milk pumpers to your udders or you'll get kicked back. So they didn't. They just sat there and let us clamp electric milk suckers to them.

Breakfast came after chores. Ham, bacon, sausage, cereal or oatmeal, bran, apple juice, orange juice, grapefruit juice, French toast or pancakes or waffles, toast, jams—strawberry blueberry grape—and even orange marmalade.

Work. Jeez, there was a lot of it. Feed the animals, move them from one pasture to the next, fill the low spots outside the barn with dirt, and pull the weeds there while you're at it.

Lunch. Sausage, sandwiches—bacon lettuce and tomato as well as tuna fish as well as chicken salad as well as roast beef as well as ham with cheese—chicken dumplings, stew meat on buns, Jell-O salad, regular salad, Jell-O molds, tuna salad, soup: bean and broth, chicken and mushroom, and finally dessert—homemade pies—every variety.

Unexpected events too. Gene got a call. One of his cows was grazing in a neighbor's backyard. Either somebody had left a gate open or there was a break in the fence somewhere.

I never opened or closed any gates but I still felt responsible. I hadn't mended any fences either.

The cow was down the road a piece grazing near the neighbor's swing set. The neighbor was out there too. Gene went back to get the pickup and a trailer. It was too far for the animal to walk.

Get up that ramp and stand still in the back so we can drive you home peacefully. Then get out and join the rest of them so we can wire you up in a while: thwock-thwock-thwock-thwock-thwock.

Dinner. Steak or pork chops or ham or roast beef or stew or even more sausage (The Kozels were Polish. They shortened their name a while back. That's why there was so much kielbasa.), salads, rolls, butter, Jell-Os, beans, vegetables, fruits, butter, margarine, milk milk milk, and Pepsi.

Dessert.

Feed the cows, bale the hay, watch TV, and maybe even take a short walk along the road with Bradley while the evening wind pushed the sun away.

Bradley pointed to the distant textured drops of clouds spattered above us.

"They look like light blue clouds," he said.

It seemed Bradley was confused. They *were* light blue clouds, softly tinted from the sky and floating above us as light blue clouds ought to.

Yet as we walked and the day's work dissipated into comfortable aches of satisfaction, I looked up and also saw distant textures that looked "like light blue clouds." Reality is simply too harsh a concept for innocence and wanderlust walking along a gravel road toward sunset.

I never really knew what the two girls thought of my being there. We never spent much time together except in passing. Young teenage women are very hard to relate to. They are women, but they are still girls; they giggle sometimes when they should laugh.

Best to respect that special privacy that their brothers always seemed to be infringing upon, I thought. Still, I wondered what they thought of my being there.

Sometimes there were hints to go on. Like the morning William and Dave tried to have a jam session thirty minutes before my alarm was to go off. Those moments of sleep before feeding the cows were especially precious. Imagine my dismay when I rolled over that morning to find William struggling to keep a loud beat with Dave, who was increasing volume rather than chord variation on his electric guitar.

Placing both pillows over my head didn't get the message across to the Kozel brothers, who were hell-bent on fame at six in the morning. I didn't feel as though I had the right to tell them to shut up in their own house, either.

Then Jane appeared at the door throwing a wad of socks at each musician.

The noise stopped.

"Can't you see how selfish and inconsiderate you're being? He's trying to sleep!"

My eyes caught hers for a very brief moment with nothing but "thank-you" in them. She turned away, looking a little embarrassed, while I rolled over for a particularly special half-hour of slumber.

Whenever he got the sticks in his hands, it was only a matter of time before William became overcome with the desire to hit every drum and every cymbal as loud as he possibly could.

"Just concentrate on getting the beat first," I said. "Boom-tick, boom-tick, boom-tick."

William went boom-tick, boom . . . tick, boom . . . . . . CRASH BANG SPLASH RAT–TAT–TAT BOOM.

Try again.

"Why can't I play it like they do on the record?"

"Because you can't play it like they do on the record."

"Yeah I can, listen . . . "

" . . . that's not how they play it on the record."

"It's close."

"The point is, William, you're never going to learn how to play like they do on the record until you learn how to keep a simple beat."

"That's not what they do on the record."

I unplugged the record player.

"I guess we'd better forget about the record then," I said. "Now the first thing we're going to learn how to do is count: one, two, three, four, one, two, three . . ."

Standing on his chair at the dinner table, Bradley looked down at his plate, then side to side, down at his plate again and finally at William, who, he realized, had stolen one of his hot wieners.

"You sow!" he yelled, reaching across the table at his brother's plate.

"Bradley!" Gene yelled in disbelief.

Bradley recoiled and looked at his dad with eyes crunched up from the injustice that had been done.

"William took my wiener," Bradley explained before breaking into tears.

There were just enough wieners for some to have two, and at the moment William did and Bradley didn't.

"William you jerk, give him back his wiener," Dave said, while punching his younger brother in the arm.

William grabbed his arm and opened his mouth in a silent expression of pain, then screamed back, "I didn't *take* his wiener, you idiot!"

Pat just rolled her eyes while Jane surveyed the situation.

"William, you know you did it so why don't you just admit it and give it back to him," Jane said finally.

"I didn't do it, you fat pig," William yelled, with a sudden swing of his arm that couldn't possibly reach his sister across the table.

Meanwhile, Bradley was crying so loudly I could see his tonsils.

"Here," said Mrs. Kozel, who had been too busy at the stove to be concerned until Bradley's decibel level had reached a certain point. "Take the wiener and give it to Bradley and I'll give you an extra piece of corn."

She did as she said, taking the wiener off William's plate and setting it on Bradley's, while plopping the ear of corn onto William's plate — splashing a bit of hot water onto his arm in the process. William, of course, overreacted to the burn.

As soon as the wiener hit his plate, Bradley began studying it in silence. William started buttering his corn and Mrs. Kozel took off her apron and sat down at the table.

"Bradley," Gene said, "say grace."

*   *   *

"One, two, three, four; boom, tick, boom, tick."

One, two . . . three, four; boom . . . tick . . . b-boom, boom.

"Try it again. One, two, three, four; boom, tick, boom, tick."

One, two, three, four; boom, tick, boom . . . t-tick.

"That's it, William! Now do it again."

One, two, three, four; boom, t-tick, boom . . . tick.

Rain provided a vacation from farm work. You couldn't work in the rain and stay healthy, so instead everyone remained inside and played cards or flipped channels, thinking, maybe, someone might stop by just any time.

A boy and his parents arrived in a steady rain. The boy wore a number 14 jersey. He looked about fifteen or sixteen years old, but he sat awkwardly upon his mother's lap and held her neck like an infant that had been brought into a room full of strange, scary people.

He never said a word, but studied William, Dave, and me while we remained in the kitchen for lack of anyplace better to be. The rain's interruption of the daily routine somehow magnified the boy's abnormality. It seemed almost horrifying.

"Don't think it's gonna stop for a while," the boy's father broke a long silence.

"Glad I got my hay up when I did," Gene said.

Mrs. Kozel dropped a lid from a pot.

Nothing was said for five, ten, then twenty minutes. Finally the boy's father told his wife to dress their son because they were going home.

The boy had a poncho he couldn't seem to manage over his head, even with his mother's help.

"Here, let me get it," the father snapped, grabbing the raincoat from the mother and violently jerking it onto his son.

The boy grunted once in pain.

This was to have been the father's son who could drive the tractor by now. Instead, this was the father's son who could not even put his poncho on.

The father pushed his family out the door toward home, while Gene looked out the window for a hint of clearing.

There was only one Markham listed in that particular suburb of Minneapolis. While I was enjoying my stay at the Kozel farm, I looked forward to taking a rest from this trip. I figured that I had better call her sometime to let her know that I was planning on stopping by.

Gene's brother Zack and his nephew Chuck had come to visit. Both wore shiny black shoes, white socks, white button-down shirts, and black pants that were too short. Both had black hair slicked down with what looked like more than just a dab of Brylcreem.

Gene worked under his tractor as Zack spoke to him and Chuck listened.

"Heard McDaniel almost lost his field the other day," Zack said.

He didn't seem to mind talking to the lower half of Gene's legs.

"What was it he had growing there anyway?" Zack asked.

Gene popped out to search for a new tool.

"Clover," he said, trying to match a wrench with a bolt he held in his hand.

"No, it was, let's see . . . "

"Clover," Gene said.

"No, it was sort of a green grass like . . . "

"Clover."

"No, it was . . . "

Gene stopped what he was doing and waited for his brother.

"Clover!" Zack exclaimed.

"Yeah, that's it," Gene said, before going back to working on his tractor.

Mrs. Kozel came outside and complimented Chuck on his "nice shiny shoes," which had a way of calling attention to themselves seeing as they were far below the hems of his pantslegs.

"I got them and the pants for free," Chuck bragged.

Mrs. Kozel said something like, "Well, that's very good, Chuck," and added that wieners were ready inside.

Chuck and his dad hurried in while I waited for Gene to finish working. In a moment he was wiping the grease from his hands.

"Awhile back Zack fell off a building and hadda have a plate stuck in his head," Gene explained. "He's had a rough time of it ever since.

"The boy just wasn't right from the beginning. They try and keep a farm going, but it seems like every year they gotta get help from the government or from the local folks. The crops die somehow, or the cows don't get fed right. We try and help him as best we can. After all, he *is* my brother."

After wieners, the boys and I went down to the basement, where, surprisingly, there was a pool table. I hadn't played the game in about three years, but remembered getting very frustrated the times that I had, possibly even throwing a stick once or twice.

Yet as I chalked the end of my stick, I noticed the others eyeing me as if they were waiting for me to light one end and swallow the thing.

I blew the chalk off the end a few times.

They watched intently.

I rechalked a particular spot that looked a bit chalkless, and blew some dust off a few more times.

They thought that was just the neatest thing.

The best explanation that I could come up with was that *hitchhiker* was the same sort of word as *poolshark* in a rural Minnesota teenage vocabulary.

"Got any powder for the stick?" I asked.

Dave and William looked at each other in amazement. Of course they didn't have any.

"Maybe Dad will let me go buy some," Dave offered.

"Don't bother," I said, wiping the moisture of my dry pool stick off with my shirt. "Let's just play."

They argued about who was going to be on my team until William finally won out.

The three of them missed almost everything they shot at, and so did I, the difference being that I always had an explanation. "Not enough English on that one."

But something began to catch as the game went on. The balls started lining up better as my muscles relaxed. I got real close to the "cha-boop" of the ball dropping in the corner pocket and felt myself becoming the role that I had been playing.

Perhaps my entire system was adapting to my mode of travel. Whatever, it was real hard to break from the table when Bradley came downstairs to announce that juice and popcorn were ready.

I told Dave that I'd be there in a little while and that I had to use the phone in the barn to call a girl. He winked at me like it was some big deal. When he went upstairs, I could hear him tell everyone that I was going to call one of my girlfriends.

There was an exhilaration in the wind whipping through the corn beneath the crescent moon. It was blowing toward Minneapolis that night, where an acquaintance waited to show me a city I had always wanted to visit since the first time I'd seen "The Mary Tyler Moore Show."

Popcorn-eating silhouettes cast shadows on the long white side of the barn like a movie projection: "After-dinner Snacks" was showing on the main barn from 8:45 till the food ran out. Inside, there was a single light next to the phone. The smell of cows and hay greeted me as I fumbled in my back pocket for the number.

"Hello, may I please speak to Lynn?"

"Lynn? Lynn's not here."

"Do you know when she'll be back?"

"Not really, who is this?"

"My name is Tom DeTitta, I went to school with Lynn and was going to be in town in a few days and was hoping to see her."

"I'm sorry, but Lynn just moved to New Jersey with a friend a couple days ago. I don't think she'll even be back to visit for a few months."

Outside, the light from the kitchen drilled through the darkness to remind me that I was expected inside for popcorn and drinks. I was not prepared for the feelings that overcame me. There would be no break from this journey: the last person I knew between these cornfields and the Pacific Ocean had fled to New Jersey.

The lights from the kitchen called, but the long gravel road beckoned. The darkness there smirked at my newfound understanding of it. There were not to be any distractions along this route.

Much later, I found my way back to the group that had become worried when they had found the barn empty.

"We saved you some popcorn, but it's not hot anymore."

I stepped into the hall for a moment, where William cornered me to say how everybody thought my girlfriend dumped me and that they thought I was going to commit suicide. They probably believed that only a disaster could keep someone away from hot popcorn and cherry Kool-Aid.

There was nothing wrong, I said. There was nothing wrong at all.

Explanation was too much of a risk. Their friendship was the only type I would know for a long while. I could not afford to test its depth.

I was surprised to be awakened by Jane the next morning.

"Cut it out, William!" she screamed as something—or someone—klunked against the wall.

"What did I do? I didn't do nothin'!"

"Hey, you two, knock it off," Gene yelled up the steps. "William, come down here!"

"What! I didn't do nothin', Dad, not a thing! What's wrong with you anyway, Jane?"

At the breakfast table, I found out that tomorrow was the first day of school for Foley, Minnesota, and Jane had gotten braces on her teeth over the summer.

Bradley was complaining about everything he didn't want to eat—which was everything. He couldn't just say he didn't want it, either; he had to toss it across the table and scream, "Bleah!"

"Bradley!" Gene yelled.

Eventually Bradley got down to the real issue at hand: "Do I have to go to school tomorrow, Mom?"

"Come on, Bradley," Mrs. Kozel said, leading her youngest son away from the table, "Let's start getting your things ready so you'll be all set to go."

The cows were supposed to have been in one small pen that morning, waiting for the old "thwock-thwock-thwock." But instead, we found them in a larger pen that didn't lead to their stalls.

"Dammit, Dave, who left the gate open?" Gene yelled.

The question apparently contained the answer. Donning rubber boots to wade through the manure, it was time for us to move cows.

"Jeez, how stupid can you get?" Gene yelled over and over.

Dave grumbled to himself, and once snapped back at his father, more to defend his pride than his actions.

Dave began punching the cows in the back, telling them to get into the stinking barn. Gene smacked the animals with his pitchfork, and William just screamed at them. The net result of these actions was a large ball of cows clumped tighter and tighter in the middle of the pen and going absolutely nowhere.

Gene hit harder, Dave hit harder, and Pat, William, and I stood in front of the openings the cows weren't supposed to go through. Every once in a while, a cow would break loose from the pack and run at Pat, see the pitchfork, feel the pitchfork, come to a screeching halt, then run at William and get away.

"William, what are you doing over there?" Gene screamed.

"It's not my fault!"

Eventually, they all sort of fell through the one opening that was provided for them and began their morning "thwock-thwock-thwock." We continued the chores amidst the smell of spattered manure on sweaty clothing, and I could not figure out why those kids didn't want to go to school.

After chores, Bradley took me to his room to show me all the things he "didn't" want to bring to school the next day, as well as all the things he "didn't" want to wear.

"These are my crayons—you see, red, yellow, orange, blue, green, and this color (purple). These are the socks I'm gonna wear and this is the shirt . . . "

"I don't know, I just don't feel like playing," William said. "I just don't feel like it."

"You want to try and play to the record today?" I asked. "Now that you've got the beat down we can try to put it to music."

"Nah, I just don't feel like it. I just wanna go outside for a while."

*   *   *

The kids were up an hour earlier than usual, combing hair, washing faces, brushing teeth, and dividing up "Foley" notebook covers.

Their departure — bright, shiny, and ready for a new year — meant trouble for me. The manure pen needed cleaning that morning, and Gene and I were the only ones around to do it.

I supposed my experience on the farm wouldn't have been complete otherwise. We decided that after the unpleasant chore we would take the "Gene Kozel for County Commissioner" campaign to the streets. I wondered if there was some sort of symbolic connection involved.

The game plan for our first campaign — "Operation Cow Manure" — was that Gene would come through with a bulldozer and scrape the stuff up, and whatever he couldn't pick up I would shovel into the dozer's cup.

At first glance, the job didn't look so bad. The sun had baked a crust on the manure field, making it look like the type of thing you buy in bags at a nursery for organic gardening.

But my first step into it proved otherwise. A wet sludge oozed out from my boots, releasing a stench pent up beneath the cover that was so strong it reached down my esophagus and tried to pull my stomach out. I was throwing up little bits of my breakfast as I worked, gagging over and over while searching for air that wasn't directly in the path of the fumes.

Still, I'd rather have gagged than listen to any more city-boy jokes. I turned my head away from Gene, and continued to shovel the manure.

We each took forty-five minute showers after the proceedings. I washed myself thoroughly, even scrubbing the insides of my ears and between my fingers.

It was time to meet the man on the street.

Gene came decked out for the event, wearing his cleanest overalls, a sparkling white shirt, white socks, and, of course, his finest International Harvester.

On the kitchen table, there was a stack of posters picturing Gene with his family and announcing "VOTE FOR KOZEL." There was also a stack of cards that pictured Gene's face and a little of Pat's elbow. The message was the same.

"It doesn't cost as much if you let them use the same picture for both," Gene explained.

"How many of these things do you want?" his wife asked.

"Not too many. Ten of the big ones and thirty-five of the little ones — no, maybe thirty-eight in case we hit a lunchtime crowd and fifteen of the big ones. But then I don't want to use them all up at once. Better give me thirty-two of the little ones and . . . "

Frances grimaced and stuffed both stacks into her politician husband's gut. I think she just wanted to know if he wanted the whole stack, half the stack, a bunch, or a few. Gene didn't realize that his wife had not yet signed up to be his official aide.

He hugged her, then looked over at me.

"Ready to go, Sidekick?"

The name on the grain silo said that we were in Rice — our first stop to meet the people. The town was on the very edge of Gene's county, and he figured it would be the least costly place to start honing his politicking skills. Rice was a "four-stores-two-gas-stations-and-a-post-office" kind of town.

We parked along the street and walked into the first grocery store, hoping the owner of Hamby's — or Handle's — would allow us a window space to announce Gene's candidacy. It looked like one of those family-owned grocery stores that never quite had enough room for everything.

Sensing by our lack of movement in any particular direction that we were on official business, the owner, "Fred," came over to find out what was up.

"Yes, what can I do for you?"

He wore a white shirt, white apron, black bow-tie, and had a gun hanging off his belt that was loaded with twenty-five-cent stickers. He combed each of his few grey hairs directly back over his scalp, and glared hard, stained eyes over the top of half-rimmed glasses.

"Hi, I'm Gene Kozel and this is my sidekick, or, er, helper, Tom."

Gene pointed at me with his arm as if displaying a side of beef, waiting for me to say:

"Hi, I'm glad to meet you."

Gene sort of forgot to talk after that. Fred looked as though he had some pricing to do.

"I'm running for county commissioner," Gene finally said.

He extended his hand toward Fred, but drew it back when he realized that the three of us had been together long enough for Fred to have pinned 150 bananas on the tree with the paper lady on top of it. The handshake should've come at the beginning. We both made a mental note of that.

Then nobody said anything for a while.

Finally, Gene just went for it.

"Can I hang one of these in the front of your store?"

Fred snatched the one away from Gene and looked it over. He checked the back too, just in case we were trying to put up a "Fred's a Jerk" poster disguised as a political ad.

"All right," he said, "just keep it low and it'll be all right. I like people to be able to look in the window if they want," and off he went stamping individually wrapped apples.

At the window, Gene and I had a choice. We could either pretend like we thought Fred was kidding when he told us to keep the thing low, or we could do a slight injustice to the Firemen's Benefit Pancake Breakfast, something to the tune of a fifty-percent reduction that would leave "efit ... till noon ... hall."

We decided that interested people would know what that meant.

After that blissful rendezvous, the rest of the storefronts were easy. Soon we had a picture of Gene's family in almost every store window in town. I would have thought the law of "diminishing returns for amount of county commissioner posters per block" would start to take effect after the number two. But apparently Gene hadn't heard of that law, because he used up all fifteen posters along the town's three blocks.

With no posters left (and no storefronts left, either), Gene decided it was time to "meet the people." He distributed the cards between us—thirty-one for him, nine for me—explaining that I was to use my cards only if he had to kiss a baby.

With instructions laid out and cards in hand, we stood on the street corner in Rice, Minnesota, and waited for somebody to show up.

Twenty-five minutes later, Gene decided we'd have better luck in front of the post office. Sure enough, not ten minutes after establishing our new territory, we nabbed a few unsuspecting Riceonians who thought they were going to the post office just to mail their letters.

"Hi, I'm Gene Kozel, and this is my campaign manager, Tom (I'd smile), and I'd like to ask you for your vote."

Gene extended both arms to his victims, one with a "Vote for Kozel" card, and the other with a large handshake.

Gene's abrupt approach left many people startled at first. But they'd soon notice the way every muscle in his body was straining to give the voter all the attention he could muster. They'd notice the International Harvester hat, the white socks, and the way he'd smile when he said "campaign manager" or "sidekick." Then, they'd shake his hand, knowing that Gene Kozel was having the time of his life that day campaigning for Benton County commissioner.

We ran out of cards after Gene decided to do a table-to-table campaign at a Shoney's Restaurant during lunch hour. Actually, we had one card left, but it was hidden away in my back pocket.

"You know, I kinda like this campaigning, there, Sidekick," Gene said as we drove off for a lunch spot closer to home. "I wish I had more time for it."

"Do you think you'll have time to work as commissioner if you don't have time to campaign?" I asked.

Gene slowly took his cap off and held it with his fingers while scratching his head with his knuckles.

"I'll worry about that after I win," he said.

The skating rink was over in Pell. A dollar-fifty for skating from 6 to 10:15, Bradley, Jane, Dave, William, and me.

"What size?"

"Ten and a half."

Size ten was all they had, but they looked like they'd fit, all right.

I laced Bradley's skates while he was looking over his shoulder at the skaters. At one point he turned to me and said, "Too tight," then turned away again and continued watching the action.

Bradley was getting pretty used to my helping him with things.

Jane and her friends talked among themselves to the right of me without any over-the-shoulder giggling. Dave and William were already up and skating without me, as I struggled to get Bradley's skates tied just the way he wanted them.

When they were finally tied right, Bradley was off, trying to make some headway by clinging to the rails while his tongue slipped out the side of his mouth in anticipation of falling.

I sat on the bench and watched them all go around. Dave and William kept crossing in front of a girl they knew from school—much to her delight. Jane skated between her two girlfriends, keeping a watchful eye on any new developments, and Bradley held the railing in absolute fascination of the wheels on his feet.

Drawing myself back further still, I tried to see them turning even greater circles through the spring, summer, and fall of it. I knew that I would be leaving soon, and I wondered what had happened during my two-week stay with the Kozels. I wondered if they would ever talk about the hitchhiker who had stopped off that one summer, and if so, I wondered what they would say.

Just then Bradley stood before me hugging the rail with both arms while his feet slipped out from under him.

"Do you know how to do this?" he asked.

"Skate?"

"Yahha."

"I think I do. It's pretty much like ice skating, isn't it?"

"Do you think you could show me how?"

"Sure, Bradley. Sit down here a second and let me get my skates on. I'll show you how."

The next day, Gene and I took a drive to the farm-supply store to get another part for the tractor. It had been a long time since we had made that first trip.

"You know, I was thinking that I probably had better tell you when I was planning on moving on."

Gene took off his cap and scratched his head the way he always had.

"Thinking of leaving us, are ya?"

"I guess I better go sometime. If I stayed too much longer William will be too big to fit in bed with."

"Yeah, I suppose you're right about that one, Tom. When are you thinking of going?"

"Didn't you say that you had a friend who drives cattle into Minneapolis?"

"Billy Buckman?"

"Yeah, that's the one."

"He could take you, I guess. I'd have to give him a call—but he leaves real early in the morning."

"When's the next time he's going into the city?"

"Thursday."

"That's tomorrow, isn't it?"

"Yup."

I looked out the window of Gene's pickup at the long, straight rows of corn stretching out to the horizon.

"Do you think you could give him a call tonight?"

After dinner, I presented Gene with a going-away present I'd purchased while using the truck on an errand. It was one I knew for sure Gene would use.

"Well, Mr. Jack Daniels, one of my favorite people. I guess that means we're going to have to do a little celebrating."

Gene poured a little bit for everyone at the table who was old enough. Bradley got to smell the cap.

"Here's to our hitchhiker friend, Tom. May he find whatever it is he's looking for out there, sometime soon."

Four hours later, the bottle was a lot less full than it had been awhile back.

"Let's see, what haven't we talked about?" Gene asked, wavering slightly.

The round fluorescent light shining above us was the only light on in the house, and perhaps in all of central Minnesota. It bored through the surrounding darkness the way Gene and I had bored through unfamiliarity and distrust so that we could sit up together all night and drink whiskey.

"Tell me something," I said. "Is sixteen hundred bales of hay a lot to do in one afternoon?"

"You're still thinking about that, huh?"

"My arms are still hurting."

"I suppose it was a pretty good day's work. Pretty good for a city boy."

Gene came back from the dining room with an old box that had a name written in gold script across the lower right-hand corner. He placed a towel on the kitchen table and laid the box upon it. Inside was a family portrait of the Kozlowskis of Duluth, Minnesota. Seven boys and four girls, all looking their very best for the special occasion.

"See if you can find me."

That wasn't hard to do. His sincere look remained, even though most of his hair hadn't. He was one of the oldest boys, standing in the back next to two brothers.

"Charlie and Dave," Gene said. "Dave works for the state agricultural department, and Charlie's got a good job at a lumber plant in the northern part of the state."

But Joey was the one we talked about. Joey and Zack, the brother who had been over the other day. They weren't farmers married with four kids and living near Saint Paul. Nor were they carpenters, or managers, or anything you could categorize that easily.

"Joey, he just never seemed to get on track. He'd start something for a while, then pretty soon it'd go all to pieces. Zack was doing all right until the accident. Then things changed for him. Things never got any better."

"Sometimes I wonder why God gave it to me so good and forgot about Zack and Joey."

Through a long silence, Gene was truly perplexed. In time, he placed the picture back upon its blue velvet cushion. He closed the cover, got up from the table, and put his family portrait back in the dining-room closet.

The conversation had become less talking and more yawning. Upon my eighth return from the bathroom, I found Gene napping on the table. It was clear then that the whiskey, the night, and the stay were coming to an end for me.

Knowing that it was time to go, but yet wanting to stay somehow, I picked up the bottle, which had only a few swallows left, and handed it to Gene.

"You have to promise that come election night, win lose or draw, you'll take that last bit in remembrance of our campaign."

"Win, lose, or draw," he said, "that's a deal."

Billy Buckman was honking his horn as I turned to face a little red five, four, and five on the digital alarm beside me. Pain settled into parts of my body I hadn't even known existed.

Halfway through falling about the bathroom, however, the realization hit me: I was moving on. Excitement shot through my deteriorating condition and carried me down the stairs—half-sad that it would be my last trip to the breakfast table, but mostly happy that I had been around for so long.

Frances was examining the whiskey bottle that less than ten hours ago had been full.

"No wonder Gene couldn't get his pants off last night," she said.

The others had gotten up early and were working in the barn. Two slices of French toast, bacon, and juice were waiting for me at the table.

"So you're off to the big city," she said. "Well, I hope you enjoy it as much as we've enjoyed having you."

The food rested in my stomach without having been tasted. It was the first time I had failed to savor every detail of her cooking. Billy Buckman continued blowing his horn.

We hugged each other good-bye. I'd have to write when I got to the West Coast, I thought, and every Christmas after that. Then maybe they'd know how much their company meant to me. At the moment, words just wouldn't come.

For the first time in two weeks, I hoisted the pack back onto my shoulders. I'd almost forgotten how heavy it was. A strong gust of wind was waiting on the other side of the back door, blowing hard in a single direction. It looked as though there had been a storm that night. The deep red, early morning sun was breaking through heavy grey clouds.

They all probably thought I was still drunk when I entered the barn for the final time to say good-bye. My eyes were probably moist and bloodshot. They gathered in a semicircle around me.

"Listen, I'm going to see you all later," I said through the hugs and handshakes.

"Maybe I might get a job in Minneapolis for a while, and then you could come and visit me there."

They looked like they were enjoying the spectacle of my trying to get the words out in the terrible early-morning state I was in. I heard a few "take cares", a few "don't forget to writes."

It was time to leave. Finally, I made a break for it.

"I gotta go, he's out there waiting."

I dashed past the cows and through the big sliding door at the end of the barn, leaving a couple of drops of all that had happened uncommunicated in the hay.

Billy's truck was old and tall. The passenger seat loomed almost three feet above me. Quickly, I hopped up into the cab, and pulled my backpack beside me, setting it on my lap so I could close the door. On the other side of the window, the corn shimmered from the coming of new weather, and a fresh, clean smell welcomed another day on the farm after a night of rain. I took one last look, then took a deep breath and turned to face my new companion.

"Hi, I'm Billy Buckman."

11

"Dear John..."

"Where are you going in Minneapolis?" Billy asked—again.

"I'm not really sure."

"Why are you going there?"

"I've never been there before."

The fields along I-94 grew increasingly cluttered with billboards, then buildings, as we headed southeast.

"My girlfriend and I, we like to go to the Wisconsin Dells. We've been going there for the last five years. We got a hotel that we like, and a restaurant, too. There's a boat tour that we like to go on, also.

"We set everything up about six months in advance, so we don't have to worry. That way, we can look forward to it all year long."

An animal banged against the side of its aluminum holding pen, then there were no sounds at all. The pigs in the back were going to the city to become bacon. The cargo in the passenger seat was another thing.

"You don't even know where you're staying in Minneapolis, do ya?"

"Not really."

"Got any idea what you're gonna see when you're in town?"

"No."

"Well, where are you gonna go after Minneapolis?"

"No idea."

Billy downshifted unnecessarily.

"Goddamn, a fella could lose his mind traveling the way you are!"

I thought about that for a moment.

"Yeah, you're right."

The street light at this particular corner changed exactly every twenty-eight seconds. That was probably standard. The green and white rectangles jutting from the light posts read Euclid and Ninth Streets, and that was unique. This town was the same. This town was altogether different.

There was an empty white bag lying before me. I tossed it between waiting cars, then watched it fly up and over and about in the sudden draft of "green," before finally coming to rest in an altogether different place.

I started thinking about what time Bradley was going to be home from school. Then I remembered that I had something to do in this town.

"Send me a letter to the Minneapolis general delivery to let me know how you are. . . ."

In the midst of a massive wooden hall loaded with woodwork, the station for transients' mail was a small, plain window. I had to ring the bell several times to get service.

"No, it's *D* as in Donald," *e*, capital *t, i, t, t, a.* DeTitta."

"You just made deadline. We only keep these things for a few weeks."

"Thanks."

Outside there was a long, flat row of marble that decorated the building. It seemed like a good place to read. The wind was gentle yet complete as I opened the letter postmarked New York, excited somehow, in anticipation of its contents.

Dear Tom,
I hope you understand what I am about to say . . .

An hour later, a couple approached and sat nearby on the marble slab, assuming they had found privacy, based on the faraway look that disguised the nearest inhabitant.

"I just don't understand you, Charlie, that's all. Sometimes you seem like you really do care, and then . . ."

Charlie mumbled something while caressing this woman who was about to cry.

"How can you say that, Charlie? How can you say that when you come in with your friends and act the way you do—telling them they don't have to leave a tip if they don't feel like it? How do you think that makes me feel?"

Charlie mumbled again, held her. She began crying.

"I just don't know, Charlie, I just don't know."

Charlie held her, kissed her.

"Oh, Charlie . . ."

The woman held her man as if she didn't know how to let go, at the same time crying upon his chest as if she didn't know how to stop.

I spent about seven or eight days in Minneapolis chasing around two Australian woman who were on some sort of airline tour. I could never figure out how to separate them and I didn't even know why I wanted to. When I finally did get one alone, she slapped me in the face. She thought I wanted sex. But really, there's a whole lot of other reasons for wanting to hold someone.

The next day, I ran into a guy who was on his way across the plains to the West Coast. I had no reason to stay.

"You need someone to share the driving?"

12

"There's Always Grad School..."

We stopped at the Minneapolis post office on the way out because my driver had to mail some letters. Waiting in the car, I noticed a man alone with a letter on that same long, marble slab. The words seemed to hold him in a world of their own so that everything else was superfluous.

Finally, he folded the letter into the envelope and let it lie beside him. As we drove off, the man looked up between the tall buildings and squinted toward a place in the western sky where the sun was less bright. A slight wind pushed the letter further and further away.

Leaving again, the Minnesota scenery called out to take one last look at the friend I might not see for a long time; advising me to take with me a part of the intricate patchwork fields with long, straight rows of corn, as I traveled toward the red glow they led to.

Along Interstate 94 heading west from Minnesota, the sky's massive billows of moisture bore down on an uninspired landscape like a Rembrandt along the stark white walls of a modern gallery.

"I guess this is the plains," I said.

"Yeah, for a long time."

My driver was a man about my age, about my size, who looked a lot like me. He was doing pretty much the same thing that I was—traveling around the country, going in and out of towns—although he said his purpose was to find a town for him and his girlfriend to live in. I remembered offering that same reason once to an uncle who needed to know why.

He was Tom. I was Tom.

"Did you go to college?" I asked.

"Yeah, uh-huh."

"Where'd you go to school?"

"Oberlin. I just graduated last year."

"Oh, yeah? I just graduated from Duke last year. What'd you study over there?" I asked.

"Piano mostly. Some liberal arts."

"You studied at the Oberlin Conservatory?"

"Uh-huh."

"I've been playing the drums for about fourteen years, less and less classical these days, but I began in that orientation."

"I was starting to do a lot of jazz work by the time I left the school," he said.

"Well, what are you doing now?"

"Driving around, looking for a place to live. What about you?"

"I'm not sure. Looking for a place."

"My girlfriend sent me off to try and find a city that would be good to live in."

"Is that her under the sun visor?"

"How'd you see that?"

"It slipped down once when you stopped. I noticed you sticking it back up there."

"Here, her name's Joyce."

"She's a pretty woman."

"I like her," he said.

"So what are you going to do when you find a city you like? Got a job in mind?"

"I don't know; I had a job for a few months as a chiropractic assistant. I kinda liked that. There's lots of different jobs you can get, I guess. I'd just like to find the right city, first, then take it from there.

"Get a little context."

"Yeah."

"Why don't you get a job playing piano?"

"No, I couldn't do that."

"Why, don't you like it any more?"

"Sure, it's the greatest thing in the world, but you can't get a job playing piano."

"Well, what else is there for you?"

"I'm not sure. I was thinking I might want to go back to graduate school one day," he said.

"I was thinking about that too."

"You know what you might want to go in for?"

"No idea. How about you?"

"I don't know either. But it's always a possibility."

"Right, there's always grad school."

Over the state line into South Dakota, the land offered nothing that hadn't already happened twenty minutes before.

"College was all right," he said. "Even if it wasn't, it kept you too busy to realize it. I wouldn't say I disliked college, but it's hard to figure out what it was all for."

"I remember my graduation," I said. "There was some guy who sat behind me with his arms folded, watching everyone else pop their corks and drink their booze while all the pomp and circumstance went on around him. He just sort of stood there as if he was mad about something, and I remember having a tremendous feeling toward him—as though he were some sort of hero. I don't remember a word of what was said at my graduation, I just remember that guy, sitting there, watching it all from his own distance. It was like, there he was, and he had no intention of popping a cork just because everyone—I mean everyone—was doing that at the moment."

"I remember feeling mad like that too," he said. "There I'd spent four years working my butt off and the only things the world was going to pay me to do were either become a bank manager or join the Peace Corps. A counselor at school told me that things were different now, that an undergraduate degree didn't mean as much to the job world anymore, and that it was just a stepping stone. He said that I'd have to take the next step. Something like grad school."

"But doesn't it seem like those steps just keep getting thrown at you from somewhere?"

"What do you mean?" he asked.

"It just seems like there'd be another step that would lead to another step, and then another, and they'd all make sense, and they'd all be 'the right decision,' and you'd just keep making them until fifteen years later you found yourself someplace different without knowing how you got there."

"Yeah, but you always gotta take the next step. You can't just hitchhike forever. We can't just keep looking around. Eventually, you've gotta take the next step."

"Yeah . . . next step."

"What's that?"

"What you said about steps. I just remembered some old guy that I ran into when I started way back in Kentucky."

"What about him?"

"Nothing, really. Just some old black guy that had no place to go except where he was going."

"Doesn't sound like much of a future."

"Maybe not."

But the sky that hung above it all was magnificent. Complex entanglements of moisture rose upward in layers, while long straight beams of sunlight sprayed out from the creases.

"You know, I think I've seen more in these past few months than I did in my whole life before that," I said.

"I know what you mean. Traveling is just the most incredible thing. I've got a whole notebook full of people I've met on this trip. People who I probably never would have bothered to get to know if I was working with them or went to school with them."

"Yeah, it's kind of funny the way that works. With hitchhiking, I think it's got to do with the vulnerability. It's like, when you think that someone might knife you, and then they don't, all of a sudden you want to be their best friend."

"I think it's the same thing with any kind of travel. The vulnerability has a way of bringing people together, while security has a way of keeping them apart," he said.

"If I ever settle down and get married, I've got about a million places I want to take my kid. I feel like I'd want him to see most of the stuff I did. I'd want him to spend a summer working on a farm in Minnesota."

"It's also nice being able to just up and go like this without having to worry about anything breaking down at home, so to speak," he said. "You get the feeling that you can keep going anywhere, and there's nothing holding you back."

"Yeah, and when it gets real good, you feel like you don't even *have* to go anywhere, either."

"Just keep your eyes on a sky like that and watch it come at you."

"That's the nice thing about being confused. You get a chance to notice things a lot better than if you knew where you were going."

Night drew our hunger into a town named Humbart, where a diner of the same name offered hamburger steaks with onions and gravy, iced tea, apple pie, and a jukebox.

"This is a neat place," he said. "I like these types of places."

"Me, too," I said. "It's got context."

"Where do you eat while you're traveling like this?" he wanted to know.

"Wherever. Seems like I eat a lot of tuna-fish sandwiches while I'm waiting to go somewhere. I've always got a couple cans of the stuff in my pack. I buy lots of fruits in grocery stores, too. I don't eat that well most of the time, but that doesn't seem to matter much when you're on the road. You can eat a loaf of bread on a back road in Kentucky, and you're too busy thinking about the fact that you're in Kentucky to worry about the taste."

"Yeah. You eat out a lot?"

"When I'm with people, I do. I've got to average about six dollars a day, so I can't eat out that much."

"You making it on that?"

"No problem. If I spend too much one day, I just eat tuna the next."

"Where'd you get the money for the trip?"

"I went around sealing driveways for a couple months. Sticking that black stuff on 'em. I used to go door to door trying to get business. I was getting pretty into it. Every time I'd go by someone's house I'd start looking for cracks in their driveway."

"It's amazing how easy it is to get caught up in whatever you're doing," he said.

"You know, at one time I actually considered starting my own business."

"That's kinda scary when you think about it."

"Damn right it is! It scared the hell out of me."

Night fell hard on the plains, leaving an enormous darkness above and in front, beside and behind. There were no longer any lines to follow in the sky, nor was there any flat land to become bored with. There was only a deep, still darkness that overcame, and laid bare.

"You know, it would've been nice to have at least been a hippie or something that whole while," he said. "Not that I was really into any of that stuff from the sixties, but just so I could've said I was one. Hell, the only thing to join in college was a fraternity, and that was more a parody of the type of thing I'm talking about."

"Did you have any movements on your campus while you were there?"

"No, not really. Every once in a while someone would get pretty worked up about women's rights, but I just couldn't get that excited about that," he said.

"Yeah, I know what you mean. Everyone was pretty concerned about getting into grad school, or whatnot."

"Yeah, if you weren't studying to be something, you were pretty much lost," he said.

"Do you feel that way?"

"How?"

"Lost?"

"Uh-huh. I'm trying to get back at it one step at a time. First find a city I like, then a job, then who knows? What about you?"

"I just feel confused, I guess, maybe lost. Sometimes I feel lost.

Most of the time it's a good kind of lost, like I'm curious to see where I wind up. Sometimes it gets real lonely though. I guess that just makes sense—hitchhiking alone like this."

"Get's pretty bad, huh?"

"Sometimes it gets like there's nothing at all. Nothing to hate, nothing to look forward to, no job to get back to, no life to continue on with—nothing, just me—for whatever that's worth."

"Is that what you want?" he asked.

"I don't know. Maybe it is."

"You ever try and figure out why you're doing this?"

"Sometimes. I never really come up with a reason, though. It seems I keep coming back to this feeling I had when I was a kid, driving in the back seat of my folks' car on our way to see my uncle or something. I remember looking out the window and watching all these big open fields go by, and getting a real strange feeling like I wanted to go out there and lie down in one. But I knew that I couldn't; there was no way my parents were going to stop the car for me to go out and lie down in some damned field.

"I remember feeling really trapped, like I was caught up in something that wasn't my own and that I didn't have any control over. I've felt that way a bunch of times; like I was caught up and I just wanted to lie down in a field on the side of the road for a minute. I guess maybe I thought if I stuck out my thumb and just went wherever, eventually I'd have to get out of the car. I wanted to feel like I could get dropped off anywhere and find a place to sleep. If I could do that, things would be different. Then it wouldn't be like I was caught up."

"Has that happened yet?"

"Maybe for a little bit here and there, but most of the time it seems I'm always getting in somebody else's car going somewhere else. I like that, though. That's a big part of the reason I'm traveling this way, too. But that's not all there is to it."

"I know I'll feel better when I find a place to live, then I know I'll feel even better when I find a job," he said.

"I don't see why you don't play the piano professionally."

"No, that's just not something you can do to earn a living."

"Why not?"

"I don't know, you just can't."

"I wish I could play the drums professionally. I don't think I've ever felt anything like I do when I'm playing them. There's just nothing like being 'on time,' you know?"

"Yes, there is nothing like it at all," he said.

"So why don't you play professionally?"

"I don't know, why don't you?"

"Well, it does seem like a tough way to make a living. I mean, they say that you've got insurance payments and all that stuff you gotta take care of. It seems like it'd be a tough way to send the kids to college, so to speak."

"Or the refrigerator needs repair—or you've got to get another chair for your patio set . . . "

"You think that's what lies ahead?"

"Seems that way, sometimes," he said.

"Maybe you could play music while you were chiropracting or something."

"I might do that, as sort of a hobby."

"Did I tell you that I met this guy back in Michigan who's been bumming around for nearly twenty years just going from place to place, playing the trumpet?"

"No. How does he live?"

"He just plays the trumpet and people toss him change here and there."

"That sounds neat," he said.

"Yeah. Imagine doing that—going anywhere you felt like going and playing music."

"That would be something. Sometimes I feel like I could do something like that. It's like a dream that's usually gone by the time I wake up."

"Yeah, sometimes I feel that way too."

"It'd be a nice feeling to have for a while," he said.

"Yeah. . . . Maybe you could go to graduate school in music?"

Close to 1 A.M. and nowhere near Rapid City, the night was calling two tired travelers into its bosom, hours before reaching the day's destination.

There was an exit, and the remnants of a town; a town so insignificant it was as though it used to be a town. A single light shone at a vacant filling station. We pulled into the parking lot of a restaurant that was closed.

"Let's just get out of the car for a minute," I said.

The wind had increased tremendously since dinner, and its warm, solid puffs met our eight hours of driving fatigue in an explosion of excitement.

"Holy shit!" I screamed, "This is great!"

Far away and in opposite directions, two brilliant lightning storms gave perspective to the enormity of the darkness that surrounded us, while the metallic thunk-thunk-thunk of a chain clanking against a pole was the only sound to pierce the high-pitched whir of the wind.

"We really should sleep outside tonight," I said.

"That sounds like a good idea."

We crossed over the Interstate onto a paved road that soon became gravel, and then dirt, as it made its way along some low, ragged growth that walled endless fields of nothing.

Eventually, we came to a clearing in the brush that was just wide enough to sneak the car into. In another moment, two sleeping bags lay on the far end of an endless expanse of dirt pasture heading west. The ground was cracked in slabs that peeled the first inch of soil, as though the earth was suffering from a tremendous sunburn. Its contour was smooth though; no roots, no stones, no branches to clear away.

"I feel like looking around some," I said to my companion already bedded down. "You want to check out what's here?"

"I'm pretty tired. I would if I could."

"OK, I'll be back in a while."

Not half a mile from our place of rest was a cemetery that protruded from a slight, grassy slope where everything else was brown and flat. A gate across the entrance proclaimed, "Belvedere Cemetery."

Against the endless stretch of solitary miles, the simple metal structure had the presence of a cathedral, ringing its single note like a hundred orchestras, while the moon ducked in and out of the clouds between the letters C and E.

The tall, green grass of the cemetery scratched at my ankles as I continued through the gate, moving closer to the overwhelming sky that would not let go.

The tombstones grew black along the edges from a long stillness. David Mashburn 1934–1981. "Rest in Peace." I hovered around the suggestion, until the permanence of the stone and the import of its message were too inviting to feet that had traveled so far. I took a moment to lay upon this place where another man had forever been relieved of the burden of movement.

I lay still for a long time, watching the clouds playing hide-and-seek with a moon that was two stages from full, and let my mind wander: a field beside me where wind was blowing; the twinkle of a town I once passed; a woman's touch along the side of the lake in Michigan; the flat, green moss and a view of the lake – Superior.

Closing my eyes, I saw a man hustling up and down an aisle; nervous somehow, looking toward me – beckoning. Motion continuing beneath him and me, then stillness. Absolute and complete. Forever. Thoughts of an ocean, of a house, of a woman, but then there was no woman. There was just me absolutely alone. . . .

Immediately, I jumped up, horrified to find myself lying in a graveyard, surrounded by dark. I began to run up—further into it—without a thought as to why or what for.

The motion of my legs churned images like the handle of a peep-show: the cab of a truck, a weary bus station, a telephone in a barn—so many places I had come upon, all running together, faster and faster to create a single impression that I could not yet discern.

The tombstones were fewer and fewer in the far reaches away from the road. The grass grew taller and healthier there.

Then I saw a motion; a tall and narrow motion approaching slowly. The image of a man, his face thin and his feet sore, continuing toward me, one step after another. A black man on a back road in Kentucky.

"You ain't gonna get around that bend—dere's BEARS on da hill! Dey's tellin' everyone to go back!"

I was running hard up the slight grade, running as fast as I could as if that were all that mattered. At the top there was only grass to stand on as the unending vastness of the plains continued on toward horizons that were too deep and too distant.

This motion wanted only to continue. It wanted to run across a wind-blown prairie for all it was worth, until it reached what would forever be beyond its grasp. In vain, I searched for a horizon that was closer, but saw only a space that was too far and without relief. And so I stood absolutely still, with the fear of all existence blazing through every inch of my body: Where was the comfort? Where was the relief in a life that offers unreachable horizons?

"You ain't gonna get around that bend. . . . Dere's BEARS."

Until the man continued away, one step in front of the other, on and on, and the vastness of the clouds that were so much taller, and the wind that was so much stronger, settled in to carry off my trembling. Into the open space it flew. Like a feather in a great ocean of air, I watched it fly.

I lay awake for several hours, watching the moon hide and the lightning dance, wondering what it would take to walk alone in this life without fear.

Morning brought a deep, red sun that shone orange across a herd of cattle less than fifty yards from where we slept. Their proximity startled me and I jumped, which frightened the animals and sent them away in a cloud of dust.

It felt good to have so small an action yield such a tremendous effect—especially on the plains. My existence reaffirmed, I watched as the sun grew brighter, making its way above that elusive spot where the sky met the land.

Toward the western end of South Dakota, what once was an Interstate became one long commercial runway for a place called Wall Drug.

"FUN LIKE A CIRCUS – WALL DRUG."

"WALL DRUG SINCE 1931."

"EAT UNDER THE TREE AT WALL DRUG."

"RIDE THE BUCKING HORSE (STUFFED) AT WALL DRUG."

I remembered seeing similar signs as far back as Minnesota. They had appeared about every thirty miles or so, until nighttime spared us of the information. Now, in the morning light, they seemed to appear every sixty-five seconds.

"WALL DRUG IN 10 MINUTES."

"COWBOY ORCHESTRA LIFE SIZE ANIMATION AT WALL DRUG."

"STALL AT WALL'S WALL DRUG."

"WALL DRUG STRONGLY RECOMMENDED."

Being as we were college sophisticates, we got a good laugh over this place's tremendous attempt to capture those more easily swayed.

"I bet you they've got a special parking lot for Winnebagos," I said.

"They probably sell those ceramic pink flamingos in their gift shop."

"TAKE PICTURE ON A BUCKING HORSE – FREE AT WALL DRUG."

"FREE ICE WATER WALL DRUG."

"Now that's a deal. I can remember paying up to fifteen dollars a glass for ice water at some places," I said.

"I know, and every time I try to get my girlfriend to take a picture of me on one of those horses at the supermarket, we usually get charged."

"COFFEE STILL 5 CENTS – WALL DRUG."

"FIVE MINUTES TO WALL DRUG."

"Have you ever been to South of the Border in South Carolina?" I asked.

"Yeah – I mean I passed by it."

"ONE MILE TO WALL DRUG."

"Do you know that people actually have honeymoons there?"

"At Wall Drug?"

"No, South of the Border. They've got a brochure and everything: 'Have your Honeymoon with Little Pedro,' or something like that. Can you believe it?"

"WALL DRUG ½ MILE."

"That's really something."

"Yeah."

"WALL DRUG EXIT."

We were about ten feet past the exit ramp when each of us asked simultaneously, "You wanna just stop to get a five-cent coffee?" and Tom swerved into the exit, nearly sending a Winnebago with New Jersey tags to an early roadside rest.

The green and white water tower in Wall, South Dakota, proclaimed, "Wall S.D. Home Of Wall Drug."

In fact, most of the town was done in the same green and yellow or green and white that had colored the warnings for this drugstore for the last four hundred miles.

"I guess they don't want to upset anybody's expectations," Tom said.

"What do you suppose this is, a drugstore or what?" I asked.

"Got me."

One quick left prompted by a green and yellow sign, and we found ourselves on a street lined with a long, "let's-pretend-we're-a-pioneer" storefront, above which loomed the message "Ted and Bill Hustead's Wall Drug Store." In the parking lot beneath it, it seemed as though no two license plates had the same colors.

There were about three entrance ways that looked capable of yielding the five-cent coffee we sought. The word *Café* was all over the place. Inside of the largest "café" the place was full of plastic everything: a prospector with a pipe in his mouth, a cowboy smoking a cigarette, even a Butch Cassidy and a plastic Sundance Kid. Signs pointed every which way: the gift shop was in this direction, the Buckboard Clothing Store in another, don't forget to see the "Hole in the Wall" on past Ted Hustead's fake cowboy orchestra, and then there were about six different lines toward the five-cent coffee.

"Which looks the shortest to you?"

"Let's just go to this one."

Had we had much more trouble than that, there was a man whose specific job was to guide us followers of green signs toward breakfast with the least amount of psychological peril. Still, I noticed one couple in the line next to ours shift places three times before settling on the right one. Fortunately there weren't many of those types or breakfast could have been very confusing.

"Bacon, eggs, sausage, pancakes, or oatmeal?"

"I'll just have the five-cent coffee," I said.

The man in the green and white chef's hat seemed worried. He knew the five-cent coffee was in exchange for twenty-five dollars in pancakes, gifts, and film. Suddenly things were not working right.

"That's it?"

"No."

He looked very relieved.

"I want sugar, too."

My friend Tom ordered the same, but fortunately, some guy in a straw hat with a Nikon dangling from his neck ordered both French toast and oatmeal along with side orders of bacon, sausage, and hash browns.

I looked all around at people eating eggs and reading pamphlets that were handed to them as they came in the place: "Welcome to Wall Drug, the Ice Water Store in the Badlands" or "WALL AND WATER, It's One of America's Most Surprising Success Stories." Meanwhile, some guy was taking a picture of his wife next to Butch Cassidy and the Sundance Kid.

I thought of the moon that night from the spot where we lay on the long, flat earth, and a depression began to take hold that I had no control over. I thought of the commercial campground in Kentucky, and then of all the things that had happened beyond it.

"Let's get out of here," I said to Tom.

"What, and waste five cents on a cup of coffee?"

He could see I was upset.

"All right," he said, "let's go."

In Rapid City, I asked the gas station attendant if he knew of a good place to eat.

"There's a McDonald's down the strip here a-ways, and a Burger King about . . ."

"But where's a *good* place to eat," I interrupted. "Where do *you* eat?"

The man smiled as if he were getting ready to tell me about the time he'd seen the president with his zipper down.

"Well, it don't look like much, but right down the road a-piece, there's a little place called Ma's that's got the best breakfast in town."

Hitchhiker Rule Number 19: Sometimes you've got to ask twice to get beyond the chamber-of-commerce persona we all have on tap for the questions of a stranger.

Hitchhiker Rule Number 20: Humanity thrives around the answer to the second question.

Ma's was a long U-shaped counter with a roof over it and tightly surrounded with glass walls. The menu was written on the chalkboard hanging over the opening for the kitchen, through which you could see Ma cooking whatever it was that she felt like cooking that morning.

We had to wait for a couple of truckers to leave before we could even get in the place. There were a lot of blue-collars around the table, a lot of three-piece suits too, all shoveling down the same food next to conversations that ranged from air brakes to divestitures. There weren't any fake Indians or souvenirs. Ma just sold Lifesavers at the door.

"What'll it be, gentlemen?"

"I'll go with the two eggs and a biscuit."

"Number six for me."

I heard the eggs crack and sizzle upon a greasy clean grill. I ordered a cup of forty-cent coffee, spun a bit back and forth on the linoleum-covered stool, and felt like I was getting back on track at Ma's Diner in Rapid City.

"It takes a while to get over a place like Wall Drug," I said to Tom. "But a place like this sure helps."

13

"I Think I'll Drop You Off in Deadwood"

"You sure you want to stop here?" Tom asked.

"Yeah, I really am."

"Spearfish, South Dakota?"

"I just need to get out of the car for a while."

"You can come with me to Oregon if you'd like."

"No really, this is as good a place as any."

"Are you sure you're going to be all right?"

"Positive."

Tom thought I was kidding when I suddenly asked him to pull over near the signs for Spearfish. He thought we were just passing through. When he drove off, he looked back as if he were afraid for me—alone in some strange place.

But we're all just a quiet moment from Spearfish, South Dakota, I thought; no matter where we happen to be at any given time.

Without warning, black clouds from the east blanketed what had been a sunny day, sending painful pellets of wind-driven rain onto my hands and face. A sign about forty yards from my spot on Main Street offered "Public Library." In the few moments it took for me to accept that invitation, I had become completely soaked.

I set my pack against one of the many unoccupied wooden tables, set myself in one of the many unoccupied wooden chairs, and gazed out the window at the violent interruption to a beautiful day.

This "Spearfish" is a confusing place, I thought. It is not plain nor mountain nor prairie. It is some part of all three. The traveler from the East finds the first change of topography in the slight hills surrounding the town, but to the traveler descending from the lush Black Hills to the south, these same short hills mark the beginning of the flat land.

Immediately to the north and west, the rolling prairie stretches toward the Rockies with smaller hills, greater space, and more grass.

Earlier, at 12:45, the bank on Main Street had said the temperature was ninety-two degrees. As the rain tried its best to tear down the roof above me, the bank proclaimed 12:55 and seventy-five degrees.

Ten minutes later, the weather broke into another beautiful, but cooler, day. With one eye to the sky and the other constantly reassessing the position of the nearest shelter, I took to hanging out. From the library, I went to the gift shop across the street.

"Can I help you with something?"

"No thanks, I'm just looking."

"We've got cards on sale."

"Thanks, I'm just looking."

To the Roy Rogers near the Interstate: "Is that $1.99 salad bar all you can eat?"

To the chamber of commerce: "There is a campground at the corner of Oak and Maple where you can spend the night, and we have a map that will get you there."

To the police station: "Is there a place to camp in town? I'm traveling through and I wanted to sleep out tonight; maybe a Boy Scout camp? I'm a former Boy Scout, you see."

(Hitchhiker Rule Number 21: Whenever possible, let the police in a small town know who you are, so they don't feel obligated to arrest you to find out.)

To another gift shop: "No thanks, I'm just looking."

To the laundromat:

"Jeez Jughead, don't you think you could've gotten me a better date than that?"

"I'm sorry Arch."

Toward an orange sunset, and the search for a chamber-of-commerce map rolled up somewhere in my back pocket.

The homes were dark and too close together, as I moved closer to an "X" on a white piece of paper. Old cars and rusted swing sets decorated ragged homes that clung to the backside of Main Street. The sporadic neon street lights made too much noise as they needlessly blared fluorescent yellow onto empty streets.

I walked the distance drawn for me along the designated streets. Finally, trees overrun with shabby vegetation broke the monotony of decrepit homes. Teenage music rose faintly from this place, along with the occasional slamming of a car door. Listening harder, I heard the reckless laugh of an adolescent girl and the quick-spray pop of a beer can opening.

This was not the "X" I had counted on. I hesitated to continue for fear that I would be intruding. While I considered, reconsidered, and grew less and less sure, a shadow approached. She had long dark hair and an even stride. The yellow light from above shone on a pretty face that smiled briefly as it followed legs intent on continuing.

"Excuse me, but do you know where the campground is?" I called out.

"Campground?"

"The lady at the chamber of commerce said there was a campground near here where I could spend the night."

I handed her the map.

"Campground? I think the only people that spend the night at this park are in Chevys," she laughed. "It doesn't look like you're equipped to pull that one off."

She continued laughing until she realized I was not amused. Only yesterday I had been in Minnesota. I craved a simple sleeping experience.

"Well, maybe you could," she said.

I probably could have managed better if I hadn't held the map. But misinformed and misdirected, I had become lost.

"I guess the lady from the chamber of commerce hasn't been back this way in a while," I said.

"Hey look, don't worry about it. You can spend the night at my place," she said. "I've got plenty of room."

With those words, I watched my spirit fly through the air and land in the hands of a woman whom I had met less than two minutes ago.

Jane occupied two rooms of a large house on the plains side of town.

"Would you like tea?" she asked.

"Sure."

"Peppermint or Midnight in Missoula?"

"Either one would be fine."

I sat in a chair at the far end of the room while the woman made tea around the corner of my vision. I entertained myself by watching how the ceiling and the walls came together to form shelter.

"Be careful, it's still hot," she said, offering me a steaming ceramic mug.

"Thank you, that's very nice of you to do this."

"It's nothing I wouldn't have done for anyone else in your shoes. I can't believe they told you there was a campsite there."

Jane had been to four colleges in the past four years, searching for the answer to "What am I going to do with my life?" Her quest had begun at a four-year liberal arts school in Vermont. She had been in Spearfish for three weeks.

"But I really like what I'm doing now," she said. "I feel something different this time, like I am finally doing the right thing."

She was currently enrolled in an Indian Studies program.

"When I spent a week on the reservation one summer and saw all the houses without floors, all the poverty and all the drinking, I knew there was something I could do to help. We've really treated the Indians terribly. This whole country used to be theirs."

Then she began talking about something Jim Morrison once said about Indians, and I realized everything she had on was made out of cotton gauze.

"You can live on just potatoes," she was continuing. "A friend at a health food store back east showed me how they contained all the vitamins you need, and ever since then . . ."

But beneath the cotton gauze lay soft contours of stillness I had not known since Michigan. Suddenly, I wanted to hold her—just hold her. At the same time, I was greatly indebted to her for offering me a place to stay, and didn't want to do anything to offend her, as she began reading from a book of Jim Morrison's poetry.

Eventually, the issue was settled without me. Jane announced that she had "a lot of planning" to do the next day, and shortly thereafter, we each had our own separate nighttime space on a couch and on a floor. (No, please—you sleep on the couch; I'd like to see what it's like for the Indians.)

I had a place, I had a shelter, but I was not at all still. My inability to express this newfound longing kept me awake most of the night. This woman held me in her uncomfortable grasp while she slept on the floor and I slept on the couch.

The next morning there was a note waiting for me on the kitchen cabinet beside the potatoes:

> Well, it was nice having you here. I really shouldn't have, though, because I'm trying to get my act together and I need to work hard so you can't stay anymore. Lock the door when you leave.

That sounded funny: "Trying to get my act together." As if life were a ten-minute vaudeville routine about to be taken to Kansas City. For some reason the eviction notice bothered me. Nobody had ever asked me to get out before—at least not directly. I needed a hitchhiker rule to deal with it.

Hitchhiker Rule Number 22: No matter how good it feels to watch yourself soar through the air and land in the hands of another, you never really can.

The blatant violation of the last hitchhiker rule set me adrift into the center of town, where I stood a good while, waiting for something else to come along.

Eventually, it did, in the form of a wooden backpack that was the same genus as my own. It had a short, stocky man with a mustache attached, and the entire unit was heading from north to south along Main Street. I heard my pack cry, "Mother," and quickly I ran toward it.

Perhaps too quickly. I had not considered that the person attached would not be as excited to see me as I was to see him.

"Oh, I thought you were a hitchhiker, too," I said.

"No, I'm just carrying some tomatoes and bread home for my wife the best way I know how."

So there we were, two unrelated strangers with backpacks standing on the prairie side of Main Street in Spearfish, South Dakota. The temperature stayed the same, but the bank's digital time switched from 10:45 to 10:46. Soon it would be 10:47, then 10:48.

"Well, I'm a hitchhiker," I said.

"Really?"

"Uh-huh . . . what do you do?"

"I teach English at the college, but right now I'm taking time to write a book."

"No kidding, well, I'm a writer too . . . "

Although it was still morning, I felt the night already on its way. That hitchhiker rule about subtly letting people know was about to go into effect once again since that shaky start back at a Kentucky campground.

"How long have you been hitchhiking?" Bill Jackson asked.

"Not too long. Tell me what your book is about."

"Oh, I don't know; it's hard to say really. I know I'm spending a lot of time on it."

"That's interesting. I've written for a lot of newspapers, but my real interest is in fiction. All I know about fiction, though, is what the publishers tell me."

"Publishers?"

"Just the ones I know."

"Well, if you're not doing anything tonight, we've got a small group that meets at the Little Professor Restaurant to talk about our work. You might find it interesting."

"Sure, that sounds like fun!"

"I could even give you a copy of a short story that I'm working on so you can have some input into the discussion."

"I'd like that. What time will you be meeting?"

"About eight; we usually go till eleven or so."

"Oh . . . "

"I guess that's pretty late to be finding a campsite?"

"Yeah, it gets pretty dark around then."

"Well, we've got an extra room—why don't you stay at our house tonight?"

"Hey, that's a great idea!"

Bill really didn't have anything to say to the rest of humanity, but his prose did reveal a certain keenness for the title of the profession, as if being a writer were an intellectual fashion he had grown fond of.

"A Night Far Away" was set in medieval times and had something to do with an alchemist and a time machine, and of course, two people falling in love, making the escape back to their modern-day lives just in the nick of time. About half of the words appeared to be very large typographical errors. I'm sure an unabridged dictionary would have proved me wrong.

Fashion-conscious writers have a fondness for big words and exotic settings. Words like *persiflage,* when placed in the early 1500s, provide the appearance of inspired creation that the narrative simply cannot offer.

Alone at the Roy Rogers Salad Bar Special, I decided that I would be a gracious guest and ignore my feelings on the matter. Surely someone else would point out what I was really thinking.

At 7:45 I found Bill at his home reading the second volume in his set of *The History of the World.*

"I'm up to the Holy Roman Empire," he said, "I'm trying to finish all twenty-eight volumes while I'm writing my book."

"What was that book on, again?" I asked.

"Well, it's really hard to say."

A soft-looking woman came in from an adjoining room of screaming infants. Bill introduced me to his wife, Rebecca.

"Tom is going to be spending the night with us tonight."

Bill offered a moment for his wife to respond, but she only smiled.

"We decided that having a baby-sitting service was the best way to keep an income going while I was out of work," Bill added. "None of them are ours."

Bill showed me the room I would be staying in and the bed that was there, and together we were off to the writers' conference at the Little Professor Restaurant in Spearfish, South Dakota.

The Little Professor was decorated in books. Rows of classics offered semiprivacy between tables in much the same way that ornamental planters or wooden dividers serve in more proletarian institutions.

The Merchant of Venice and *A Tale of Two Cities* were two of the selections that kept us from seeing exactly what the couple in the next booth was up to.

Each of the four people at the writers' conference chose one of the more than twenty brands of herbal tea listed on the menu. Bill had Ginseng; Charlie, who also taught at the school, had Orange Mandarin; and Sally, who taught English at the high school, had Sleepy Time. I warily stirred a Peppermint Zinger.

"OK, where should we begin?" Sally began.

Charlie looked about twenty-seven years old and smoked a pipe.

"Since Bill's friend Tom has read only his story, why not start there?" Charlie reasoned.

"Yes, that sounds like a good idea."

"Well," Charlie said—and I began to feel a little sorry for my newfound friend—"I thought some of the language used in this was exquisite."

"Yes, Bill, that was something that I felt as well; you really used some very complex terminology here."

"Thank you, I'm glad you both noticed."

Exquisite?

"When I saw *perorate* and *enswathe* in there, I was very impressed. What did you think, Tom?"

"Well . . . there were certainly some incredible words there."

"I think writers should make an extra effort to make use of the language—the whole language, and not just the first words that come to mind," said someone.

I thought that writers should always use the most understandable word that best expresses their idea. I believed this devoutly.

"We too often get caught in trivial phrases and meanings when we have so many words at our disposal, isn't that right?"

I looked up and saw the *Iliad* perched diagonally against a row of books to make it look as though it had just been read.

"The language is an end in itself, I think, and we need to keep stretching its uses even if it means our readers have to go to the dictionary once in a while to exercise their minds. Don't you agree, Tom?"

Intellectual elitism, I thought, while my mouth just said:

"Uh-huh."

"I think it was absolutely brilliant of you to take us into a time so far away, too. Imagine the Middle Ages in the streets of Calcutta. It just sets the mind to wandering. Why did you pick that, Bill?"

"Well, it was always a place I thought was fascinating from what little I've read . . ."

The bed was comfortable, as were the many hospitable gestures found at the end of a thumbnail. But its soft, cotton sheets could not silence the twelve-syllable words resounding over and over in my mind — and my going "uh-huh."

Walking softly in another person's life because it was not my own; afraid to offend, afraid to approach, while my essence demanded to be heard. I could no longer find comfort in another person's bed. The lure of a distant radio station had gotten me out and into so many things. But now, where was I?

Past the north end of town lay the mountains. It was an area to walk alone through; an area to follow my own curiosity. I had finally gotten out of the car ("Are you sure you don't want to go to Oregon with me?"), and now I needed to stay out. Tomorrow it would be the Black Hills of South Dakota — alone. I was determined to avoid all interesting experiences.

There were more cans of tuna fish in my pack than there were dollars. Only necessity was allowed to accompany my isolation. Everything else remained in Spearfish in the room next to the *History of the World*.

With someone else's coffee and homemade biscuits in my stomach, I was dropped at the base of a road that headed up. Bill said there was a place called Rimrock Campground about ten miles further along. The bank clock in town had read eighty-nine degrees at 9:35.

I began the climb toward a campground with both hands in my pockets.

The rumble of a car approaching is one of the world's most seductive noises. It starts with a faraway whisper that makes you wonder where it has been. As it draws closer, the sound conjures images of all those that had come before, and suddenly there is a baseball cap, a roll of Lifesavers, and a girlfriend's picture falling from behind a sun visor.

When the noise is almost upon you, a nervous twitch develops in your thumb from wanting to know who, what, where, and why, as if you had a duty to know the intimate contents of each passing vehicle.

When it passes, you wipe the sweat off your brow and continue upward, while the good times linger from the various makes and models that all began with the same sound.

A few hours later, I could look down the road and still see where I had started. My water container was already three-quarters empty, and I estimated that nine and a half of the ten miles still lay ahead. The temperature wasn't dropping any either.

The grass shook to my immediate left on a windless day. A large black snake slithered away about twelve inches from my feet. I jumped into the road without regard to traffic, but the snake had disappeared.

A logging truck climbed slowly, slowly upward, giving me time to consider and reconsider: a logger would not have any great adventure to distract me. He could just give me a little help getting up this hill. From there, I could continue my own way amidst the more scenic—more level—country. Still, something told me to trust no one. The driver may have been recently divorced and ready to cut loose in town.

Perhaps he'd let me ride on the back of the truck. I stuck my thumb out and waited. The air brakes came on, and I ran ahead toward another fix for my moving addiction.

While the weathered old man behind the wheel seemed glad to have the company, he didn't really know what to say to me. He mentioned that he was hauling logs to Newcastle, Wyoming, then mumbled something else, but I couldn't tell what.

"Newcastle, that must be pretty far from here," I said.

"No, nothing like it! Newcastle's only twenty miles or so."

"I thought you said it was in Wyoming."

"It *is* in Wyoming."

"Wyoming's only twenty miles from here?"

"No, Newcastle's only twenty miles from here. State line's only about five miles west. Newcastle's a good ways south."

"No kidding! Wyoming five miles away. . . . That's pretty much considered the West, isn't it?"

"Come again with that?"

"Oh—nothing; just thinking out loud."

As he dropped a gear to relieve his straining motor, I noticed the increasing presence of reds and yellows in the trees at the higher elevations.

Fall in the West, I thought. Somehow, I'd come a long way.

About halfway along the drive I wasn't going to take, Hitchhiker Rule Number 23 was created: Never abandon a ride that is going uphill, especially when the temperature is nearing ninety.

"You wanna go to Rimrock Campground, you gotta go down this road here for 'bout three miles," the driver said. "Good luck to ya."

The mountain peaks at this higher elevation broke out of the dense pine forest in lofty rock columns that looked like Gothic church spires. Gone were the subtle landscapes of the Midwest that required effort to notice; gone too were the vast spaces of the plains that allowed one's sight to wander unobstructed. The Needles — as they were called — surrounded me wherever I turned, and it was impossible to look away without feeling the shadows they cast.

Five miles away from the state of Wyoming, the West was ripping through my eastern sensibilities, admonishing me for not knowing where I had been only moments before.

With half the day given back to me by a truck driver, I slowed a pace that had questioned ten uphill miles by sunset to one that now hoped not to finish three by noon. My stride had become open to suggestion.

After a quick detour through a picnic area, I noticed two guys drinking beer on the hood of a black Camaro bursting with heavy-metal music.

They looked like an interesting pair. One had a surfer-type air about him, wearing mirror sunglasses beneath a tanned physique, while beside him, a short, skinny runt in dilapidated jeans and a black T-shirt eyed me suspiciously.

Why was he doing that, I wondered? Who were these two people?

I nodded hello. Then, before I could catch myself: "Hey, you wouldn't happen to know how to get to Rimrock Campground, would you?"

By then it was too late.

"Dammit Bones, I know it's not near Deadwood. Why the hell would he be over here if it were twenty miles away?"

"Because he's lost, that's why; either that or he's a nark."

"Why would a nark be walking around out here with a backpack?"

"Surveillance equipment. He's probably taping every word we're saying."

The short suspicious guy talked from beneath a cap bearing the Confederate flag, although his words lacked the corresponding drawl. His rolled-up black T-shirt revealed a few tattoos on arms that were too narrow for "MOTHER" and had to settle for "MOM."

"Don't mind him," the other guy said. "You want a beer?"

"Well, really I think I ought to be heading out to . . . "

"He's just naturally lousy. He don't mean nothing by it. Go ahead, Bones, and get the guy a beer."

Soon there was a Michelob in my hand, then another, then another.

It's really tough for a hitchhiker to walk aloof through the world. That was Hitchhiker Rule Number 24.

"Bones" felt obligated to tell me right off that he was carrying a concealed weapon. There were no bulges anywhere along his skintight clothing, and somehow I managed to keep myself from speculating out loud as to where the weapon must have been concealed.

He also told me that he belonged to a bikers' club, but he made it a point not to let me know the club's name. I didn't know what to say to all that. This was at the stage of a relationship when you're expecting to hear stuff like "What are you doing?" "How do you like it here?" or "Boy, these beers are good."

I tried to get the conversation back to a more manageable level.

"So where are you guys from, anyway?" I asked.

Suddenly, Bones jumped off the car and stood in a ready position just three inches from my neck—looking up.

"Who's wantin' to know?" he asked real slow.

His friend grabbed him by the scruff of the neck and knocked him back against the car.

"Dammit Bones, when are you ever gonna smarten up?"

"Hey watch it man! Don't fuck with me—remember?"

"Yeah, I know, I know."

"You don't fuck with people around here. You don't ask no questions and you don't get hurt; that's just the way it is."

"Dammit Bones, please shut up."

"I'm just telling him like it is so he don't get hurt. You remember what happened to Smith don't you?"

"Yeah, right, I remember what happened to Smith. Just shut up for about three minutes though, would ya?"

Bones found a place back on the hood to brood, leaving his friend named Dave some time to talk about how the mines were on strike and how they'd both been out of work for about five months.

"They said they wanted to lower our pay and increase our hours, and we said no way. That's where it stands; that's where it's been standing for a long time. All that's left for us to do is lie out in the sun and drink beer and wait for the management to see it our way."

"A lot of mean bikers out of work too," Bones chimed in. "You go into a bar at night and start asking questions, they'll throw you through a friggin' wall—just like Smith."

"Why is it I can't take you anywhere?"

"What happened to Smith?" I finally had to ask.

Again, Bones flew off the hood of the car to within two inches of my neck.

"Now just why is it that you want to know that?"

Again his friend smacked him up against the car.

"Bones, you stupid little moron."

*   *   *

I tried my best to shake off the effect of five beers in the heat of the day, but the Gothic spires that surrounded me were looking more and more like Victorian bedposts.

After some good hard walking, though, I felt as though I could get over it. The desolate dirt road ahead looked promising. There was no way another distraction could find me there, I thought. It was just a matter of a few steps before I would be back on track.

Just then, a red Buick with a very attractive woman pulled up alongside of me.

"Excuse me, but do you know where Alman Lake is?"

I should have dropped my pack and run into the woods. Instead, I followed every urge swelling within me except for the right one and walked over to talk with this woman.

"What was that again?"

"My map here says that the lake should be right about here (she pointed to a spot on the map), and I figure we're about here (she pointed to another spot on the map), but I'm not sure."

I didn't know what to say.

"Why don't you just hop in and be the navigator," she suggested. "I'm sure you don't have anything against a quick dip at a nice secluded lake, do you?"

Yes, as a matter of fact, I had several objections to getting in her car and taking a quick dip at a secluded lake, but they just could not make their way out of my mouth.

"My name's Jill," she said, sticking a soft hand into the back seat for me to shake, "and this is my sidekick, Dave."

She pointed to a four-year-old I had not noticed before.

"We're from Belle Fourche and we like sex, drugs, and rock and roll. You want a beer?"

I wanted to say yes, but somehow I had forgotten how to talk.

Jill kept passing warm beers back to me, which I swallowed one after the other, hoping their five-percent alcohol content would eventually lead me to my voice.

"You're not a cowboy, are you?" she asked me.

"No," I said.

"Well, that's too bad, because cowboys are the rip-roaringest, partying, good-timing people on this earth, and I just love to chase 'em."

I thought about that for a moment and finished off a beer that had been half full.

"Well," I said, "I used to play hockey in college."

There were far too many people at the secluded beach. In a

moment, I was in the back seat with the map, trying to navigate toward another such beach Jill knew about.

Within a few minutes, we were in the middle of a cow pasture.

"How old do you suppose that thing is?" I asked, trying to blame the whole thing on Rand McNally.

Jill took the map.

"So where were you planning on going tonight, Tom?" she asked.

"Oh, just anywhere; nowhere in particular. Don't really have any place to stay; nowhere in particular."

My form was way off.

"You need a place to stay, huh?"

"Yeah! Uh-huh."

"Well, don't worry about it. Don't you worry about it one more minute."

The last of my resistance lay somewhere on the floor beside the empty beer bottles. I swallowed another two beers in rapid succession, and surrendered the last of where I was going to this woman who had picked me up when I wasn't even hitchhiking.

"There's a bar about ten miles from here that I like going to. What'd ya say we quit driving for a little bit and get a real drink or two?"

Along a dirt road that led to more liquor, I noticed a place that seemed quiet, peaceful, and without any people.

"RIMROCK CAMPGROUND" were the only words being spoken there.

Maybe tomorrow, I thought. I quickly opened another beer to keep from having to think about that hitchhiker rule I had left at Jane's house the day before.

A chronic South Dakota cloud cover was developing as we arrived at some bar/restaurant that had more beer-lights than customers. The temperature began to drop and so did a piece of rain—right on my nose—as I opened the door.

"They've got good Margaritas in here," Jill said.

I ordered a whiskey straight up to compensate for the fact that I wasn't a cowboy. I wondered if I had brought enough money to pay for my drink, Jill's drink, and the next round that was inevitable.

"Would you like something to eat?" the frumpy waitress wanted to know.

"No thanks, I'm not hungry."

I hadn't eaten a thing all day. I counted only ten dollars and change.

Jill's little sidekick wound up with a hamburger plate that he was too young to manage. I felt like one of those starving Biafrans as I watched each French fry sail onto the floor, and a hamburger become a plaything.

Jill had been quiet, studying the little fold-out sign with strawberries all over it that said "Why Not a Daiquiri?"

"Wait here for a second," she said abruptly, "I've got to make a phone call."

While she was gone, I picked four French fries off the table, and might have taken a bite of the recreational hamburger, had I not noticed the interest of the frumpy waitress.

Jill returned with an altogether unhappy look.

"Who were you calling?" I asked.

"His father," she said.

I hadn't considered that: there must have been a man involved for her little sidekick to have happened.

"We were going to go by his house a little later," she continued.

I took a hard gulp of whiskey.

"We were?"

"Uh-huh."

"His house isn't your house?"

"No, we're not married."

"You mean you're divorced?"

"No we're just not married."

"Separated?"

"We've never been married."

I began studying the little fold-out sign that had strawberries all over it and the words "Why Not a Daiquiri?"

"We had been going together for a long time," she continued. "When I got pregnant, I just figured marriage would be the thing to do. But he never did. I'm lucky if I can get him to keep the kid on weekends."

Jill became lost in an angry stare that completely engulfed her view of the world. Her little David hobbled off without generating any concern from his mother. I realized then that Jill had not done a lot of the "Here, let me cut your hamburger"-type things that would be expected from their relationship. In a moment, the little boy was at the base of the next table, holding the edge of the tablecloth—about to pull a table setting for four onto himself.

Jill looked once in that direction, but didn't seem to notice. The frumpy waitress, who had been in limbo around her only customers, immediately ran over and grabbed the kid before he could do damage to himself. She brought him back to our table.

"You've got to watch this little fella," she said in a fun sort of way. "He almost had all of our dishes over his little head."

"Thanks," Jill said, as she watched her fatherless son dump the rest of his hamburger plate onto the floor.

"OK, he's done—let's get out of here."

It was raining hard outside and the temperature had dropped considerably. Darkness was about a half-hour ahead of schedule because of the ominous cloud cover. As best as I could tell, I was about fifteen miles from anywhere I knew and at least thirty miles from my money. Signs began appearing along the side of the road for places like Lead and Deadwood.

The day of too much alcohol and no food began to work angrily against me. A dry numbness grabbed hold and left me incapable of any kind of motion. I felt beaten. I hoped that the car's motion would soon lead to a nice warm bed—with or without company.

David was more antsy in the front seat than he had been.

His mother noticed.

"Cut the shit—now!" she yelled.

The boy began to scream. Jill reached over and slapped him.

I felt as though I needed to intervene.

"So, what's next on our agenda?" I asked, trying to sound whimsical.

"I think I'll drop you off in Deadwood."

. . . drop you off in Deadwood . . . Deadwood?

"You mean, drop *me* off and you're going somewhere else?"

"You got it."

"I thought you said I didn't have to worry about a place for the night."

"You don't. You can get a room in Deadwood."

"I don't have any money to get a room in Deadwood."

"Then you can pitch your tent on Main Street."

I realized then that I had been used in a symbolic hostile gesture toward all the people in the world who carried a Y chromosome.

I barely managed to get my pack out of the back seat.

"Well . . . thanks for the ride, I think."

I looked past her to the other person who had recently been dropped off in Deadwood. What can you do about a bum ride, little guy?

Inside a bar called the Wooden Nickel, I was surrounded by a theme that had become abhorrent. Guys walked up to girls and asked if they could buy them drinks. Girls tossed hip movements into watchful male eyes on their way to the ladies' room. It was like watching a bad movie. A girl gave me the eye from across the bar and I almost shot her the finger.

A bar was not the place I needed to be. Still, it was warm and dry. I tried to concentrate on the warm and dry.

"What can I get you?"

"Coffee."

"Irish?"

"Black."

"Anything in it?"

"Sugar."

Next to me, in an equal state of detachment, sat an older man who looked as though he'd spent the last forty years of his life going through what had just happened to me. He wore two shirts, neither of them clean, and had his cap turned sideways on his head. He looked like a friend.

"Women," I sent off in his direction, "they can really get you off track sometimes."

"Boy, I'll tell you something, I don't even go near them anymore."

He perked up around his Miller's and primed for an extended conversation. Evidently, I had pressed the right button.

"The second time I got married, I was living here cutting wood and had a lot to drink at a party one Friday night. Well, as best as I can remember it, I wound up at some hospital taking a blood test with my first wife's sister. I guess she wanted to get married.

"They should've thrown me in jail after the blood test. It would've been better for everyone. But they didn't. Next day, the woman threw me in the back seat and we tried it again. Just as soon as I passed this one, I was standing in front of a justice of the peace in a town called Missoula, who was pronouncing us man and wife. That's when I finally started sobering up.

"She divorced me in a couple of months. Never could figure out why, but then I never could figure out why we got married in the first place. The wedding cost me $27.50 with a picture; the divorce, close to $300. Then there's the payments. . . .

"I tell you, I learned my lesson. I'll never get drunk and let a woman marry me again. No sir, costs too much."

He told me about a place that he thought was a campground. I followed his directions through the back roads until I came to a wooded area that was just beyond the street lights' reach.

I draped my tent loosely over myself, planted a stake here and a pole there, and tried to ignore the cold rain that splattered through my feeble attempt at resistance. If it wasn't a campground before, it would be now, and I would forcefully designate it so to any fool who tried to tell me otherwise.

I awoke the next afternoon to what seemed like the whole of Deadwood staring me in the face: A cold and wet face. A cold, wet, miserable face that was generally pissed off.

The campground that had seemed a good ways out of town, was, in fact, a vacant lot on the side of a hill only a few blocks up from Main Street. Everyone doing business in town would soon be able to watch me crawl out of bed in my underwear.

My teeth had been clattering incessantly and I had only just realized it. Nothing was dry. The tent faltered completely and was clinging to a sleeping bag that had collected all the night's rain.

I tossed about in a frigid, sopping dankness. I tossed about until I realized how uncomfortable it was to do that. Then I refused to move. Water is wetter when you move, I reasoned. In stillness it has less of an opportunity to be wet. Where was I going to go, anyway? Stillness helped me ignore my lack of options. I hoped that someone would come along and arrest me.

But in the desperate throes of my mind, there shone a dim, dim ray of hope shrouded within a bad memory from Michigan. That janitor, Jim, and the address he had given me of a friend who lived in some strange sounding town in South Dakota—Deadwood?

It was enough to inspire motion. First, out of a saturated sleeping bag—who cared what the town thought—then toward a backpack that was wet through the second layer of clothes. Then, into a side flap and past a toothbrush rarely used, and beyond dental floss that had never been. Finally, onto a little scrap of paper—wet, written on in ink partially smudged: Bobby Davis; 202 Mockingbird Lane—Deadwood, South Dakota. 555-4562.

"You don't know me, but I'm a good friend of your friend Jim from Michigan, and he told me that I had better make sure to look you up when I came through here."

"Where are you now?"

"At a pay phone in town—Deadwood."

There was a hesitation laden heavily with the sound of sports through a television. The day was Saturday.

"Jim gave you my name, huh?"

"Said I should definitely look you up."

"Well, OK, why don't you come on out to the house if you get a chance."

"Where do you live?"

"Didn't Jim give you the address?"

"Yeah, but I'm not sure where it is."

Through a long pause, an announcer's voice screamed to be heard over the roar of the fans: Touchdown.

"Just come on up Main Street out of town until you get to Mockingbird Lane. It's on the right side about two miles out. Ours is the second house on the left."

"I don't have a car."

"It should only be about a forty-five-minute walk."

"The last time I saw Jim was about seven years ago. We had all decided to take a bike trip across the country, and when we got to Minnesota, Jim had had trouble with his bike. He told us to go on ahead and said he'd meet us in Spearfish in about four weeks. We got there in about two, and started living it up while waiting for Jim. Of course, Jim never showed up. We decided that we were having too much fun to leave, so we got jobs and stayed. So here we are, and as far as I know, Jim's still in Minnesota fixing a flat.

"Actually, in a way . . . "

"My wife sends him a Christmas card every year. That's all we've really heard from him."

Bobby Davis wandered into a construction business, a wife, and a six-year-old. The wife had said hello at my entrance, then had gone into another room to fix something. The boy just kept popping in and out and around.

After explaining to me how insignificant Jim had been in their lives, Bobby was watching the television. Make no bones about it, he was watching the game.

They didn't seem as excited about having a hitchhiker around as the Kozels had been. The little boy didn't even acknowledge my title. I had waited for him to retreat into his mother's apron, or even start telling me some stories about his little-league team, but instead, he nonchalantly wandered in and out, in and out, and finally in for a while, holding a game he presented to his father.

"Daddy, will you play with me?"

"Not now, Michael, Daddy's watching television."

"Please, Daddy."

"Go ask your mother."

"She already said no."

"Well then go read a book, or maybe ask Tom if he wants to play with you."

"Who's Tom?"

"He's that man sitting right over there with the beard and the green shirt."

"Will you ask him for me?"

"No, you can go ask him."

I was about three feet away.

"Please Daddy, will you ask him?"

"Michael, Daddy is watching television."

"Michael," I chimed in, eager to gain a purpose, "I'll be glad to play with you. Why don't you come over here and we'll play."

"You come over here."

Sure, why not.

Little Michael was cheating the hell out of a game called "Little Red Riding Hood and the Wolf." It wasn't so much that I minded losing the game, but when the kid went one-two-three-moves and wound up sixteen spots closer to Grandma's house—and then thought that I didn't notice—that started to bother me.

"No, you're not counting right," I said, taking his piece away from him and starting it again. "It's one, two, three, like that."

Michael looked like he was going to cry, and called out to his dad, still watching TV.

"Michael, play the game right, Sweetheart."

The next turn Sweetheart avoided a "Go back seven spaces" by moving six spaces past the three he rolled.

"You're cheating."

Little Michael started crying, and suddenly I realized where I was and what I had done.

"I was just kidding," I said to little Sweetheart, cuddled up in Daddy's arms. "Come on and let's finish the game."

"Go ahead, Sweetie, finish the game and see who wins."

The next roll, Sweetie moved twenty-seven spaces in one roll of a single die and won the game.

"Boy, that was really good," I said, trying to gain some credibility. "That kid's really a good player."

"Please pass the ham, Dear."

"Certainly, Dear."

"Do you want some more potatoes before I put them away, Dear?"

"No, I'm fine. Michael, how many times have I told you to sit up straight at the table?"

My plate held exceptionally small servings of ham, potatoes, and salad. I felt funny about taking any food at all. I didn't feel as though I was giving anything to justify taking: no excitement, no conversation, no thrill of adventure. Things were not working right.

I watched as the potatoes passed by, then the ham, then the salad, and knew that soon I would be leaving on an empty stomach.

Outside, the sky that could not remain still was heading toward grey, as clouds steadily collected themselves for another night of cold and rain. I wore three shirts to ward off the plummeting temperatures, and kicked gravel in front of me, leaving dust behind me, while searching for a place beside me.

A systematic arrangement of equities and exchanges had gotten me to that dirt road: excitement for lodging and an ear for listening; signs tilted this way or better off that way; and bright clothing — always use bright clothing. Hitchhiker rules that enabled me to drift further and further away, while the Kozels, Spencers, and Big Joes kept me from realizing just how far.

But the vehicle had left; the system had quit working.

Hitchhiker Rule Number Final: At any point in time, all hitchhiker rules are susceptible to total failure.

The night's approach into darkness cast a dim light on open areas between trees and level spots along the hillside. Several cold drops of rain urged me toward a place on the side of the road that had been following me since I had begun.

Soles of shoes that had been over more than three thousand miles slipped again and again on wet pine needles. For every two steps forward, I advanced one. And so I took twice as many steps until I didn't need to anymore, then I dropped my backpack to the ground.

A chorus of unrecognizable sounds tried to convince me that I had no right to be there: something metal was dragging someplace that I did not know; other things settled and crunched in places that I had no idea about. There were no shelves in my mind on which to place these noises.

Yet if I looked right into the spot where I had laid my tent — if I looked directly into it — there was peace. Deep into the grass, stones, and twigs, there was solitude. I tried to narrow my focus.

Sounds unrecognizable and feared faded into meaningless noise as the stillness of my place on the earth seeped from beneath me and beckoned me to listen. The quiet I heard was my own. The stillness there depended on no one. Without forward or reverse, its soft melody would continue alongside of wherever I was going.

Eventually, the only noise that remained was a familiar thud, thud, thud, that would soon disappear until morning claimed me from the conductor wanting me to get off the train.

It wouldn't even rain as I drifted along the roadside the next morning; it wouldn't even be so definite. Instead it drizzled, and the drizzle slowly collected on my face and hair to form drops that fell and then began again. Behind me, the familiar drone of the highway sent a cold twitch toward a thumb that had grown numb.

That night, the rain had found the holes in my resistance and sent every bit of cold and wet rushing through. I slipped again and again on the gravel of the road's shoulder—finding more energy than I thought I possessed in righting myself each time.

I tried to think of someplace where things would be better—perhaps California? I searched my mind for a name or phone number. But each time I tried to look up, the penetrating mist soaked my eyelids closed and forced my vision back down.

Yet, I continued.

And so for the first time ever, I turned from following thoughts and dreams to following whatever it was that kept my feet moving, one step in front of the other—on and on—righting me from stumbles and helping me along, without ever needing to know where.

EPILOGUE

The road continued through thousands of western miles from Wyoming to Washington before ending behind a pretzel cart on Fisherman's Wharf in San Francisco. Each morning I wheeled my cart into the street, cranked up the burners, spread the salt along the bottom, and tried to anticipate how many pretzels I would have to cook to meet the day's demand.

It took me about four weeks to earn enough money to fly home safe and sound for Christmas. Hitchhiker Rule 25–A: At any time, all hitchhiker rules are susceptible to complete failure; *therefore – don't press your luck.*

The plane sailed over the whole six months and eight thousand hitchhiking miles in less time than it took me to catch a ride out of Thunder Bay. It seemed obscene to look down on it all like that; it seemed arrogant. Closing my eyes, I forced my way back to Oregon, where Route 101 flirted with, but had not yet come upon, the Pacific Ocean.

"They were saying there's good jobs in Seattle. But you know, I've been cutting up these woods for twenty-one years now. Anything else would be like starting over."

With the logging industry along the coast at a standstill, it was too early for the bars, too late for filling out job applications. Fall was firmly ensconced in the crisp golden feel of the rain forest. My driver was killing time with a hitchhiker and a six-pack of Rainier Lagers.

"Did you cross the Plains coming out here?"

"Yeah, for a long while."

"It's funny, I've always wanted to see the Plains. Here in Washington we've got the mountains and we've got the ocean, but we don't have any plains."

"At this point, I'd kinda like to see the ocean."

"You mean you haven't seen the Pacific yet?"

"No, someone was telling me 101 just sort of goes near it, but doesn't actually get there until a place called Aberdeen. That's where I figure we'll meet."

"Aberdeen's a lousy place to see the ocean for the first time."

"That's where the road goes."

"Well, look, as late as it is, you're not going to get to Aberdeen today. I've got to turn off pretty soon, but I know a trail that leads to this real nice camping spot in the woods. We'll have to drive off the highway a little ways, but you can hitch back to 101 in the morning."

"Sounds great."

That night, someone would be racking them up at that same bar; racking them up so he could smash the cue ball right through them. Then, he'd watch the balls splatter toward so many different places, directed by a random energy that even the pros couldn't control.

When the table was cleared that last time, he'd look into the flat green plane and see the hitchhiker walking along the trail. For the first half-mile or so, the pines were as thick as in the rain forest. But over a hill and completely unexpected, there'd be a sparkle through the trees unlike anything the hitchhiker had seen for thousands of miles.

"You don't have to know my name or nothing. Just remember me as someone who helped you get a little closer to that ocean," he had said.

"Yeah, I will. . . . Thanks a lot for the ride."

Appendix

HITCHHIKER RULES

1. There are things you can do that make a difference.
2. Don't mess up people's basket-making sessions for a lousy clarification.
2½. If a woman displaying half the nation's flora and fauna on her head misinterprets your existence, there's probably a good reason for it.
3. You've got to let people know your needs without sounding pushy. You've got to make it their idea.
4. It is difficult to get beyond a place that is designated for your use — even a place you don't like.
5. You just never know.
6. No matter how comfortable you may feel at any given time, every ride has always got to end.
7. Always talk to your driver before getting in the car so you know something of what he is about before the locks of his burgundy Impala go "kerplunk."
8. Beneath every huge wave that looks like it is about to knock you over, there is a still pool of water that remains unaffected.
9. Sometimes you can't look the way you feel.
10. It's awfully difficult to lie in bed when the world is moaning outside your window.
11. Feel yourself a part of what you are afraid of. Keep close contact; never let there be any distance.
12. Taking a big chance is the only way to escape a big problem.
13. Don't destroy your driver's sense of reality before he drops you off.
14. In the general sense: You've always got to be on the lookout for the potential because the actual doesn't always present itself. In the specific sense: Where there are students, there are beds.
15. For all the time you spend alone in this world, it's really difficult to get some privacy.

16. If you ever do happen to come upon a private type of alone, lock it up and hide it.

17. When you never know, you just never do.

18. When your ride says go, you must, especially if you're in grizzly-bear country north of Superior.

19. Sometimes you've got to ask twice to get beyond the chamber-of-commerce persona we all have on tap for the questions of a stranger.

20. Humanity thrives around the answer to the second question.

21. Whenever possible, let the police in a small town know who you are, so they don't feel obligated to arrest you to find out.

22. No matter how good it feels to watch yourself soar through the air and land in the hands of another, you never really can.

23. Never abandon a ride that is going uphill, especially when the temperature is nearing ninety.

24. It's really tough for a hitchhiker to walk aloof through the world.

25. At any point in time, all hitchhiker rules are susceptible to total failure.

25-A. At any point in time, all hitchhiker rules are susceptible to total failure—therefore, don't press your luck.

About the Author

A hitchhiker, newspaper editor, playwright, producer, and former ice hockey goalie, Tom DeTitta finds comfort in the thick of things. Correspondingly, his writing reflects a complete dedication to and immersion in his subject matter.

He wrote most of *Deadwood* in the southern Appalachian Mountains, where he had retreated to find the quiet space of a rural area devoid of any familiarity. He soon became fascinated with the place he had come upon, and began writing about it both as editor of a local newspaper and as freelance correspondent for several national publications. This interest eventually culminated in his writing and producing "The Reach of Song" drama—an epic celebration of the southern Appalachian region as seen through the life and works of native writer Byron Herbert Reece.

A 1982 magna-cum-laude graduate of Duke University, Mr. DeTitta has written freelance articles for many newspapers, including the *New York Times*, the *Atlanta Journal-Constitution*, and the *Raleigh News and Observer*.